Modern English

SECOND EDITION

VOLUME TWO

Modern English

SECOND EDITION

VOLUME TWO

William E. Rutherford
UNIVERSITY OF SOUTHERN CALIFORNIA

HARCOURT BRACE JOVANOVICH, INC.

NEW YORK   CHICAGO   SAN FRANCISCO   ATLANTA

© 1968, 1977 by Harcourt Brace Jovanovich, Inc.

All rights reserved. No part of this publication may be reproduced or transmitted in any form or by any means, electronic or mechanical, including photocopy, recording, or any information storage and retrieval system, without permission in writing from the publisher.

ISBN: 0-15-561062-7

Library of Congress Catalog Card Number: 76-47907

Printed in the United States of America

PREFACE

This book is intended for use by learners whose native language is not English. Volume One, designed for those with little prior exposure to English, gives students fundamental abilities to communicate in both the spoken and the written language. Volume Two enables learners to extend those skills to English of greater complexity and sophistication. Although the two volumes are about equal in size, Volume One contains fifteen units, Volume Two nine. Each of these nine units provides instruction and practice in speaking, understanding, grammar, sound and spelling, word formation, punctuation, reading, and writing.

The present revision retains some features of the original edition but otherwise departs from it in fundamental ways. Most significantly, the book now devotes as much attention to language *use* as to language *form*, and it assigns primary importance to the function of language as a vehicle for communication and expression. Accordingly, exercises are contextual wherever possible, facts of grammar are frequently explained with reference to social situations, principles are taught for choosing among alternative grammatical structures, and much of the material in the book focuses on English beyond the sentence level. In addition, the previous proliferation of new vocabulary has been brought under control; the major areas of grammar are treated in depth and revisited in later units; the writing exercises are both more comprehensive and more numerous; information and exercises on sound-spelling correspondences have been added; most of the dialogs have been replaced; and the basic format of the book has been completely altered for the sake of clarity, convenience, and flexibility. Purely manipulative exercises are no longer to be found in the text. However, those instructors who favor the use of such drills will find them sketched out in the Instructor's Manual accompanying this volume. Generalizations about the language display eclecticism rather than theoretical orientation to a particular linguistic model.

What has not been revised, however, is the notion that it is still worthwhile to make language generalizations for purposes of classroom teaching and learning. Those instructors familiar with the first edition will also note that a dialog and a reading selection in each unit are still the source for all the structure presented in that unit, that a number of the original exercises have been kept, and that supplementary lists of structurally similar lexical items are still an important feature of the book.

I wish to thank the critics, too numerous to cite individually, of the original edition of *Modern English*, including, especially, the many students and instructors who have had occasion to use the book in recent years at the American Language Institute, University of Southern California. Among the instructors who have experimented with the present volume, special thanks go to Marvin Coates for having given unstintingly of his time in offering many valuable insights and suggestions. Similar help has come from Esther Blake, James Butler, Virginia Heringer, Noel Houck, Martin Mould, Donald Pederson, and Ronald Shook. I am grateful to my colleague Professor Jacquelyn Schachter for many stimulating discussions of matters both theoretical and practical concerning the teaching and learning of English for international students.

W. E. R.

CONTENTS

Preface

Preparatory Unit   1

Unit 16

A	Dialog: "Close Quarters"	19
	Sound Patterns: intonation	20
	Phrasal Verbs: vocabulary equivalents	22
	Speech Act: *What?*	22
B	Pronoun reference	24
C	Reading: "Psychological Space"	26
	Vocabulary Relations: verbs of change	28
	Punctuation: general	29
D	Substitution and shortening	30
E	Reflexives and reciprocals	32

Writing Exercises   35

Unit 17

A	Dialog: "The Classroom"	45
	Sound Patterns: tense and lax vowels	46
	Phrasal Verbs: particle/preposition	47
	Speech Act: summonses	47
B	More on nouns and noun phrases	49
C	Reading: "Missing Piece Found in Continent 'Puzzle'"	52
	Vocabulary Relations: verbs of ascent	54/64
	Punctuation: initial capital letters	55
D	Possessive form	55
E	*'s* vs. *of*	58

Writing Exercises   61

Unit 18

A	Dialog: "The Accident"	73
	Sound Patterns: affix (*-ize, -ify*)	75
	Phrasal Verbs: verb-particle + object	75
	Speech Act: *How come . . . ? / What . . . for?*	76
B	Cause and effect	77
C	Reading: "Highway Dinosaurs"	80
	Vocabulary Relations: verbs of causation	82
	Punctuation: the period	83
D	Assignment of cause	84
E	Reason and purpose	87

Writing Exercises 91

Unit 19

A	Dialog: "A Letter from Down Under"	105
	Sound Patterns: sentence stress	106
	Phrasal Verbs: with *take*	107
	Speech Act: presupposition	107
B	Other uses of comparatives; comparison with other forms	108
C	Reading: "Australia and the United States: A Comparison"	110
	Vocabulary Relations: opposites	112
	Punctuation: the comma	113
D	Complex comparison	114
E	Comparison and contrast	117

Writing Exercises 121

Unit 20

A	Dialog: "The New York Times"	135
	Sound Patterns: affix (*in-, im-, il-, ir-*)	137
	Phrasal Verbs: verb-particle + long object	137
	Speech Act: *fairly, rather*	138
B	More on modals	139
C	Reading: "A Great News Story"	142
	Vocabulary Relations: verbs of possession	144/154
	Punctuation: the semicolon	145
D	The past in the past	146
E	The past for the present	148

Writing Exercises 151

Unit 21

A	Dialog: "The Personal Letter"	163
	Sound Patterns: contraction	166
	Phrasal Verbs: with *back*	166
	Speech Act: exclamations	167
B	Relatives with verb-*ing* and *to* verb	169
C	Reading: "The Formal Letter"	172
	Vocabulary Relations: *ask*	174
	Punctuation: the dash	175
D	References for *which*; relatives within units	176
E	Other -*ing* clauses; the use of nonrestrictives	180
Writing Exercises		183

Unit 22

A	Dialog: "Other 'Americans'"	195
	Sound Patterns: double letters	197
	Phrasal Verbs: verb-preposition + sentence	197
	Speech Act: extensions, clarifications, and changes	198
B	More on complementation	199
C	Reading: "French Canada"	202
	Vocabulary Relations: verbs of deprivation	204/216
	Punctuation: parentheses	205
D	Simple complements; object movement	206
E	Weight and focus	209
Writing Exercises		213

Unit 23

A	Dialog: "The Television Studio"	225
	Sound Patterns: corresponding consonants	227
	Phrasal Verbs: with *out* and *off*	227
	Speech Act: *this* and *that*	228
B	Condition: *if*	230
C	Reading: "The Conversation"	233
	Vocabulary Relations: *come* and *go*	235
	Punctuation: quotation marks and inverted commas	238
D	Condition: *only if*; negative condition	239
E	Condition, wishes, and the subjunctive	242
Writing Exercises		245

Unit 24

A	Dialog: "The Science Seminar"	259
	Sound Patterns: word stress (learned vocabulary)	261
	Phrasal Verbs: stress contrast	262
	Speech Act: qualifiers	263
B	Sentence rearrangement: adjective complements; *-ed* vs. *-ing*	265
C	Reading: "Zero"	268
	Vocabulary Relations: affix (*in-/un-* vs. *non-*)	270
	Punctuation: the colon	272
D	Choosing among sentence rearrangements	273
E	More on sentence rearrangement: inversion	277

Writing Exercises   283

Appendixes   297

Index   311

Modern English

SECOND EDITION

VOLUME TWO

Preparatory Unit

This unit, consisting entirely of writing exercises, is designed to serve either of two purposes: (1) to provide a review of the major areas of English grammar for students who have worked through Volume One or (2) to provide a sample of the kind of knowledge presumed to be in the possession of the student who is starting out with Volume Two. For such students this unit also serves as an introduction to the various conventions of exercise format and language representation that are a feature of both volumes. The numbers in brackets at the end of each exercise explanation designate the parts of Volume One where the relevant grammar points are discussed.

a • Write a very brief solution to each of the following riddles.[1] [2-9]

1. What table has no legs?
   a time table

2. What is the difference between an old penny and a new dime?
   nine cents

3. What has four legs and flies?
   _____

4. What is it that only dogs have?
   _____

[1] From *Encyclopedia of Humor,* copyright © 1968 by Joey Adams. Reprinted by permission of the publisher, The Bobbs-Merrill Company, Inc.

5. What is full of holes, yet holds water?
   _____

6. What is all over the house?
   _____

7. Who wears the biggest hat?
   _____

8. What gives milk and has one horn?
   _____

9. What is it that never asks any questions, yet requires many answers?
   _____

10. Should a person stir his coffee with his right hand or his left hand?
    _____

11. What do you sit in, sleep on, and brush your teeth with?
    _____

b • Learners of English sometimes make mistakes with certain kinds of questions. Instead of saying **What does "apron" mean?**, for example, a student might say *****What means "apron"?** or *****What "apron" means?** or *****What does mean "apron"?** (The sign * always indicates that something is wrong.) The correct form, therefore, is **What does X mean?** What is the "X" part of the question accompanying the following cartoon? What does it mean? [2-8]

"What does hanging on to one's mother's apron strings mean?"

Reprinted by permission of Newspaper Enterprise Association.

c • In each of the blank spaces of the dialog below, write one of the following: **(i)s, (a)m, (a)re, do, did, can, (wi)ll, may, must, should, could, happens to, would, have to.** In some cases more than one choice is appropriate. [3-9, 11, 20; 4-9, 10, 11, 22, 23, 29, 30]

ETHEL   It *must* be time to get on the plane, *do* n't
               1   2
you think, Harry?

HARRY   No. _____ n't be nervous, Ethel. They' _____ call us
                    3   4
when it' _____ time.
                 5

LOUDSPEAKER   All passengers for flight number 51 _____ now board.
                                                      6

Preparatory Unit

HARRY   There. You _____ n't believe me, _____ you? We
                    7   8
        _____ board now.
          9

ETHEL   We _____ show the tickets to the stewardess, I sup-
              10
        pose. You _____ have them, _____ n't you?
                    11   12

HARRY   Of course. How _____ I forget an important thing like
                          13
        that?

ETHEL   Frankly, Harry, it _____ n't be the first time. I guess
                             14
        these _____ be our seats.
                15

STEWARDESS Attention, please. You _____ fasten your seat belts
                                     16
        and observe the "no smoking" signs.

ETHEL   You heard that, _____ n't you, Harry? You _____
                           17   18
        fasten your seat belt.

HARRY   Yes. I' _____ not deaf, you know.... What _____
                 19   20
        you doing, Ethel?

ETHEL   What _____ you think? This _____ my first flight,
                21   22
        _____ n't it? I' _____ praying.
          23   24

HARRY   It _____ n't your turn, Ethel. You' _____ likely to
              25   26
        live to a hundred.

ETHEL   But suppose it _____ be the pilot's turn?
                          27

d • The following sets of descriptions refer to the occupational potential of different people. Within each set the pieces of information or "clues" move from the general to the particular. After each such clue, speculate on the occupational possibilities using the modals **could, should,** and **will,** as in the models.[2] [4-9, 10, 11]

1. A   George is very good with his hands.
   B   *Perhaps he could be a carpenter.*
   A   He likes to work with clay.
   B   *Maybe he should be a sculptor.*

[2]This exercise is an adaptation of one by Virginia Heringer appearing in a forthcoming issue of *TESOL Newsletter*.

Preparatory Unit

- A But he's learning how to repair cars.
- B *Then he'll probably be a mechanic.*

2.
- A Sally has a good eye for detail.
- B _____
- A She likes to take pictures of people.
- B _____
- A But she's finishing a degree in art history.
- B _____

3.
- A Barry is well developed physically.
- B _____
- A He likes to ride horses.
- B _____
- A But he's finishing his training with the Forestry Service.
- B _____

4.
- A Martha has a good way of relating to other people.
- B _____
- A She likes to help those who are in trouble.
- B _____
- A But she just declared her candidacy for the next election.
- B _____

e • This exercise is similar to d, except that the person in each set already has a job. Again, taking the clues supplied, guess at the occupations, this time using the modals **might (possibly)**, **may (very well)**, and **must**. [4-9, 10, 11]

1.
- A Linda's job requires her to sit at a desk.
- B *She might possibly be an editor/accountant/ teacher/executive/and so on.*
- A She has to make a lot of notations and corrections.
- B *She may very well be an editor/teacher/ and so on.*

Preparatory Unit

A She reads other people's manuscripts.
B *Then she must be an editor.*

2. (The rest of the clues are to be found in the Instructor's Manual.)

f • In the blank spaces write the form of the verb that seems most appropriate. [5-21, 22, 23]

The story *is told* of a young boy who *attempted* to lift out of
       (1) tell   (2) attempt

the way a heavy stone that _____ his car. His father _____
                  (3) block   (4) happen

to come by and _____ his son's failing efforts. The father
          (5) notice

_____ to him, "Son, I don't think you _____ all your
 (6) say   (7) use

strength."

"Yes, I _____," the boy _____ impatiently.
      (8) be   (9) reply

"No, you _____ not," _____ the father. "You _____
       (10) be   (11) say   (12) ask

me for no help whatsoever."[3]

g • **Already** vs. **yet.** Correct the false impressions contained in the following questions by writing answers according to the models. [10-25, 26]

1. When do we do exercise b?
We've already done it.

2. When did we do Unit 16?
We haven't done it yet.

3. When does class begin?
_____

4. When did we finish the course?
_____

5. When will (name) have a chance to speak?
_____

6. When did you finish learning English?
_____

---

[3]Adapted from *A Complete Treasury of Stories for Public Speakers,* by Morris Mandel. Reprinted by permission of Jonathan David Publishers.

7. When will we do some writing?

   _____

8. When did the period end?

   _____

9. When will the teacher speak to us?

   _____

h • In each of the blanks below write **a(n), the,** or **X** (for nothing), as required. [7-7, 8, 9]

__*A*__₁ certain very rich woman decided she needed __*a*__₂ little culture. She walked into _____₃ famous art shop. _____₄ first painting she saw was from _____₅ brush of one of _____₆ masters. It was _____₇ beautiful study of _____₈ vagrant in _____₉ ragged clothes sitting on _____₁₀ park bench. _____₁₁ woman became very angry. "I'll never give _____₁₂ beggar _____₁₃ cent again," she said. "He's too poor to buy _____₁₄ suit of clothes, but he's got _____₁₅ money to have somebody paint _____₁₆ picture of him."[4]

i • Convert the following representations into sentences using **-er/more . . . than.** [8-26]

1. France produces [X+] coal [Italy produces [X] coal]
   France produces more coal than Italy (does).
2. France produces [X+] coal [France produces [X] oil]
   France produces more coal than (it does) oil.
3. There is [X+] coal in France [There is [X] coal in Italy]

   _____

4. There is [X+] coal in France [There is [X] oil in France]

   _____

[4]Adams, op. cit.

5. People find television [X+] entertaining [People find radio [X] entertaining]

_____

6. People find television [X+] entertaining [People find television [X] educational]

_____

7. [X+] people find television entertaining [[X] people find radio entertaining]

_____

8. [X+] people find television entertaining [[X] people find television educational]

_____

9. It is [X+] easy to speak English [It is [X] easy to speak Latin]

_____

10. It is [X+] easy to speak English [It is [X] easy to write English]

_____

j • Convert the following representations into a paragraph containing **as . . . as** and **-er/more . . . than** constructions. Try to avoid the unnecessary repetition of words. [8-19, 26]

There are many [X+] languages spoken in the world. [There are [X] countries in the world]. In some countries, for example, [X] many different languages are spoken [There are [X] many provinces in some countries]. On the other hand, [X+] people speak certain languages [[X] people live in the countries where those languages originated]. There are [X] many English speakers in the world, for instance, [There are [X] many people in England, France, and the Soviet Union combined]. It is [X+] easy today to identify all these languages [It was [X] easy several centuries ago to identify all these languages].

k • Rewrite the following groups of sentences by changing the sentences in brackets into relative clauses. Make any further possible alterations that you wish: relative clause reduction, substitution of an **-ing** form, use of **with**. [12-6, 7, 8]

1. Sandra Cobb is *a woman* [*The woman* has *problems* [*The problems* need attention]]
   Sandra Cobb is a women with problems needing attention.
   (who has) *(that need)*

2. Yesterday she saw *a doctor* [*The doctor* advised her to have an operation]

_____

3. The day before that she got *a message* [*The message* was from her husband's lawyer [*The message* said that her husband wanted a divorce]]

_____

_____

4. The week before that she was fired from her job by *a company* [*The company* had employed her for ten years]

_____

_____

5. Now she is looking for *a lawyer* [*The lawyer* can help her [*The lawyer* doesn't charge a lot]]

_____

_____

6. Sandra Cobb is *a woman* [*The woman* has a lot on her mind]

_____

I • Rewrite the following groups of sentences by changing the sentences in brackets into relative clauses. Make any further possible alterations that you wish: deletion of relative marker, substitution of **where**. [12-18, 19, 24]

1. Mark Ellis is *a man* [People find it hard to understand *the man*]

   Mark Ellis is a man (that) {whom/who} people find it hard to understand.

2. He is often unkind to *the friends* [He really cares about *the friends*]

_____

3. *The letters* [He sends *the letters* to his friends] are short and businesslike.

_____

4. The door of *the apartment* [He lives in *the apartment*] has three locks on it.

_____

5. He refuses most of *the dinner invitations* [People occasionally send him *dinner invitations*]

_____

_____

Preparatory Unit

6. Mark Ellis is *a man* [The world in general is a hostile place for *the man* and very little brings joy to *the man*]

_____

_____

m • Write the following as a complete paragraph by changing the sentences in brackets into relative clauses. Make any further possible alterations that you wish. The presence of **AND** indicates a nonrestrictive relative clause. [12-23]

Cotton [AND *cotton* came originally from the Arab world and *cotton* derives its name from the Arabic word "qutun"] is now grown all over the world. Cotton contains *delicate seed hairs* [*The delicate seed hairs* consist of *a single long cell* [*The single long cell* has *a thick wall* [AND *The thick wall* allows cotton to be spun into strong yarn]]]. *The first process of manufacture* [AND the industry refers to *the first process of manufacture* as "ginning"] is the separation of the hairs from *the seeds* [AND they in turn crush *the seeds* for cottonseed oil]. The cotton is then compressed and shipped in this form by *the chief cotton export countries* [AND *the chief cotton export countries* are the USA, the USSR, China, Egypt, India, and Brazil].

n • **A high-school diploma** is **a diploma from a high school** (The high school gives a diploma). **A sheepskin diploma** is **a diploma (printed) on sheepskin.** With this kind of distinction in mind, do you have any comments concerning the following cartoon?

Used by permission of Chicago Tribune-New York News Syndicate.

Rewrite each of the following compounds as a noun + prepositional phrase [1-D]

1. a dinner invitation

   an invitation to dinner

Preparatory Unit

2. a dinner guest
   a guest for dinner

3. theater tickets
   _____

4. a ticket line
   _____

5. health articles
   _____

6. a post-office box
   _____

7. hearing difficulty
   _____

8. a fruit cake
   _____

9. birth dates
   _____

10. a river bank
    _____

11. a plane trip
    _____

12. a doctor bill
    _____

13. unemployment insurance
    _____

14. a job interview
    _____

15. arm and leg pains
    _____

16. hotel information
    _____

17. the growth rate

    _____

18. bank accounts

    _____

19. teaching methods

    _____

20. the whole world

    _____

o • Rewrite each of the sentence sketches below as usable English by changing the bracketed sentence into the proper form: **for-to, that**-S, or **-ing**. Make any other desirable alterations: deletion of **for** element, use of an **it** construction. [13-8, 9, 17, 18, 19, 23; 14-8, 17, 24]

1. My friend Jim cannot afford [Jim owns a car]   **for-to**

    My friend Jim cannot afford to own a car.

2. [He maintains a car] would be too expensive for him.   **for-to/-ing**

    _____

3. He even regrets [He bought the motorcycle that he rides to work on]   **-ing/that-S**

    _____

4. He expects [He will have to get another job soon]   **that-S/for-to**

    _____

5. He assumes [The economy isn't going to improve]   **that-S**

    _____

6. He wouldn't even mind [He works at night], if it paid well.   **-ing**

    _____

7. [One supports a family on such a small salary] just isn't possible any more.   **for-to**

    _____

p • Write out the following sketch as a complete paragraph by changing all sentences in brackets into usable English. [13-18, 19; 14-8, 17, 24]

When Franklin Delano Roosevelt became president in 1933, he knew [*The economic crisis requires a strong hand*]. He decided [*He requests* [*Congress creates new job programs*]]. Although he failed [*He reduces unemployment significantly*], he succeeded in [*He creates new confidence in the government*]. Roosevelt did not intend [*Roosevelt sees America become isolationist*]. [*He improves relations with the countries of Latin America*] was his wish, therefore, and he insisted [*The British receive America's support at the beginning of World War II*]. Roosevelt risked [*Roosevelt plunges the country into war on several occasions*], but after the attack on Pearl Harbor in 1941 he did not hesitate in [*He asks Congress* [*Congress declares war*]]. [*He died only one month before the war ended*] is sad.

that-S
for-to, that-S
for-to
-ing
-ing
for-to/it
that-S
-ing
-ing, for-to
that-S/it

q • Most of the examples of verb + complement from the previous exercise are repeated below. Rewrite each of these as noun + complement. [14-25]

1. Roosevelt *knew* that the economic crisis required a strong hand.

    Roosevelt had *knowledge that the economic crisis required a strong hand.*

2. He *decided* to request something.

    He made _____

3. He *requested* that Congress create a new job program.

    He made _____

4. He *failed* to reduce unemployment.

    _____ was his.

5. He *succeeded* in creating new confidence.

    He experienced _____

6. He did not *intend* seeing America become isolationist.

    He had no _____

7. He *insisted* that the British receive America's support.

    He made known his _____

8. He *risked* plunging the country into war.

   He ran _____

9. He did not *hesitate* in asking Congress to declare war.

   He showed no _____

r • Look at the cartoon below and then write out your own definition for "the secret of success in life." [13-23]

CROCK   by Rechin & Parker

"CROCK" by Bill Rechin and Brant Parker. Courtesy of Field Newspaper Syndicate.

   In my opinion, the secret of success in life is _____
   _____

s • Each of the items below is the representation of a sentence. Since the first element of each set is a verb, something else needs to be moved to the left of the verb (subject position) in order to make a usable sentence. Many of the noun phrases to the right of the verb will require prepositions. Choose an appropriate tense for the verb. [15-8, 9, 18]

1. happen — an accident

   An accident happened.

2. report — the accident

   The accident was reported.

3. involve — the accident — a car and a truck

   _____

4. drive — the car — a university instructor

   _____

5. travel very fast — the truck

   _____

6. notify — the police

_____

7. call to the scene — an ambulance

_____

8. arrive half an hour late — the ambulance

_____

9. take to a hospital — the truck driver

_____

10. suffer — the driver of the car — only minor injuries

_____

11. see — the whole drama — a crowd of people

_____

12. not put on page one — things like that

_____

t • Write the proper form of the verb in each of the blanks of the following paragraphs. [15-8, 9, 18]

WASHINGTON—The president of the American Geophysical Union ___*said*___ Wednesday that thousands of lives could ___*be saved*___ in
    (1) say   (2) save

Southern California if the state would _____ from the earthquake
                                       (3) learn

prediction techniques that _____ successfully in the People's
                                 (4) use

Republic of China.

   It _____ at a special session of the Union that the Chinese
         (5) report

accurately _____ an earthquake that _____ the city of
             (6) predict   (7) strike

Haicheng in February, 1975. It _____ that more than a million
                                       (8) believe

people _____, which probably _____ tens of thousands of
        (9) evacuate   (10) save

lives.

Preparatory Unit

Chinese scientists _____ intensive study of the Haicheng area
                      (11) begin

after they _____ an uplifted area near the city that _____ a
            (12) discover   (13) resemble

bulge in California that can _____ along a one-hundred-mile stretch
                                  (14) see

of the San Andreas fault near Palmdale.

The report _____ that the Chinese, who _____ a high
           (15) say   (16) place

priority on earthquake research, _____ a major investigative effort
                                  (17) concentrate

in the Haicheng area from 1970, when the bulge _____, until 1975,
                                                    (18) discover

when the earthquake _____ the city. Such intensive efforts have yet
                        (19) destroy

to _____ in this country.[5]
  (20) see

u • The following sentences have mistakes concerning the relationships between verbs and noun phrases. Rewrite each sentence in such a way as to remove the error. [15-8, 9, 18]

1. *Crime in many countries has recently reduced.

2. *Nobody knows who this book is belong to.

3. *Something may be happened after four or five years.

4. *Since graduation my friend has been worked in a law office.

5. *It was a party that enjoyed everybody.

6. *I have never been met this kind of situation.

---

[5]Adapted from an article by Richard C. Paddock in *The Los Angeles Times,* Part 1, page 1, April 15, 1976. Copyright, 1976, *Los Angeles Times.* Reprinted by permission.

v • Rewrite the following sequences as a full paragraph by moving something into subject position, changing the form of the sentences in brackets, and choosing an appropriate verb tense.

operate — the university computer facilities — University Information Processing

locate at the University Computer Center — the computers themselves

and

request to inquire there — *students and staff* [*The students and staff* wish to use these facilities]

feature — the Center — *an IBM computer system* [*The IBM computer system* provides local and remote processing]

Furthermore,

support — the computer — tabulating equipment and a knowledgable staff

Hopefully,

can soon use — a large number of terminals — students and faculty

Unit 16

16-1 DIALOG

CLOSE QUARTERS

ETHEL   [calling] Harry!
HARRY   What?
ETHEL   There's a reptile in the bathtub!
HARRY   What?
ETHEL   There's a reptile in the bathtub . . . . I think it's a lizard.
HARRY   Well, where <u>else</u> would she take a bath?
ETHEL   Don't be funny. And how do you know it isn't a "he"?
HARRY   "He" lizards don't lay eggs, and this one did. One of Jody's playmates gave it to him.
ETHEL   Harry, this apartment is already small enough with just the three of us, let alone with a lizard. And I don't care if he, I mean she, does wash him . . . uh, herself.
HARRY   But they like each other . . . Jody and the lizard, I mean. And she doesn't take up much space.
ETHEL   Well, I'm not putting up with any reptiles in this apartment. Little lizards get bigger, you know.
HARRY   So do little boys, but <u>that</u> doesn't seem to bother you.

CULTURAL NOTES   Though "he" and "she" can generally be used only with reference to "higher animals" (that is, those larger than rodent size), the gender pronouns can also refer to any creature (animal, insect, reptile, bird, and so on) performing the function of a household pet.

VOCABULARY

lay/laid quarters take a bath
wash reptile
take up bathtub
put up with lizard
  bath (bathe)
  space (spacious, spatial)

16-2 ■ DIALOG VARIATION

1. *There's a reptile in the bathtub!*
   The bathtub has a reptile in it!
   In the bathtub there's a reptile!
2. *Where <u>else</u> would she take a bath?*
   Would she take a bath anywhere else?
   She wouldn't take a bath anywhere else, would she?
3. *One of Jody's playmates gave it to him.*
   It was given to Jody by one of his playmates.
   Jody was given it by one of his playmates.
   Jody had it given to him by one of his playmates.
4. *I'm not putting up with any reptiles in this apartment.*
   I'm not tolerating any reptiles in this apartment.
   I won't stand for any reptiles in this apartment.
5. *So do little boys. . . .*
   Little boys do too.
   The same goes for little boys.

16-3 ■ QUESTIONS

1. What information does Ethel have for Harry?
2. What is Harry's response? Is he upset?
3. Is the lizard a "he" or a "she"? How do you know?
4. Who do you think Jody is? About how old do you think he is? What pieces of information tell you?
5. How many occupants does the apartment have?
6. How big is the apartment?
7. Why doesn't Ethel want the lizard?

16-4 SOUND PATTERNS

In speaking, intonation conveys an important part of the meaning. English has a number of different intonation patterns, some of which were studied in Volume One, and almost any word or group of words can carry any of these patterns. Quite often, however, the social situation in which the language is used will determine the choice. The use of **what** in the dialog at the beginning of this unit is a good example of this:

A1 *Harry!*
B1 *What?*
A2 *There's a reptile in the bathtub.*
B2 *What?*

What? in B1 means something like **What is it?** or **What do you want?**, which a speaker says in responding casually to someone who has just addressed him. **What?** in B2 means something like **What was that you said?**, which a speaker says in response to something addressed to him that he doesn't understand or that he can't believe he heard correctly. Information questions with rising intonation, such as B2, are often called *echo questions*.

The meaning of a single isolated sentence, then, is often ambiguous or incomplete; it is the social situation in which the sentence is used that gives it its final definition:

(HUSBAND *My boss asked me if I'd take a pay cut.*)

FRIEND *What did you say?*
(to him)
[information question]

WIFE *What did you say?*
(to me)
[echo question]
= *What was that you said?*
(to me)

16-A • (See page 35.)

16-5 ■ From the looks of the following cartoon, what do you imagine that the customer has just said? Try to imitate the intonation of the clerk's response.

Section A   21

Copyright, 1976, Universal Press Syndicate

"Size what?"

16-6   PHRASAL VERBS

—But they like each other . . . . And she doesn't *take up* much space.
—Well, I'm not *put*ting *up with* any reptiles in this apartment.

Take up and **put up with** are *phrasal verbs,* which are extremely common in English. Notice that the meaning of a phrasal verb is very seldom the sum of the meanings of the words that make it up. For each phrasal verb, however, there is usually a one-word verb with nearly the same meaning: **take up** = *occupy,* **put up with** = *tolerate.* This is the first of a series of phrasal verb studies, with another one in each unit to follow.

16-B   • (See page 35.)

SPEECH ACT

—Harry!
—What?

16-7 ■ The single question word **what** with falling intonation, as suggested in 16-4, usually implies a full question of some kind. In the sample dialog above, for example, **What?** really means something like **What is it?** or **What do you want?** Act out the following mini-dialogs, and after each **what** let another student supply a reasonable paraphrase.

1. A Somebody said something.
   B What?
   C **What did they say?**
2. A Somebody say something.
   B What?
   C **What do you want us to say?**
3. A Hey, Joe!
   B What?
   C and so on.
4. A. There's only one thing we can do.
   B What?
5. A Can you do me a favor?
   B Sure. What?
6. A Pssst . . . Mary!
   B What?
7. A I know what you're thinking.
   B What?
8. A You know what?
   B No, what?

16-8 ■ DIALOG IMPROVISATION

(Try to re-create or even improvise a variation of the Dialog at the beginning of this unit, as you remember it.)

A Harry!
B . . . ?
A There's a reptile . . .
B . . . ?
A There's a reptile in the bathtub. I think . . .
B One of Jody's playmates . . .
A This apartment is already . . .
B She doesn't take . . .
A Well, I'm not putting . . .

Section B

Pronoun reference

—And how do you know *it* isn't a "he"?
—"He" lizards don't lay eggs, and *this one* did. One of Jody's playmates gave *it* to him.

16-9 In Unit 7 we saw that the "definiteness" of a noun phrase is often determined more by rules of discourse than by rules of grammar. The same applies to noun phrase substitutes, *pronouns*:

                                                                             it
    A I live in *an apartment*.   B Do you like ~~the apartment~~?

The pronoun **it** (or **him, her,** when appropriate) replaces a noun phrase referring to something identifiable for speaker and hearer. The pronoun **one** replaces noun phrases that are examples of a class of items:

                                                                           one
    A I live in *an apartment*.   B I live in ~~an apartment~~ too.

In the first example, with **it**, the speakers have to be talking about the same apartment; in the second example, with **one**, the speakers cannot consciously be talking about the same apartment.

16-10 "Indefinite" nouns are replaceable by **one** or **ones**; entire noun phrases can be replaced by **one** for the singular, **some** for the plural or noncount:

A **We have** *a very small apartment*.

             one
B **I have** ~~a very small apartment~~ **too.**

                      one
C **We're six, so we need** *a large* ~~apartment~~.

              one
D **I'm looking for** ~~an apartment~~ *on the ground floor.*

                    some
B **I think there are** ~~apartments on the ground floor~~ **in our building.**

                           ones
D **I'll have a look. I don't like** *the* ~~apartments~~ **I've seen so far.**

16-11 ▪ The response to each of the following is to take the form **I think I saw . . .**

1. I'm looking for *a pen.*
   I think I saw one (on the table).
2. I'm looking for *a pen with my name on it.*
   I think I saw it (on the table).
3. I'm looking for a *VW.*
   I think . . .
4. I'm looking for a white 1963 VW with black stripes.
5. I'm looking for a policeman.
6. I'm looking for a policeman; his name is Sgt. Boyle.
7. I'm looking for some books.
8. I'm looking for some books that I left here somewhere.
9. I'm looking for a handkerchief.
10. I'm looking for a handkerchief with my initials on it.
11. I'm looking for a glass; a small one will do.
12. I'm looking for a glass, a small one half-filled with tea.

16-12 ▪ Act out the following conversation, supplying **one**, **ones**, or **some** in the blanks, as required.

A *We just bought a house.*
B *We're still looking for . . .*
C *There are always . . . advertised in the paper.*
D *But the best . . . never appear in the paper.*
E *You mean the cheapest . . .*
F *I know of a cheap . . . that nobody would want.*
G *How about a cheap . . . that's very old?*
H *. . . that are at least a hundred years old are the hardest . . . to find.*
I *And . . . of those are kept as museums.*
J *I just want an ordinary . . .*

16-13 ▪ Read the following dialog, carefully noting the use of pronouns. Then improvise dialogs of the same structure based on the situations described below.

1. (Two people discover that they're looking for the same apartment.)
   A *I'm looking for* an apartment.
   B *I'm looking for* one *too.*
   A *What number is* it?
   B 203B.
   A *That's* the one *I'm looking for!*
2. (Two people discover that they're trying to find the same book.)
   A *I'm trying to find* a book.
   B *I'm . . .*

Section B   25

3. (Two people discover that they have scheduled appointments with the same person at the same time.)
   A *I have* an appointment *for three o'clock.*
   B *I . . .*
4. (Two people discover that they're looking up the same words in the dictionary.)
   A *I'm looking up* some words *in the dictionary.*
   B *I'm . . .*
5. (Two people discover that they have to catch the same bus.)
   A *I have to catch* a bus.
   B *I . . .*

16-14 ■ Look at this cartoon strip, and see if you can say why it's supposed to be funny.

"CROCK" by Bill Rechin and Brant Parker. Courtesy of Field Newspaper Syndicate.

16-C • (See page 36.)

16-D • (See page 37.)

16-E • (See page 37.)

16-15   READING (223 words)

PSYCHOLOGICAL SPACE

Not everyone in the world requires the same amount of living space. The amount of space a person needs around him is a cultural preference, not an economic one. Knowing your own psychological space needs is

important because they strongly influence your choices, including, for
example, the number of bedrooms in the home. If you were reared in a
two-child family and both you and your sister or brother had your own
bedrooms, the chances are, if you have two children or more, that you
also will provide separate bedrooms for them. In America they train
people to want their own private rooms by giving them their own rooms
when they are babies. This is very rare in the world. In many cultures the
baby sleeps in the same bed with his parents or in a crib near their bed.

The areas in the home where people gravitate also reveals a lot about
psychological space needs. Some families cluster, and the size of their
house has nothing to do with it. Others have separate little niches where
family members go to be alone.

Although it is true that psychological space needs are not determined
by economic factors, they sometimes have to be modified a little because
of economic pressures. It is almost impossible, however, to completely
change your psychological space needs.[1]

VOCABULARY

influence (influence, influential)
rear
provide (provision)
train
gravitate (gravitation)
reveal (revelation)
cluster
determine (determination)
modify (modification)

chance
parent (parental)
crib
niche
member
pressure (press)

separate (separate, separation)
private (privacy)
rare (rarity)

strongly
alone

16-16 ■ INCLUDED MEANING

(For each of the following passages pick the one statement whose meaning is part of the meaning of the passage.)

1. *Not everyone in the world requires the same amount of living space.*
   a. No two people need the same amount of living space.
   b. Living space requirements are not always the same.
   c. The world requires the same amount of living space.
   d. Nobody needs a required amount of living space.
2. *Knowing your own psychological space needs is important because they strongly influence your choices, including, for example, the number of bedrooms in the home.*

[1]Adapted from "Apartment vs. House Living: 'Need' is Psychological" by Linda Lee Landis, from the *Chicago Tribune*. Reprinted by permission.

Section C

a. Psychological space requires influence.
   b. Psychological space needs importance.
   c. Space needs are influenced by choice.
   d. The number of bedrooms is influenced by psychological need.
3. *In America they train people to want their own private rooms by giving them their own rooms when they are babies.*
   a. People want the Americans' private rooms.
   b. Babies get the people's private rooms.
   c. Babies get their own private rooms.
   d. People want the babies' private rooms.
4. *Although it is true that psychological space needs are not determined by economic factors, they sometimes have to be modified a little because of economic pressures.*
   a. Economic factors do not determine psychological space needs.
   b. Economic factors sometimes have to be modified.
   c. Economic factors are not determined by psychological space needs.
   d. Economic factors sometimes have to modify economic pressures.

16-17 ■ QUESTIONS

1. What determines how much living space a person needs?
2. Why do so many Americans want their own private room?
3. Is this the way it is in other countries as well?
4. Where does the baby sleep in your country?
5. How can economic pressures affect psychological space needs?
6. Can psychological space needs be changed in any way?
7. What are your own psychological space needs?

16-18 VOCABULARY RELATIONS

For almost any verb in English it is not hard to find additional verbs that have very similar meanings. Yet it is almost never the case that such verbs are freely interchangeable. This is because they do not all occur in the same kind of grammatical construction. For example, two verbs appearing in the Reading for this unit, **change** and **modify**, can both occur in the following sentence:

It is almost impossible to completely $\begin{Bmatrix} change \\ modify \end{Bmatrix}$ your psychological space needs.

Yet only **change** can occur in the following, where the verb has no object:

You've $\begin{Bmatrix} changed \\ *modified \end{Bmatrix}$ quite a bit since I last saw you.

This is the first of a continuing series of studies, one per unit, in which you will have a chance to examine the relationship of vocabulary words to the contexts in which they can occur.

16-F • (See page 38.)

16-G • **COMPOUNDS** (See page 39.)

16-H • **RESTATEMENT** (See page 40.)

16-19 PUNCTUATION

English punctuation serves, among other things, to mark degrees of separation among the elements of the written language. These degrees of separation extend all the way from adjacent letters to the paragraph itself. The common punctuation marks, some of which will be focused on in the units to follow, are listed here:

hyphen	-
dash	—
parentheses	( )
comma	,
colon	:
semi-colon	;
period	. [In British English **period** = **full stop**.]
question mark	?
exclamation point	!

16-I • (See page 40.)

16-20 ■ **READING IMPROVISATION**

(Complete each of the following sentences with what you remember from the Reading.)

1. Not everyone in the world requires . . .
2. Knowing your own psychological space needs is important because . . .
3. If you were reared in a two-child family . . .
4. In America they train people to want . . .
5. In many cultures the baby . . .
6. Some families have separate little niches where . . .
7. It is impossible to completely change . . .

> Substitution and Shortening
>
> —How do you know it isn't a "he"?
> —"He" lizards don't lay eggs, and this one *did*.

16-21 All communication, spoken or written, contains a lot of reference to what has been mentioned previously. This reference takes the form of either a *substituted* word ("pro" form) or a *shortening* of the original. Here are some examples of this from previous units:

>   (6-1) **A thank-you note is customary,** *but a gift isn't.*
>   (*... but a gift isn't customary.*)   [shortening]
>   (11-12) **In Hollywood there is a company that publishes children's books** *with the aid of computers.* **Although other book companies also publish** *that way, ...*   [substitution]
>   (14-22) —**How do you know** *it won't rain this evening?*
>
>   —**The radio said** $\begin{cases} \text{it won't.} & \text{[shortening]} \\ \text{so.} & \text{[substitution]} \end{cases}$

16-22 Substitution and shortening can involve other elements of the repeated verb phrase as well, often with stress contrasts:

> **They didn't want me to rent the apartment,** $\begin{cases} \text{but } \underline{I} \begin{cases} \text{did} \\ \text{wanted to (rent...)} \end{cases} \\ \text{but I} \begin{cases} \underline{\text{did}} \\ \text{rented it} \end{cases} \text{anyway.} \end{cases}$

16-23 ■ Respond with surprise to each of the comments below. Follow the models.

1. A There's water on the floor.
   B **There is?**
2. A Yes. The roof leaks.
   B **It does?**
3. A Yes, and the toilet won't flush.
4. A Yes, and the stove doesn't light.
5. A Yes, and the phone's dead.
6. A Yes. We never paid our phone bill.
7. A Yes, and the kitchen tap drips.
8. A Yes, and one light in the bedroom isn't working.
9. A Yes, and you forgot to put out the rubbish.
10. A Yes, and we owe two month's rent.
11. A Yes. We have problems, and don't act so surprised.

16-24 ■ Choose the response of speaker B which you think fits the statement of speaker A. Only the stress pattern of speaker A can tell you.

1. A My wife didn't think I could find a house, $\begin{cases} 1. \text{ but I } \underline{did}. \\ 2. \text{ but } \underline{I} \text{ did}. \end{cases}$

   B **You mean** $\begin{cases} 1. \textbf{ you found a house?} \\ 2. \textbf{ you thought so?} \end{cases}$

2. A I thought she'd like the house, $\begin{cases} 1. \text{ but she } \underline{didn't}. \\ 2. \text{ but } \underline{she} \text{ didn't}. \end{cases}$

   B **You mean** $\begin{cases} 1. \textbf{ she didn't like it?} \\ 2. \textbf{ she didn't think so?} \end{cases}$

3. A She doesn't think I try very hard, $\begin{cases} 1. \text{ but I } \underline{do}. \\ 2. \text{ but } \underline{I} \text{ do}. \end{cases}$

   B **You mean . . .**

4. A She thinks I always need help, $\begin{cases} 1. \text{ but I } \underline{don't}. \\ 2. \text{ but } \underline{I} \text{ don't}. \end{cases}$

   B **You mean . . .**

5. A She thinks I smoke too much, $\begin{cases} 1. \text{ but I } \underline{don't}. \\ 2. \text{ But } \underline{I} \text{ don't}. \end{cases}$

   B **You mean . . .**

6. A She thought I had too much to drink yesterday, $\begin{cases} 1. \text{ but I } \underline{didn't}. \\ 2. \text{ but } \underline{I} \text{ didn't}. \end{cases}$

   B **You mean . . .**

7. A I didn't think she could find anything else to criticize, $\begin{cases} 1. \text{ but she } \underline{did}. \\ 2. \text{ but } \underline{she} \text{ did}. \end{cases}$

   B **You mean . . .**

16-J • (See page 41.)

16-K • (See page 41.)

E

16-L • **CLOZE** (See page 42.)

> Reflexives and Reciprocals
>
> —I don't care if she does wash *herself*.
> —But they like *each other*.

16-25 A noun referring back to another noun within the same simple sentence will take the form of a *reflexive pronoun*:

                herself
Ethel taught ~~Ethel~~ **how to cook.**

                himself
Harry looked at ~~Harry~~ **in the mirror.**

                              themselves
Ethel and Harry bought a house for ~~Ethel and Harry~~.

                itself
The motor turned ~~the motor~~ **off.**

                      myself
I found an old photograph of ~~me~~.

16-26 When a subject-object relationship is a mutual one, the *reciprocal pronoun* **each other**, or **one another**, is used:

(Ethel bought a gift for Harry and Harry bought a gift for Ethel.)
Ethel and Harry bought gifts for *each other*.

With reciprocals, therefore, the reference must always be plural:

They bought presents for *each other*.
(*He bought a present for each other.)

16-27 ■ Answer each of the following with a reflexive pronoun, according to the models.

1. Who trained him?
   Nobody. He trained him<u>self</u>.
2. Who helped them?
   Nobody. They helped them<u>selves</u>.
3. Who invited her?
4. Who reminded you?
5. Who turned it off?
6. Who taught him?
7. Who asked them?
8. Who woke her up?
9. Who corrected you?

16-28 ■ Ask a question with **each other** after each of the following.

Lewis and Maria have been married a short time, but they don't get along very well.

1. They seldom have a kind word for each other. (hate, like)
   Do they hate each other? / Don't they like each other? / and so on.
2. One speaks English and the other speaks Spanish. (understand)
3. Yesterday they passed on the street. (see, look at)
4. They were both wearing a hat and dark glasses. (recognize)
5. They both shout at the same time. (hear, understand)
6. They recently had a big fight. (hurt)
7. They both work at the same job. (help)

16-29 ■ The choice between regular and reflexive pronoun is often tied to the complexity of the sentence. The reflexive is used for reference only inside a simple sentence, whether or not it forms part of a larger sentence:

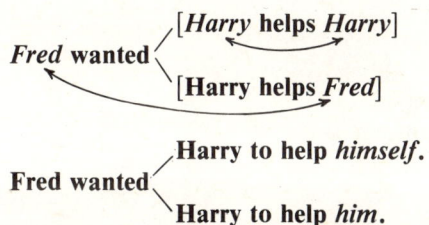

With this and other principles in mind, pass on the acceptability of the following sentences by saying either "yes" or "no" after each one. If you say "no," give the sentence in some corrected form.

1. John helped me.
   Yes.
2. John helped himself.
   Yes.
3. John helped myself.
   No. (John helped me/himself. I helped myself. and so on.)
4. Mary asked John to help her.
5. Mary asked John to help himself.
6. Mary asked John to help herself.
7. Mary helped him.
8. Mary helped himself.
9. Mary and John helped themselves.
10. Mary and John helped each other.
11. Mary helped each other.
12. Mary and John helped himself.
13. Mary and John helped him.
14. Mary and John helped her.
15. Mary's father helped her.
16. Mary's father helped himself.
17. Mary's father helped herself.

18. Mary and John wanted each other's help.
19. Mary and John wanted themselves' help.
20. Mary and John helped themselves and each other.

16·30 ■ The word **own**, used to intensify the fact of belonging, always occurs with a possessive:

He now has his *own* house. (He doesn't have to live in somebody else's.)

Respond in each of the following situations with a suggestion using **own**, with stress.

1. Let me see your answers to that last exercise.
 Do your <u>own</u> work. / **Write your <u>own</u> answers.** / and so on.
2. Here, let me have a piece of your cake.
 Eat your <u>own</u> cake.
3. Do you mind if I call London from your apartment?
4. I'll just put your signature on this check.
5. Bring me your newspaper, will you?
6. You don't mind if I use your toothbrush, do you?
7. I need your handkerchief a second.
8. Can we hold a meeting at your house?
9. Let me borrow your car a couple of days.

16·31 ■ Do you have any comments about the following cartoon?

the CIRCUS of P.T. BIMBO   **by Howie Schneider**

Reprinted by permission of Newspaper Enterprise Association.

16-M • (See page 42.)

16-N • (See page 43.)

16-O • (See page 44.)

16-P • (See page 44.)

WRITING EXERCISES

16-A • For each of the following mini-dialogs write what you think the intonation should be for speaker B, based on the context. Then act out the dialog in class.

    1. A   I just met somebody you know.

e.g. B   Who?↗

    2. A   I just met the President.

e.g. B   Who?↗

    3. A   Somebody say something.

       B   What?

    4. A   Somebody said something.

       B   What?

    5. A   Somebody said "no."

       B   What?

    6. A   I just answered the door.

       B   Who was it?

    7. A   It was . . . [unintelligible]

       B   Who was it?

    8. A   Operator.

       B   Yes?

    9. A   Is this the operator?

       B   Yes.

   10. A   I told him to take the money.

       B   What did you tell him?

   11. A   I told you to take the money.

       B   What did you tell me?

   12. A   I told you.

       B   What did you tell me?

16-B • The sentences below have all been taken from Dialogs and Readings in Volume One. For each phrasal verb substitute a verb with the same meaning from the following list. Look up the meanings in the dictionary whenever you need to.

Writing Exercises   35

> appear   lower
> awaken   require
> disintegrate secure
> encounter   telephone

1. I'll probably either send a note or { call them up. / _telephone them_ }. [6A]

2. I { woke up / _____ } this morning with a pain in my left leg. [7A]

3. Bert would { show up / _____ } for work on Sunday, thinking it was Monday. [4C]

4. The hearing aid's fine. I { turned down / _____ } the volume that's all. [9A]

5. The old British Empire began to { break up / _____ } even before World War II. [14C]

6. Tim Walker was standing in line at the bank one day when his friend, Paul Katz, came in to { take out / _____ } a business loan. [5C]

7. A woman from a foreign country goes grocery shopping and { runs into / _____ } some problems. [13A]

8. This is thought to be an area where further exploration is { called for. / _____ } [15C]

16-C • For each word in *italics* in the following sentences, circle the word(s) that it refers to and draw a line conecting the two.

1. If you buy (an old house) you should be sure *it* is in good condition.

2. Get advice from someone *who* has experience in housing construction.

3. Purchase of a house is always an important event, so you don't want to buy *one* with a leaky roof, a poor foundation, or defective floors.

Unit 16

4. If you find some defects in an old house, or a newer *one that* is in need of repair, *which* the seller agrees to correct, get a written agreement *that* says *he* will correct *them*.

5. Be sure you know what the seller will do and then insist on *it*.

6. Check the rooms; make sure there is enough space in *them* for the purposes for *which they* were intended.

16-D • Pronouns with following modifiers take the form of **that** and **those** rather than **it, they,** or **them**. Compare these sentences:

Homeowners in New York pay higher taxes than *those in New Jersey.*
In New York people pay higher taxes than *they* do in New Jersey.
People in New York pay higher taxes than *they* ever have.

In the following sentences write **that, those, it, they,** or **them** in the blanks, whichever is called for.

1. The houses in the city are cheaper than *they* seem.
2. The houses in the city are cheaper than _____ in the suburbs.
3. The problem of providing enough housing is serious, and so is _____ of producing enough food.
4. The problem of providing enough housing is serious, and _____'s getting worse.
5. People renting flats or apartments don't pay as much as _____ renting houses.
6. People renting flats or apartments don't pay as much as _____ would if _____ were renting houses.
7. For people with more money to spend than _____ know what to do with and for _____ who worry about how _____ will be able to make ends meet there is at least one feeling that _____ both share: _____ dislike being taxed.

16-E • Each of the following sentences, all taken from student compositions, contains an error concerning the misuse or absence of pronouns. Change each sentence in such a way as to remove the error.

Writing Exercises

1. *The houses in this block are older than that block.

2. *I needed money, so I asked them to send me right away.

3. *My country is the one of the modern industrial nations.

4. *This course is harder than my former university.

5. *Tokyo has the only one formal concert hall in all of Japan.

6. *After we left the party went home.

16-F • The verbs listed below have somewhat similar meanings but different grammatical restrictions. Study the sample paragraph carefully, and then in each of the exercise sentences that follow cross out whatever verbs you think render the sentence unacceptable, as in the example.

alter *switch*
change *transform*
convert *turn (into)*
modify

When the rent went up he decided to {*change* / *switch*} apartments. Then he {*changed* / *converted* / *transformed* / *turned*} part of his new apartment into an office. He wasn't satisfied with the appearance, however, and decided to {*alter* / *change* / *modify* / *transform*} it. His concern {*changed* / *turned*} to pleasure when the work was finished.

(1) Do you think you might
  a. ~~alter~~
  b. change
  c. ~~convert~~
  d. ~~modify~~
  e. ~~switch~~
  f. ~~transform~~
  g. ~~turn~~
your mind and buy the house

after all? Or is (2) { a. altering / b. changing / c. converting / d. modifying / e. switching / f. transforming / g. turning } houses too much trouble right now? You could probably improve the kitchen by just making a few (3) { a. alterations. / b. changes. / c. conversions. / d. modifications. / e. switches. / f. transformations. / g. turns. } The original white walls have (4) { a. altered / b. changed / c. converted / d. modified / e. switched / f. transformed / g. turned } yellow over the years, but that's a small problem. As far as the coal furnace is concerned, it wouldn't be very difficult to (5) { a. alter / b. change / c. convert / d. modify / e. switch / f. transform / g. turn } to gas. This house could actually (6) { a. alter / b. change / c. convert / d. modify / e. switch / f. transform / g. turn } into a real asset.

16-G • COMPOUNDS

(Rewrite the following sentences rearranging the words in *italics* into a compound.)

1. Not everyone requires the same amount of *space for living*.

   not everyone requires the same amount of living space.

2. Others have niches where *members of the family* go to be alone.

   _____

3. Were you reared in a *family with two children*?

   _____

4. How much does a *house with three bedrooms* cost?

   _____

Writing Exercises

5. It is almost impossible to make changes in *needs for psychological space*.

   _____

6. It is almost impossible to make *changes in needs for psychological space*.

   _____

16-H • RESTATEMENT

(Complete the restatement by supplying the correct form.)

1. Psychological space needs *strongly influence* the choice of a house plan. *(have)*

   Psychological space needs *have a strong influence on the choice of a house plan.*

2. Not everyone in the world *requires* the same amount of living space. *(have)*

   Not everyone in the world _____

3. Economic pressures sometimes *modify* psychological space needs *a little*. *(make)*

   Economic pressures sometimes _____

4. It is almost impossible to *completely change* psychological space needs. *(make)*

   It is almost impossible to _____

5. Some people *definitely prefer* a lot of space around them. *(have)*

   Some people _____

16-I •
Find examples in this unit of all the different punctuation marks. Look especially at the Dialog and the Reading. On a separate sheet of paper write down a sentence or word-group that contains each of the punctuation marks.

16-J • In the following sentences write out the full form of the part in *italics*, crossing out any words that are no longer needed. Then draw a line under the word in each sentence that gets the heaviest stress.

1. I helped as much as they *wanted* ~~me to help~~.
2. I helped as much as they ~~did~~ *helped*.
3. We'll leave whenever you *prefer* _____
4. We'll leave whenever you *do* _____
5. She didn't give the answer that he *expected* _____
6. She didn't give the answer that he *did* _____
7. You can sit wherever you'*d like* _____
8. You can sit wherever I *do* _____
9. I don't believe he works as hard as she *thinks* _____
10. I don't believe he works as hard as she *does* _____
11. I want us to succeed just as much as you *do* _____
12. I want us to have just as much as you *do* _____

16-K • For each word in *italics* in the following paragraphs, circle the word(s) that it refers to and draw a line connecting the two.

After *they* saved a little money, (Howard and Ellen) wanted to buy a house. So they *did*. The floor plan was almost exactly the same as *that* of Ellen's parent's home, where *she* was reared. Buying *it* was not easy for *the young couple*, but Ellen was determined to go through with *it*. *She* could not stand living in their small apartment any longer. She wanted the kind of space *that* she had always lived with.

Howard couldn't quite understand *his* wife's insistence on moving to more spacious quarters. *Their* small apartment was big enough for *him*. In fact *it* was almost like the *one* he had lived in as a child. But *he* could remember his mother saying almost daily, "If only *I* had more room."[2]

---

[2]Landis, op. cit.

16-L • CLOZE

(In each blank space write a word that you think fits naturally.)

Problems arise when _____ (1) *needs of family members are in conflict with each* _____ (2). *A father needing a few quiet moments when he* _____ (3) *home from the office is in conflict with his* _____ (4) *who are eager to play with him or who* _____ (5) *simply missed him all day. A mother who cannot* _____ (6) *the noise level in the kitchen at dinner time* _____ (7) *a stewardess who becomes irritated with her roommates' laundry* _____ (8) *in the bathroom are defining their own needs for* _____ (9) *space.*[3]

16-M • Write the following representations as full sentences, without brackets, changing all second occurrences of nouns to pronouns.

1. I noticed Mary [looking at John in the mirror]

    I noticed Mary looking at John in the mirror.

2. I noticed Mary [looking at Mary in the mirror]

    _____

3. John told Mary [not to criticize Mary]

    _____

4. John told Mary [not to criticize John]

    _____

5. Mary wanted [John to prove to Mary [that Mary could win]]

    _____

6. Mary wanted [John to prove to Mary [that John could win]]

    _____

7. Mary wanted [John to prove to John [that John could win]]

    _____

8. John admitted to John [that Mary would probably do anything to avoid [Mary's inconveniencing John]]

    _____

[3]Landis, op. cit.

9. John admitted to Mary [that John would probably do anything to avoid [John's inconveniencing Mary]]

_____

10. John admitted to John [that Mary would probably do anything to avoid [~~Mary's~~ inconveniencing Mary]]

_____

11. John admitted to Mary [that John would probably do anything to avoid [Mary's inconveniencing John]]

_____

12. John admitted to John [that John would probably do anything to avoid [~~John's~~ inconveniencing John]]

_____

16-N • For each word in *italics* in the following paragraph, circle the word(s) that it refers to and draw a line connecting the two.

People can often live in a (household) *that* is very crowded without *it* adversely affecting their lives. *This* is possible if *they* spend most of *their* time outside the house, one investigator found. A particular family living in an apartment *that she* studied had twelve members, but for long periods of time only one of *them* was there. *One* worked a night shift; the youngest child would go to spend time with relatives; an older *one* often did *the same*; and the varying family members' schedules permitted *their* limited amount of space to be sufficient. *In this way* the family was still able to function as a unit, and they *did*.[4]

_____

[4]Landis, op. cit.

Writing Exercises

16-O • DICTATION

Listen to the reading of the following passage, and at the same time write in the blank spaces either **him**, **them**, **one**, **in**, or **and**, whichever you think you hear. Since these words usually carry weak stress, they will tend to sound alike. Therefore, let the context help you select.

*David went to the real estate office and asked _____ if they could
                                                     1
give _____ some help. He was ready to give up his apartment for a
        2
house _____ wanted to find _____ as soon as possible. The
         3   4
agent who talked to _____ told _____ they had several houses
                           5   6
_____ that part of town _____ showed _____ some pictures
    7   8   9
of _____. David told _____ he wanted to see _____, so
         10   11   12
they drove over to _____ of _____ that afternoon _____ the
                          13   14   15
agent's car. When David saw the house it almost made _____ faint.
                                                                16
The _____ he chose to look at was _____ he had lived _____
          17   18   19
years before _____ his youth.*
                    20

16-P • In 150 words or so describe the house or apartment in which you were reared. Write about the size of the house or apartment in relation to the size and needs of your family.

Unit 17

17-1 DIALOG

THE CLASSROOM

MR. KLEIN I think we'll start right out by discussing that reading on geology. Is there anybody who . . .
SINA Teacher!
MR. KLEIN Whose hand is that? I can't see you.
SINA Mine. About the reading . . . Some of the vocabularies are very hard.
ESMAT I think so too. I had to look up some words. What means "jigsaw puzzle"?
MR. KLEIN We'll look at all the new words in a minute. And it's "What does 'jigsaw puzzle' mean?" Esmat.
ESMAT Oh, I forgot.
MR. KLEIN By the way, Sina, you mean "Some of the *words* are very hard." "Vocabulary" is a collection of words.
SINA Then "words" and "vocabulary" work like "people" and "population."
MR. KLEIN That's right. And Sina, before I forget, in English you don't usually get the teacher's attention by calling "teacher."
SINA You don't? Well, what do you say? "Professor?"
MR. KLEIN No. Use the teacher's own name. Or, if you don't know it, say "sir" or "ma'am." You know my name by now, don't you?
SINA I didn't catch the question, sir.

VOCABULARY

look up	geology (geologist, geological)	usually
work	collection (collect)	

17-2 ■ DIALOG VARIATION

1. *I think we'll start right out by discussing the reading.*
   I think we'll start out right away by discussing the reading.
   I think we'll begin right away by discussing the reading.
2. *We'll look at all the new words in a minute.*
   All the new words will be looked at in a minute.
   We'll have a look at all the new words in a minute.
3. *You mean "Some of the words are very hard."*
   What you mean is "Some of the *words* are very hard."
   "Some of the *words* are very hard" is what you mean.
4. *You know my name by now, don't you?*
   I'm sure you must know my name by now.
   You certainly must know my name by now.

17-3 ■ QUESTIONS

1. What does Mr. Klein want the class to do first?
2. Does anyone interrupt him? Who?
3. How is the interruption made? Why?
4. How many corrections does Mr. Klein make?
5. Does he give the meaning of "jigsaw puzzle"?
6. Can you think of other word relationships like that between **words** and **vocabulary**, **people** and **population**?
7. What information does Sina's last sentence give us?

17-4 SOUND PATTERNS

In the Sound Patterns section of Unit 6, Volume One, we looked for the first time at the differences between tense and lax vowels in English and some of the spellings that represent these vowels. As we saw then, the presence or absence of written **e** in association with a preceding written vowel indicates the tense or lax form of that vowel:

lax			tense
not /nŏt/	+ e	=	**note** /nōt/
plan /plăn/	+ e	=	**plane** /plān/
quit /kwĭt/	+ e	=	**quite** /kwīt/
them /thĕm/	+ e	=	**theme** /thēm/
us /ŭs/	+ e	=	**use** /yūs/

The pairs of words above are related to each other only by sound; they are not connected in meaning or in function. Elsewhere in the language, however, the tense/lax distinction is often intricately bound up with meaning and grammatical function. For example, the **i** of **drive** is tense /drīv/, but the **i** of **driven** is lax /drĭvən/; the **a** of **nation** is tense /nāshən/, but the **a** of **national** is lax /năshənəl/.

17-5 ■ Without thinking very much about the "reasons" for the tense or lax vowel pronunciation, pronounce the following pairs of related words. See if you can "feel" which item of the pair should have the tense vowel, which one the lax vowel. The vowels in question are all in *italics*. (All pairs have been taken from the vocabulary lists in Volume One.)

1. gr*a*de / gr*a*dual
2. expl*a*natory / expl*a*in
3. n*a*ture / n*a*tural
4. l*a*ter / l*a*tter
5. b*a*th / b*a*the
6. m*ee*t / m*e*t
7. l*ea*ve / l*e*ft
8. f*e*lt / f*ee*l
9. rec*ei*ve / rec*e*ption
10. *e*quitable / *e*qual
11. l*i*ve / l*i*fe
12. dec*i*sion / dec*i*de
13. s*i*gn / s*i*gnature
14. prescr*i*ption / prescr*i*be
15. r*i*se / r*i*sen
16. m*o*de / m*o*dify
17. kn*o*w / kn*o*wledge
18. harm*o*nic / harm*o*nious
19. cl*o*set / cl*o*se
20. hypn*o*tic / hypn*o*sis
21. ass*u*me / ass*u*mption
22. prod*u*ctive / prod*u*ce

17-6 PHRASAL VERBS

—I had to *look up* some words.
—We'll *look at* all the new words in a minute.

Among phrasal verbs a basic distinction is made between verb + *particle* (e.g. **look** *up*)[1] and verb + *preposition* (e.g. **look** *at*). The two groups have some very different grammatical characteristics. One of these differences concerns the possible positions of the direct object:

I *looked up* a word in the dictionary. ~ I *looked* a word *up* in the dictionary.
I *looked at* a word in the dictionary. ≁ *I *looked* a word *at* in the dictionary.

17-A • (See page 61.)

SPEECH ACT

—Teacher!
—In English you don't usually get the teacher's attention by calling "teacher."

[1] For a list of verb + particle constructions, see Appendix A.

Section A

—What do you say? "Professor?"
—No. Use the teacher's own name, or "sir" or "ma'am."

17-7 ■ When summoning a person engaged in a particular occupation, you don't always call out his or her occupational title. As we have seen with "teacher," you often use "sir," "ma'am," or "miss."[2] Listed below are some occupational titles followed by some summoning situations. Act out the summons, and see if you can guess correctly whether or not you use the occupational title.

doctor	officer	usher
driver	porter	waiter
flight attendant	salesperson	waitress
nurse	teacher	

1. You're in a restaurant, you have your dinner in front of you, but you don't see a fork.
   Waiter! / Waitress! / Miss! (Would you bring me a fork, please?)
2. You're on a plane and you want to know if the plane is on schedule.
   Miss! (Are we on schedule?)
3. You're in a hospital and you want to know if it's all right to get out of bed.
4. You walk toward a police officer with the intention of asking directions to the nearest post office.
5. You're in a store and you want to ask the price of a sweater.
6. You want a taxi and you suddenly see one.
7. You're at a train station and you need help with your bags.
8. You've just sat down in a concert hall but you think you have the wrong seat.
9. You're on a crowded bus and you want to know if the bus stops at the next corner.
10. You're in class and you want to know how to address the school director.

17-8 ■ **DIALOG IMPROVISATION**

(Try to re-create or even improvise a variation of the Dialog at the beginning of this unit, as you remember it.)

A   Whose hand . . .

   [2]Notice especially, however, that the two most common forms of address, "Mr." /mĭstər/ and "Mrs." /mĭsəz/, are seldom used alone for summoning: *Oh Mister! *Oh Mrs.! "Mister" is used only by a child addressing a male stranger.

B Mine. About the reading . . .
C I think so too. What . . .
A It's "What . . .
C Oh, I . . .
A By the way, _____, you mean, "Some of the . . .
B Then "words" and "vocabulary" work . . .
A That's . . .

> More on Nouns and Noun Phrases
>
> —I think we'll start right out by discussing that reading on *geology*.

17·9 Many different factors determine the choice of article for a noun: **a(n)**, **the**, or nothing. Selection is based on the context of the sentence as well as on properties within the noun itself, such as countability (see 7-7) and genericness (see 7-27). Another such property of nouns is the uniqueness of reference; that is, whether the noun is *common* or *proper*. Note the following contrasts:

common	proper
I've never seen *a queen*.	I've never seen *the Queen*.
She's taking *geology*.	She's taking *Geology 132*.
They live in *a white house*.	They live in *the White House*.
The separate states became *united states*.	The separate states became *the United States*.

Notice the effect of relative clause formation on the form of a proper noun:
  —They live in *Córdoba, which* is a town in southern Spain.
  —No, they live in *the Córdoba* { *which* / *that* } is in Argentina.

17·10 The name of a country (e.g. **Arabia**) is usually inflected to produce the corresponding adjective (**Arabian**), the name of an inhabitant (**Arab**), and the name of the native language (**Arabic**). The regularity of this process, however, extends no further than sets of countries, each set having its own rules of inflection.[3] For example:

country	adjective	person	language	
China	Chinese	a Chinese	Chinese	(also **Japan, Portugal, Viet Nam, Malta,** and so on)
Russia	Russian	a Russian	Russian	(also **Italy, Hungary, Brazil, Australia,** and so on)

[3]See Appendix B for a complete list of these correspondences.

17-11 ■ Complete the sentence "We're going to read about . . ." with each of the items listed below. Supply **a(n)**, **the**, or nothing, as required. (Most of the vocabulary is taken from the Reading in Section C of this unit.)

1. sea
   We're going to read about the sea.
2. seawater
   We're going to read about seawater.
3. earth
4. Earth
5. moon
6. geology
7. geological discovery
8. ocean
9. oceans
10. Atlantic Ocean
11. missing continent
12. Gondwanaland
13. continent of Gondwanaland
14. missing continent of Gondwanaland
15. rocks
16. geological past
17. geological jigsaw puzzle
18. geology of the ocean

17-12 ■ Refer if necessary to the lists in Appendix B while acting out the following mini-dialogs:

1. Spain
   A **He's from Spain. He's a Spaniard.**
   B **Then he must speak Spanish.**
2. Japan
   A **He's from Japan. He's Japanese.**
   B **Then he must speak Japanese.**
3. China
4. Thailand
5. Turkey
6. Mexico
7. Poland
8. Egypt
9. Argentina
10. Germany
11. Iran
12. Israel
13. Korea

17-13 ■ Although count nouns such as **school, church, prison,** and **class** have to carry an article if they are in the singular (one of the basic principles practiced in Volume One), no article is needed if the noun reference is not a specific one: **He walked** *to school* / **He walked** *to a (certain) school;* **She attends** *church* / **She attends** *a (certain) church*. Respond to each of the following with a question beginning **Did he go to . . . ?**

1. He was tired.
   Did he go to (bed)?
2. He wanted to learn to type.
3. It was Sunday.

4. He didn't do his homework.
5. He wanted to get a degree.
6. He finished school.
7. He joined the navy.
8. He committed a crime.

17-14 ■ Look at this cartoon, and see if you can say why it's supposed to be funny.

Copyright, 1975, Universal Press Syndicate
"I think I'll sell all my jewelry. I need the five dollars."

17-B • (See page 61.)

17-C • (See page 62.)

17-D • (See page 63.)

17-15 READING (183 words)

MISSING PIECE FOUND IN CONTINENT 'PUZZLE'

NEW YORK (AP)—British and American scientists, drilling into the floor of the South Atlantic, have found the last piece of a great continental jigsaw puzzle, it was announced Thursday. It is the final piece of evidence that South America and Africa were once part of the vast supercontinent, Gondwanaland, along with Australia, New Zealand, and Antarctica.

The scientists found a finger-shaped extension of the Falkland Plateau, under two miles of water and sediment, reaching 750 miles eastward from the Falkland Islands to a point 1600 miles from the South American mainland.

Rocks dug up from the submerged continent, by scientists from Columbia University and the University of Birmingham who were aboard a research ship, are believed to be more than 600 million years old—the oldest ever brought up from the bottom of any ocean.

"It completes the puzzle," said a scientist from Columbia. "All the other points along the Atlantic contours of the two continents had been proven by various scientific means to have been joined long ago. "Now, with deep-sea drilling, we've identified a large area of submerged continent, and the last piece is in place."[4]

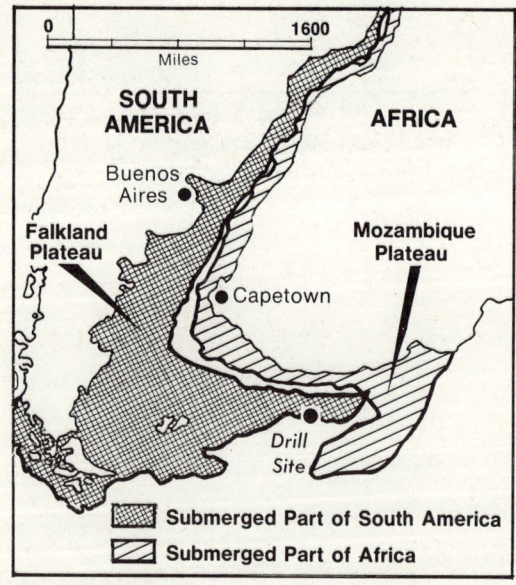

Reprinted by permission of the *Los Angeles Times*.

PUZZLE COMPLETED—*Map locates drill site that provided final piece of evidence that South America and Africa were once part of a supercontinent.*

[4]Adapted from *The Los Angeles Times,* July 19, 1974. Reprinted by the permission of The Associated Press.

VOCABULARY

drill	site	vast
announce (announcement)	piece	deep (depth)
reach	jigsaw puzzle	
dig	evidence (evident)	once
submerge (submersion)	finger	along with
bring up	shape	eastward
prove (proof)	extension (extend, extent, extensive)	in place
identify (identification, identity)	mile	
	sediment	
	point	
	rock	
	ship	
	million	
	bottom	
	ocean	
	contour	
	sea	

17-16 ■ INCLUDED MEANING

(For each of the following passages pick the one statement whose meaning is part of the meaning of the passage.)

1. *British and American scientists, drilling into the floor of the South Atlantic, have found the last piece of a great continental jigsaw puzzle, it was announced Thursday.*
   a. The jigsaw puzzle was announced on Thursday.
   b. The last piece of the puzzle was found on the continent.
   c. The drilling was done by British and American scientists.
   d. The floor of the South Atlantic found the last piece.
2. *The scientists found a finger-shaped extension of the Falkland Plateau, under two miles of water and sediment, reaching 750 miles eastward from the Falkland Islands to a point 1600 miles from the South American mainland.*
   a. The plateau extension is two miles long.
   b. The plateau extension is 750 miles long.
   c. The plateau extension is 1600 miles long.
   d. The sentence doesn't tell us how long the plateau extension is.
3. *Rocks dug up from the submerged continent, by scientists from Columbia University and the University of Birmingham who were aboard a research ship, are believed to be more than 600 million years old—the oldest ever brought up from the bottom of any ocean.*
   a. The University of Birmingham is 600 million years old.
   b. The research ship is 600 million years old.

Section C

c. The submerged continent is 600 million years old.
   d. The rocks are 600 million years old.
4. *"It completes the puzzle," said a scientist from Columbia. "All the other points along the Atlantic contours of the two continents had been proven by various scientific means to have been joined long ago."*
   a. The puzzle was complete long ago.
   b. Science has proved that the two continents were once joined.
   c. The contours had been proven by scientific means.
   d. The Atlantic has a long contour.

17-17 ■ QUESTIONS

1. What happened on "Thursday"?
2. Was the "last piece" found a long time before the article was written? How do you know?
3. Does Gondwanaland belong to the United Nations? If not, why not?
4. Would you like to live on the Falkland Plateau?
5. How do you write "600 million" using only numbers?
6. What ocean do the oldest rocks come from?
7. Is Gondwanaland a very recent discovery?
8. Do Africa and South America "fit together"?

17-E • VOCABULARY RELATIONS (See page 64.)

17-18 COMPOUNDS

—The scientists found a *finger-shaped extension* of the Falkland Plateau . . .

Many nouns can become adjectives by adding **-ed**. The meaning relationship is **A has X = A is X-ed**:

He *has talent*. = He's *talented*.
He's a *musician with talent*. = He's a *talented musician*.
He's a *musician with a lot of talent*. = He's a *very talented musician*.

Thus, **finger-shaped** = in/with the shape of a finger and **finger-shaped** extension = extension in/with the shape of a finger.

17-F • (See page 65.)

17-G • RESTATEMENT (See page 66.)

17-19 PUNCTUATION

The use in English of initial *capital letters* serves above all to specify proper nouns: names of persons (**John Brown**), places (**A**frica), works of art (**H**amlet), days of the week (**T**hursday), and months of the year (**September**), but not the seasons (**s**ummer). In addition, sentences begin with capital letters, and we use capitals in accompanying titles:

Mrs. Ward
Dr. Hall
The University of Birmingham
Columbia University

17-H • (See page 67.)

17-20 ■ READING IMPROVISATION

(Complete each of the following sentences with what you remember from the Reading.)

1. British and American scientists have found . . .
2. It is the final piece of evidence that . . .
3. The scientists found a finger-shaped extension of . . .
4. Rocks dug up from the submerged continent are believed to . . .
5. All the other points along the Atlantic contours of . . .
6. It completes the puzzles, and the last piece . . .

Possessive Form

—Teacher!
—*Whose* hand is that? I can't see you.
—*Mine*.
—You don't usually get the *teacher's* attention by calling "teacher."

17-21 In English, *possessive* form expresses many more relationships than that of mere possession. (See Volume I: 12-21, 14-25, and 15-22.) Thus, although we can say that things that a person "possesses" belong to that person, it doesn't make much sense to say, for example, that "the teacher *possesses* attention" (**the teacher's attention**) or that "the

Section D

world *possesses* problems" (**the world's problems**) or that "England *possesses* a Prime Minister" (**England's Prime Minister**). This possessive *form*, which we'll say is Noun₁'s Noun₂, can often be restated as Noun₂ **of** Noun₁: **the attention of the teacher, the problems of the world, the Prime Minister of England.** Although the two forms are interchangeable much of the time, the 's form is more likely with people and higher animals (**John's nose** ≠ *the nose of John**), the **of** form with the impersonal or abstract (**the price of peace** ≠ *peace's price**).

17-22 The information question word for possession and the relative marker for possession are the same: **whose**.

                      whose
            Is that ~~John's~~ hand?
   ***Whose* hand is that?**

                    whose
   I can't see the student [~~The student's~~ hand is up]
   I can't see the student *whose* hand is up.

17-23 ■ Complete each of the following according to the model.

1. I sat in John's chair.
   I sat in John's chair and he sat in mine.
2. John sat in my chair.
   John sat in my chair and I sat in his.
3. Mary drove my car.
4. We liked their house.
5. You took her pen.
6. They need our help.
7. John told me about his vacation.
8. I gave John my phone number.
9. Mary tried my cigarettes.
10. We believed their story.
11. You listened to her arguments.
12. They were trying to get our attention.

17-24 ■ Speaker A will inquire about the ownership of various things in the immediate vicinity. Speaker B's answer will be restated by Speaker C as indicated.

1. A **Whose book is this?**
   B **It belongs to (Esmat).**
   C **Yes, it's Esmat's.**

2. A **Whose glasses are these?**
   B and so on.

17-25 ■ The N_1 of N_2 constructions that are restatable as N_2's N_1 are generally those representing right-to-left *predication*: **the King of Spain** (Spain has a king) ~ **Spain's king**, but **the Kingdom of Spain** (The kingdom is Spain) ✝ ***Spain's kingdom**. Restate the following phrases in the 's form wherever possible. If restatement is impossible, say "No."

1. the population of Rome
   Rome's population
2. the city of Rome
   No. (*Rome's city)
3. the Queen of England
4. the news of the accident
5. the extension of the plateau
6. the arrival of the train
7. the mainland of South America
8. the tail of the dog
9. the attention of the class
10. the guest of honor
11. the importance of geology
12. the problems of the world
13. the revolution of the earth
14. the interior of the earth
15. the teacher of geology

17-26 ■ As first explained in 12-21, a phrase like **Harry's desk** can mean not only **the desk that Harry owns**, but also **the desk that Harry is sitting at/working at**, or even **the desk that Harry usually sits at (but isn't necessarily sitting at, at this moment)**. What possible meanings, therefore, can you suggest for the following?

1. Harry's answer
   the answer that Harry gave/will give/received/will receive/ and so on.
2. Harry's trip
3. Harry's student
4. Harry's life
5. Harry's bed
6. Harry's work
7. a person's opinion
8. yesterday's newspaper
9. our last argument
10. the world's problems

17-I • (See page 67.)

17-J • (See page 68.)

17-K • DICTATION (See page 68.)

> **'s vs. of**
>
> —I couldn't get *the geology teacher's attention*.
> —You mean *the attention of the geology teacher in our 1:30 class*?

17-27 Although the **'s** and **of** forms of possession are often interchangeable, there is sometimes a reason for choosing one over the other. If the **of** form were not selected in the second line of the above dialog, for example, we would have

> *****You mean *the geology teacher in our 1:30 class's attention*?

In other words, the noun phrase to which **'s** attaches has to be fairly short, otherwise we choose the form with a preposition.

Use of the **of** form, however, can sometimes result in unwanted ambiguity:

> . . . *the wife* of *our geology teacher, who* knows nothing about geology

Although a relative clause, like **who knows nothing about geology**, can modify either noun in a complex noun phrase such as the above, it will modify only the *head noun* if we switch to the **'s** form:

> . . . *our geology teacher's wife, who* knows nothing about geology

17-28 ■ Give two corresponding noun phrases for each of the following sentences, one with **'s**, the other with **of**. Do not repeat the words "something" or "somewhere".

1. The geologists discovered (something).
   the geologists' discovery
   the discovery of the geologists
2. The search continued.
3. The continent broke up.
4. The scientists believed (something).
5. The plateau extended (somewhere).
6. The expedition revealed (something).
7. The missing piece was located.

8. The puzzle is complete.
9. The plan was modified.
10. The continent was discovered.
11. The area was identified.
12. Gondwanaland was reconstructed.

17-29 ■ Titles, headlines, captions, and telegraphic English obey grammar rules that are somewhat different from those of conventional English. (See also exercise 20-Q.) Usually omitted in English of this kind, among other things, are articles. Look again at the caption under the map on page 52 and translate it aloud into conventional English.

17-L • (See page 68.)

17-M • (See page 69.)

17-N • (See page 70.)

17-O • (See page 70.)

17-P • (See page 70.)

17-Q • (See page 71.)

17-R • (See page 71.)

WRITING EXERCISES

17-A • Each of the following sentences contains a phrasal verb that you've seen before. Wherever possible rewrite each sentence with the direct object splitting the phrase (verb - object - particle); otherwise copy the sentence as it is (verb - preposition - object).

1. I *turned down* the volume on my hearing aid.
   I turned the volume down on my hearing aid.

2. She went shopping and *ran into* some problems.
   She went shopping and ran into some problems.

3. It was the noise that *woke up* the children.
   _____

4. This problem *calls for* further thought.
   _____

5. We started out to *look for* a famous church.
   _____

6. Why don't you *call up* your friends or send them a note?
   _____

7. You have to *fill out* this form.
   _____

8. It must be time to *get on* the plane.
   _____

9. Did you *find out* anything?
   _____

10. We should *get off* the bus at the next corner.
    _____

17-B • Geographical features do not always display consistent grammar, e.g. **China Lake** (California) / **the China Sea**. The use of a prepositional phrase, however, usually implies the definite article as well. Compare: **Los Angeles County** / **the County of Los Angeles**. In the blanks below write **the** wherever required, otherwise write **X** (for nothing).

1. _the_ United States
2. _X_ America
3. _____ France
4. _____ Soviet Union
5. _____ French Republic
6. _____ England

Writing Exercises   61

7. ____ United Kingdom
8. ____ New York City
9. ____ City of New York
10. ____ United Arab Republic
11. ____ British Isles
12. ____ Oxford Road
13. ____ Oxford road
14. ____ Panama Canal
15. ____ British Commonwealth
16. ____ Mount Everest
17. ____ Himalayas
18. ____ Matterhorn
19. ____ Holland
20. ____ Netherlands
21. ____ Hague
22. ____ Cairo
23. ____ Cairo, Illinois
24. ____ Cairo in Illinois
25. ____ Philippines
26. ____ Alaska
27. ____ U.S.A.
28. ____ Canadian border
29. ____ United Nations
30. ____ Caspian Sea
31. ____ Lake Tanganyika
32. ____ Mississippi River
33. ____ Ganges
34. ____ Madagascar
35. ____ island of Madagascar
36. ____ Europe
37. ____ South America
38. ____ southern part of Korea
39. ____ South Korea
40. ____ Washington, D.C.
41. ____ District of Columbia
42. ____ Cape Horn
43. ____ Cape of Good Hope
44. ____ Sahara
45. ____ Columbia University
46. ____ University of Birmingham
47. ____ Victoria Falls
48. ____ George Washington Bridge
49. ____ Queen Mary (person)
50. ____ Queen Mary (ship)
51. ____ Aswan Dam
52. ____ Bay of Bengal
53. ____ Hudson Bay
54. ____ Persian Gulf

17-C • Some nouns, called *collective nouns*, have plural force, even though they are not inflected for the plural. **People** is such a noun. Listed below are sentences some of whose subjects are collective nouns. Cross out **is** or **are** in each example, whichever is incorrect.

1. The police ~~is~~ / are coming.

2. The policeman is / ~~are~~ coming.

3. Our family is/are very small.

4. The audience is/are very large.

5. The audience is/are raising their hands.

6. Congress is/are in session.

7. Parliament is/are having a debate.

8. The committee is/are meeting.

9. The meeting is/are coming to order.

10. Your data is/are incorrect.

11. The news is/are on at 6:00.

12. The news media is/are criticizing the goverment.

13. The guests is/are each bringing something.

14. Each of the guests is/are bringing something.

17-D • One handy rule of thumb for the use of articles in English is that any count noun used in the singular will almost always have to have something with it: **a(n), the, one, this, that, my, his,** and so on. (See also 7-7.) For example,

That's { an / the / one / my / ... } answer. But not *That's answer.

The following passage contains many singular count nouns with a missing article. Put a circle around each such noun that you find and write in the article that you think is required.

We can define (sea) [the] as entire body of salt water of Earth. Sea, in which oceanographers and geologists cooperate in research, covers 71 percent of Earth's surface. Research at sea is difficult and expensive and requires use

Writing Exercises

of very specialized instruments and equipment, including specially constructed oceanographic research ships. Until recently, therefore, growth of knowledge of topography and sediments of sea floor followed behind parallel study of the lands. But, with the perfection of new devices for sounding sea bottom and for sampling its sediments, teams of seagoing oceanographers, geologists, and geophysicists have begun to put submarine geology on solid foundation. Diving geologists have photographed sea-floor areas at depths as great as 150 feet. In January 1960 two observers descended in bathyscaph to 35,800 feet, where they viewed sea floor in deep Marianas Trench in western Pacific Ocean. Feat opens way to obtaining geological information by direct observation at depths equal to average depth of sea.[5]

17-E • VOCABULARY RELATIONS

The verbs listed below have somewhat similar meanings but different grammatical restrictions. Study the sample paragraph carefully, and then in each of the exercise sentences that follow cross out whatever verbs you think render the sentence unacceptable, as in the example.

>   ascend   lift
>   bring up   raise
>   come up   rise
>   climb

The salvage company had two choices: they could either $\left\{\begin{array}{l}\textit{lift}\\ \textit{raise}\end{array}\right\}$ the sunken ship out of the water or try to find and *bring up* the cargo. They decided to $\left\{\begin{array}{l}\textit{lift}\\ \textit{raise}\end{array}\right\}$ the ship. As it began to $\left\{\begin{array}{l}\textit{ascend}\\ \textit{rise}\\ \textit{come up}\\ \textit{climb}\end{array}\right\}$, the divers had to

---

[5]Adapted from *Introduction to Physical Geology*, by C. R. Longwell and R. F. Flint. Copyright © 1962 by John Wiley & Sons, Inc. Reprinted by permission of John Wiley & Sons, Inc.

quickly { ascend / climb } the ladder. It was near high tide, and the water was still rising.

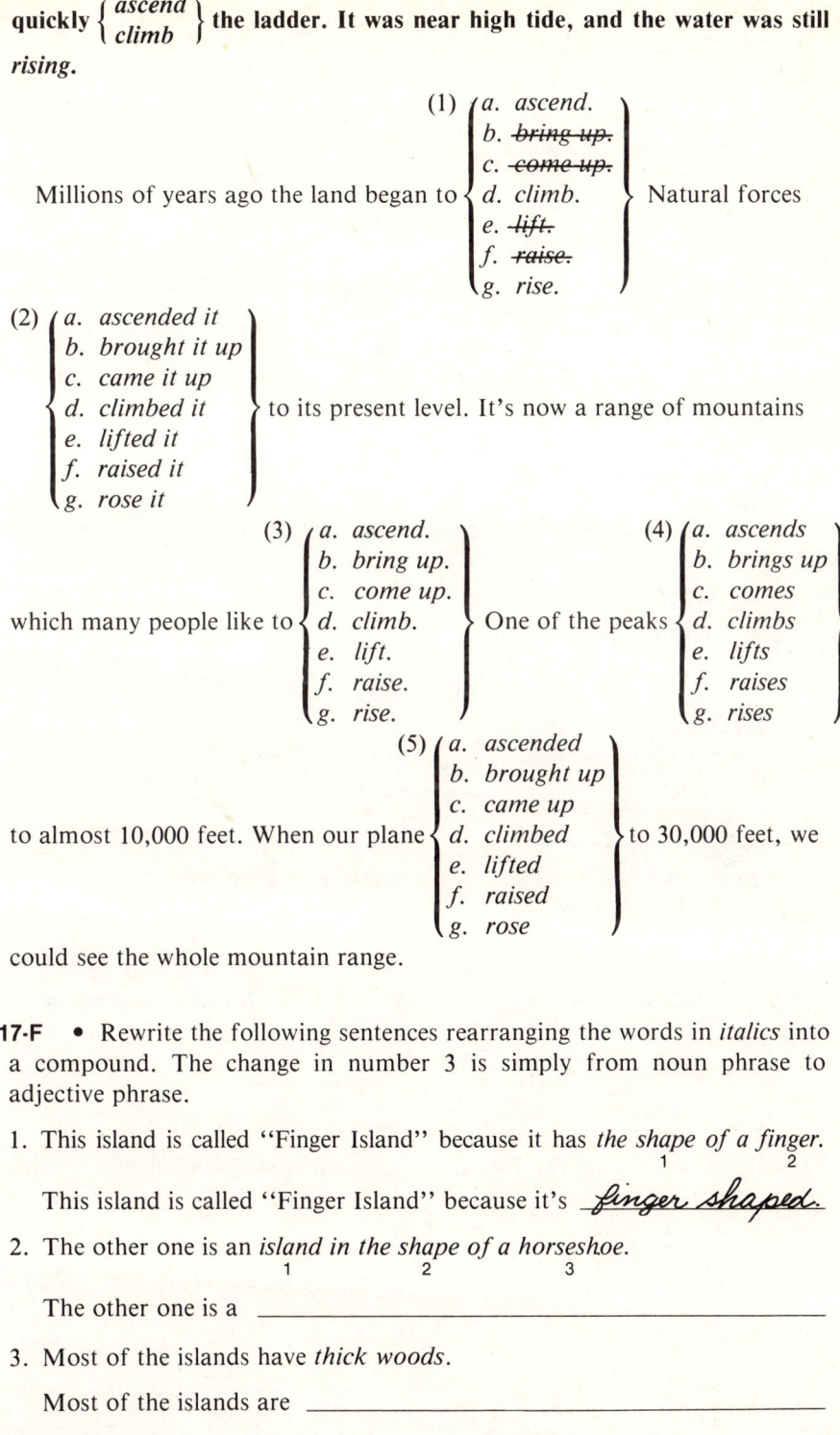

17-F • Rewrite the following sentences rearranging the words in *italics* into a compound. The change in number 3 is simply from noun phrase to adjective phrase.

1. This island is called "Finger Island" because it has *the shape of a finger*.
                                                              1   2

   This island is called "Finger Island" because it's *finger shaped*.

2. The other one is an *island in the shape of a horseshoe*.
                         1   2   3

   The other one is a _____

3. Most of the islands have *thick woods*.

   Most of the islands are _____

Writing Exercises   65

4. *Rocks with sharp edges* are everywhere.
       1   2

   _____ are everywhere.

5. Here's an island with the shape of a *star with five points*.
                                    1   2

   Here's an island with the shape of a _____

6. Here's an island with the *shape of a star with five points*.
                           1   2   3

   Here's an island with a _____

7. Here's an *island with the shape of a star with five points*.
            1   2   3   4

   Here's a _____

17-G • RESTATEMENT

(Complete the restatement by supplying the correct form. Use a compound in number 5.)

1. It was *briefly announced* Thursday that scientists have drilled into the ocean floor. *(make)*

   A brief announcement was made Thursday that scientists have drilled into the ocean floor.

2. We've *positively identified* a large area of submerged continent. *(make)*

   _____ of a large area of submerged continent.

3. There is *clear evidence* that the two continents were once joined. (—)

   It is _____ that the two continents were once joined.

4. They will *prove convincingly* that the plateau is part of Gondwanaland. *(give)*

   They will _____
   _____

5. The plateau *extends* for 750 miles eastward from the mainland. *(have)*

   The plateau _____ from the mainland.

6. The ocean is the *very deepest* at this point. *(have)*

   The ocean _____
   _____

17-H • In the following paragraph change small letters to capitals wherever necessary.

~~t~~T he author, ~~d~~D r. ~~c~~C ameron, received the b.a. and m.a. degrees from the university of north carolina and the ph.d. degree from harvard university. he has been a member of the department of geology at harvard since the end of world war II. he is also a geologist with the united states geological survey. his other books include "rocks of north america" and "outline of historical geology."

17-I • Write the sentence that corresponds to each of the following phrases. (See also Volume I, 14-25 and 15-22.)

1. the scientists' completion of the puzzle

   The scientists (have) completed the puzzle.

2. the puzzle's completion by the scientists

   The puzzle has been/was completed by the scientists.

3. the geologist's identification of Gondwanaland

   _____

4. Gondwanaland's identification by the geologists

   _____

5. Columbus's discovery of America in 1492

   _____

6. America's discovery by Columbus in 1492

   _____

7. the university's collection of the data

   _____

8. the announcement by the scientists of the existence millions of years ago of a continent called "Gondwanaland"

   _____

   _____

Writing Exercises

17-J • Use the following bits of information to write a brief description of Gondwanaland.

> hypothetical continent
> Mesozoic era
> linking of land masses
> later separation
> parts of South America, Australia, Africa, India, Antarctica

17-K • **DICTATION**

(As you listen to the reading of the following passage fill in the missing words. For some of the blanks there is nothing missing.)

_____ Professors Dalziel and Barker made their discovery as
   1

_____ cochief scientists on _____ recently completed 36th leg of
   2   3

_____ Deep Sea Drilling Project, which ended in _____ Rio de
   4   5

Janeiro _____ May 22. _____ project is being run by _____
             6   7   8

Scripps Institution of _____ Oceanography of _____ U.C. San
                           9   10

Diego for _____ National Science Foundation. _____ Falkland
               11   12

Plateau extension fills in what had been _____ unknown gap in
                                                      13

_____ reconstruction of _____ Gondwanaland, which began
   14   15

breaking up 200 million years ago.[6]

17-L • For each of the following write wherever possible the corresponding noun phrase in **'s**. If the **'s** form would result in unacceptable English, write the form that uses a preposition instead. Recall that the preposition will sometimes need to be **by** rather than **of** (Volume I, 15-22).

1. The institute initiated the project.

   the institute's initiation of the project

2. The Scripps Institute of Oceanography initiated the project.

   the initiation of the project by the Scripps Institute of Oceanogra[phy]

3. Gondwanaland has been reconstructed.

   _____

4. The submerged continent of Gondwanaland has been reconstructed.

   _____

---

[6]*The Los Angeles Times,* op. cit.

5. Scientists have reconstructed Gondwanaland.

_____

6. A group of British and American scientists have reconstructed Gondwanaland.

_____

7. The area has been identified.

_____

8. A large area of submerged continent has been identified.

_____

9. Scientists have identified a large area.

_____

10. Scientists aboard a research ship have identified a large area.

_____

17-M • For each pair below pick the phrase that avoids ambiguity and that gives a plausible meaning to the whole. Cross out the other phrase.

1. a. the reconstruction of Gondwanaland,
   b. ~~Gondwanaland's reconstruction,~~ } which began breaking up 200 million years ago

2. a. ~~the reconstruction of Gondwanaland,~~
   b. Gondwanaland's reconstruction, } which has only recently been discussed for the first time

3. a. the discovery of the continent,
   b. the continent's discovery, } which has been submerged for a long time

4. a. the discovery of the submerged continent,
   b. the submerged continent's discovery, } which scientists from two countries have claimed credit for

5. a. the completion of the puzzle,
   b. the puzzle's completion, } which was the work mainly of two scientists

6. a. the identification of the submerged area,
   b. the submerged area's identification, } which covers many hundreds of square miles

7. a. the influence of this famous institution,
   b. this famous institution's influence, } which few people are aware of

8. a. one of the criticisms of this project,
   b. one of this project's criticisms, } which will soon be dropped

Writing Exercises   69

9. a. the wives of several of the scientists,
   b. several of the scientists' wives, } who have some scientific knowledge themselves

10. a. one of the sons of the scientist,
    b. one of the scientist's sons, } who was very much like his own father

17-N • The four phrases below represent only two different meanings. Draw a line connecting each pair of phrases that have the same meaning.

1. one of the scientist's brothers
2. the brother of one of the scientists
3. one of the brothers of the scientist
4. one of the scientists' brothers

17-O • Each of the following sentences, taken from student compositions, are faulty. Change each sentence in such a way as to remove the errors.

1. *One of temple in Kyoto made from only wood and no nail.

2. *We have thirty-two alphabet in Persian's language.

3. *Regardless of their status, almost of all young men, either a prince or a poor man, will spend their time as a monk.

4. *If any countrys devaluation his currency without consult the other country we have problem.

5. *My father company is making many progresses this recent years.

17-P • In the blank spaces write **a(n), the**, a possessive, or nothing, as required. Many of the blanks allow a choice. Look up any unfamiliar words in the dictionary.

This piece of _____(1)_____ puzzle remained _____(2)_____ dry land, with _____(3)_____ Mediterranean climate, for 50 million years as _____(4)_____ continents gradually spread apart in _____(5)_____ continuing process of _____(6)_____ continental drift. Then it began to sink. "It went down rela-

tively quickly, as _____ geologist would say, and reached _____
               7   8
present depth about 80 million years ago," reported one of _____ re-
                                                            9
searchers. Not until _____ Professors Dalziel and Barker and
                        10
_____ colleagues bit into it with _____ drill did anyone know it
   11   12
was _____ old piece of _____ Gondwanaland.⁷
      13   14

17-Q • Rewrite the following sequences[8] as a full paragraph by moving something into subject position, changing the form of the sentences in brackets, and choosing an appropriate verb tense.

certain – [The ocean bottom holds the answers to important geological questions]

may reveal – *the rocks of the deep ocean floor* [AND *The rocks of the deep ocean floor* have been altered much less than the land masses] – *an extensive record of Earth's past* [AND *The extensive record of Earth's past* includes *the first two billion years* [*The first two billion years* are now so little known]]

may tell – the sea more than the land – [Why are there continents and sea bottoms?]

possible – [tell – it – [How did the world begin?] and [How will the world end?]]

17-R • How do you think the world began? Do your beliefs come from religion or from science, or both? Write your explanation in the form of one or two paragraphs. Begin with something like **I believe that the planet Earth . . .**

---

⁷*The Los Angeles Times,* op. cit.
⁸Adapted from *Rock, Time, and Landforms,* by Jerome Wyckoff. (New York: Harper & Row, 1966.)

Unit 18

18-1 DIALOG

THE ACCIDENT

MARIO Paul! What happened? How come you're limping?
PAUL Somebody smashed into my new VW. I'm not really hurt, thanks to my seat belt.
MARIO What about your leg?
PAUL Just a little sprain. I'd have broken my leg but for that seat belt.
MARIO How did it happen? The accident, I mean.
PAUL Well, you see, this big new station wagon was about three feet behind me. I stepped on the brake to avoid hitting a bicycle. But the station wagon couldn't stop, so he hit me.
MARIO It's obvious he was to blame. A new station wagon and a new VW and he smashes them up. Wow!
PAUL That's right. I emphasized that he was driving too close. But he claims it was due to faulty brakes. What do you think he'd say that for?
MARIO Why? Out of fear, or to avoid admitting that he wasn't driving the right way.
PAUL Yeah . . . in order to fool the insurance company, probably. Otherwise they'll classify him as a careless driver and make him pay a higher rate.
MARIO You know, I can't feel sorry for him and his accident. It serves him right for driving such an enormous car.
PAUL But Mario, I'm the one he happened to hit!

VOCABULARY

limp (limp)	accident	obvious
smash	sprain (sprain)	faulty (fault)
avoid (avoidance)	foot/feet	careless
hit/hit/hit	brake (brake)	enormous (enormity)
blame (blame)	bicycle	
emphasize (emphasis, emphatic)		thanks to
claim (claim)		due to
fool		probably
classify (classification)		otherwise

18-2 ■ DIALOG VARIATION

1. *I stepped on the brake.*
   I braked.
   I put on the brakes.
   I applied the brakes.
2. *It's obvious he was to blame.*
   Obviously he was to blame.
   Obviously the blame was his.
   Obviously it was his fault.
3. *What do you think he'd say that for?*
   Why do you think he'd say that?
   What reason do you think he'd have for saying that?
4. *Out of fear.*
   From fear.
   Because of fear.
   Because he's afraid.
5. *In order to fool the insurance company.*
   To fool the insurance company.
   So as to fool the insurance company.
   For the purpose of fooling the insurance company.
6. *It serves him right for driving such an enormous car.*
   It's his fault for driving such an enormous car.

18-3 ■ QUESTIONS

1. What was the value of Paul's seat belt?
2. Did Paul have a broken leg?
3. How did the accident actually happen?
4. Whose fault was it, do you think?
5. Did faulty brakes cause the accident?
6. Did Paul think the other driver was being honest?
7. Did the other driver admit that it was his fault?
8. Are Mario and Paul good friends?

18-4 SOUND PATTERNS

There are two common English verb *suffixes* or word endings that often carry *causal* meaning: **-ize** and **-ify**. Thus, **I** *emphasized* **that** . . . = **I** *made* **it** *emphatic* **that** . . . , **They'll** *classify* **him as** . . . = **They'll** *give* **him a** *classification* **of** . . . It is possible to predict to some extent whether a word root will take the **-ize** or **-ify** endings. No root whose final syllable carries the main stress can take the **-ize** suffix, which therefore rules out roots of one syllable as well: **clássize/clássify, *inténsize/inténsify*. Furthermore, almost no common roots of more than two or three syllables take the suffix **-ify**: **democratify/democratize*. Essentially, therefore, it is only with roots of two or three syllables having main stress on the first that the choice of ending cannot be predicted: **(pérson)** *personify/*personize*, **(súmmary)** *summarize/*summarify*.

The *stress pattern* of words containing the **-ize** or **-ify** suffix is regular and predictable. The addition of **-ize** to a word does not affect the stress pattern; the main stress is on the same syllable before and after suffixation: **sýmbol/sýmbolize, famíliar/famíliarize**. The addition of **-ify** does affect the stress pattern, however; the main stress, regardless of where it was in the root, will always be on the syllable preceding **-ify**: **sólid/solídify, pérson/persónify, simple/simplify**.

18-A • (See page 91.)

18-5 Virtually all verbs ending in the suffix **-ify** can become nouns by the additional suffixation of **-ation**, with one further modification: **-ify + -ation = -ification**. The **-átion** suffix always carries the main stress (Volume I, 8-6), which brings about a further stress shift for the examples cited above: **persónify/personificátion, símplify/simplificátion**. For those verbs ending in **-ize** that form nouns ending in **-ation**, the same stress-shift principle applies: **cólonize/colonizátion, famíliarize/familiarizátion**. Notice, therefore, that the process of word building in English sometimes involves more than one stress movement: **pérson/persónify/personificátion**. Failure to observe these rules of stress placement represents one of the commonest errors made by students studying English as a foreign language.

18-B • (See page 91.)

18-6 PHRASAL VERBS

—The station wagon couldn't stop, so he hit me.
—A new station wagon and a new VW and he *smashes them up*.

Phrasal verbs consist of either verb + preposition or verb + particle. The noun object of a verb-particle construction has two possible positions, as pointed out in 17-6: **He smashed** 1 up 2

the cars

However, if the object is not a noun but a pronoun, the only position possible is the first: **He smashed** 1 up 2

them

18-7 ■ Answer the following questions according to the models. The noun object in the question should be a pronoun in the answer.

1. When did she look up the information?
   She looked it up yesterday.
2. When did she look at the information?
   She looked at it yesterday.
3. When did she take out the loan?
4. When did she look for the money?
5. When did she work out the solution?
6. When did she bring up the problem?
7. When did she get on the plane?
8. When did she find out the news?
9. When did she smash into the car?
10. When did she get off the bus?
11. When did she fill out the form?
12. When did she take part in the event?

SPEECH ACT

—What happened? *How come* you're limping?
—Somebody smashed into my new VW. . . . He claims it was due to faulty brakes.
—*What* do you think he'd say that *for*?

18-8 **How come** questions very informally the cause or reason for something. (Notice the absence of question word-order in this construction.) **What . . . for** is typically the form for questioning purpose, although reason and purpose are often not distinguishable. **Why** can question either reason or purpose, as evident in ambiguous sentences such as

Why does he tell lies? = { *How come* he tells lies? (What makes him?)
{ *What* does he tell lies *for*? (What does he hope to gain?)

18-C ● (See page 92.)

18-9 ■ DIALOG IMPROVISATION

(Try to re-create or even improvise a variation of the Dialog at the beginning of this unit, as you remember it.)

A What happened? How come . . .
B Somebody smashed into my new VW. I'm not . . .
A How did it . . .
B Well, you see, this big station wagon . . .
A It's obvious he . . .
B He claims it was faulty brakes. What do you . . .
A Why? Out of fear, or to avoid . . .
B Yeah, in order to fool . . .
A You know, I can't feel sorry . . .
B But I'm the one . . .

> Cause and Effect
>
> —How did it happen?
> —This big new station wagon . . . behind me . . . couldn't stop, *so* he hit me.

18-10 The cause and effect relationship can be expressed in English through a variety of constructions. Here are some possibilities:

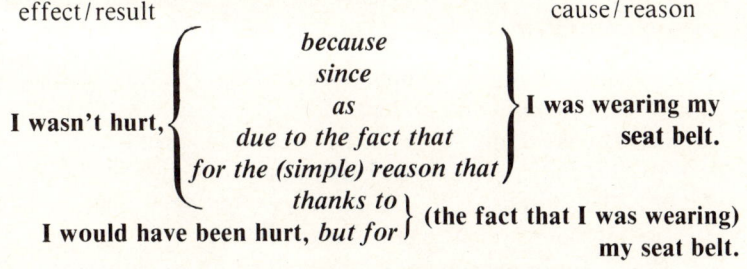

Section B

These constructions are not freely interchangeable, however, as will be seen throughout the rest of this unit. Their use is limited by certain rules of grammar and conditions of appropriateness.

18-11 Only two of the above constructions can serve as answers to the questioning of cause or reason:

A How come you weren't ⎱ hurt?
    Why weren't you ⎰

B Because ⎱ I was . . .
    For the simple reason that ⎰

Because is often dropped, however, in this kind of dialog:

A How come you weren't hurt?   B *I was wearing my seat belt.*

18-12 ■ Complete each of the following little dialogs according to the model.

1. I didn't like his face, so I hit him.
You mean you hit him just because you didn't like his face?
2. My father drinks, so I drink.
3. There was a page missing, so I threw the book away.
4. The weather was hot, so I didn't go to school.
5. My friends drive VWs, so I do too.
6. I make mistakes, so I don't talk.

18-13 ■ Each of the following items displays a cause-effect or reason-result relationship. Identify the "cause" or "reason" in each one.

1. How come I'm limping? I was in an accident. That's how come.
You were in an accident.
2. Thanks to my seat belt, I'm not really hurt.
3. But for that seat belt, I'd have a broken leg.
4. The station wagon couldn't stop, and he hit me.
5. He claims it was due to faulty brakes.
6. His insurance company will make him pay a higher rate now.
7. It serves him right for driving such an enormous car.
8/9. But since he's rich, the money's no problem. Therefore, he doesn't have to worry.
10/11/12. Are you heading down town? I need a lift. I don't have my car, of course. It's being repaired.

18-14 ■ In each of the following groups only one of the *italicized* phrases is in a causal relationship with the rest of its sentence. Identify the phrase.

1. a. *They gave me a gift*, so I gave them one.
   b. *They gave me a gift* so I'd give them one.
2. a. She turned to someone else *as I was about to say something.*
   b. She turned to someone else, *as I wasn't about to say anything.*
3. a. The medical bills weren't high, *but for the car repair* we had to pay a lot.
   b. The medical bills weren't high, and, *but for the car repair*, we wouldn't have had to pay a lot.
4. a. He has to pay higher insurance, *since he had an accident.*
   b. He's had to pay higher insurance *since he had the accident.*
5. a. *As I was talking*, someone tried to interrupt.
   b. *As I was saying*, someone tried to interrupt.
   c. *As I was shouting*, no one tried to interrupt.

18-15 ▪ **Because + S (because she died)** has the corresponding form **because of + NP (because of her death).** Give the correspondences for each of the following:

1. because he fell
   because of his fall
2. because she grew
   because of her growth
3. because he prepared
4. because he arrived
5. because he objected
6. because he helped
7. because he returned
8. because he interrupted
9. because he graduated
10. because he delayed
11. because he visited
12. because she explained
13. because she called
14. because she was patient
15. because she was married
16. because she was independent
17. because she was popular
18. because she was ill
19. because she was concerned
20. because she was enthusiastic

18-16 ▪ Respond with a comment beginning **So that's why . . .** after each of the following.

1. She was in an accident.
   So that's why (she's limping).
2. It's her birthday.
3. She's going to get married.
4. She didn't pass her exams.
5. She couldn't sleep last night.
6. She eats candy all the time.
7. She can't hear very well.
8. Her father left her a lot of money.

Section B

18-D • (See page 92.)

18-E • (See page 93.)

18-17 READING (204 words)

HIGHWAY DINOSAURS

There is increasing scientific evidence that large cars cause more highway accidents than small cars. In the news recently was the story of a woman who died of a heart attack while driving her station wagon. The car was moving so fast that it went through the highway-dividing fence, resulting in a collision in which five people died. Those unnecessary deaths are attributable in part to the woman's choice of a large automobile. A lighter and smaller car probably wouldn't have gone through the fence, because the heavier the car, the greater the force it will have in a collision. Furthermore, even if the lighter car had broken through the fence, its remaining energy would have been much less, and this would have reduced the chances of serious injury or death. Because of its small size, it might have missed the other car completely. The present design of the oversized automobile is largely responsible not only for the increasing death toll on the highways but also for the rapid depletion of our resources of petroleum, for the pollution of our environment, for urban sprawl, and for the congestion and inconvenience of our cities.[1]

[1] Adapted from "Dinosaurs on U.S. Roads," by Stanley I. Hart, *The Los Angeles Times*, March 12, 1972, Part G, p. 1. Reprinted by permission.

VOCABULARY

cause (cause)
die (death)
divide (division)
remain (remainder)
reduce (reduction)
miss (miss)

highway
dinosaur
heart attack
fence
collision (collide)
death (die)
automobile[2]
force (force)
injury (injure)
toll
depletion (deplete)
resource
petroleum
pollution (pollute)
sprawl (sprawl)
congestion (congested)
inconvenience (inconvenient)

light
serious
oversized
responsible
 (responsibility)
rapid
urban (urbane,
 urbanity)

recently

18-18 ■ INCLUDED MEANING

(For each of the following passages pick the one statement whose meaning is part of the meaning of the passage.)

1. *The car was moving so fast that it went through the highway-dividing fence, resulting in a collision . . .*
   a. The fence stopped the car.
   b. The car collided with the fence.
   c. We don't know what the car eventually hit.
2. *The heavier the car, the greater the force it will have in a collision.*
   a. Heavier cars will have collisions.
   b. Weight and force are directly connected.
   c. Force will have a collision.
3. *Even if the lighter car had broken through the fence, its remaining energy would have been much less.*
   a. We wouldn't expect the lighter car to have broken through.
   b. The lighter car had broken through the fence.
   c. The fence had less remaining energy.
4. *The present design of the oversized automobile is largely responsible . . . for the congestion and inconvenience of our cities.*
   a. Our cities are crowded.
   b. Oversized automobiles are congested.
   c. Automobile design is inconvenient.

---

[2]In British English **automobile** = **motorcar**.

Section C

18-19 ■ QUESTIONS

1. What is the effect of car size on highway accidents?
2. Was it just the size of the car that contributed to the collision involving the station wagon?
3. What is the connection of speed, weight, and force?
4. What advantages are smaller cars supposed to have? Do you agree?
5. What effect does automobile size have upon petroleum resources? Environmental pollution? Urban sprawl? Urban congestion?

18-20 VOCABULARY RELATIONS

There are a number of verbs in English that can have somewhat the meaning of "cause": **have, make, get, force,** and so on, and of course the verb **cause** itself. Among these verbs are differences that have to do with syntax:

$$\text{We} \begin{cases} \textit{had } \textbf{them} \\ \textit{made } \textbf{them} \\ \textit{got } \textbf{them to} \\ \textit{forced } \textbf{them to} \\ \textit{caused } \textbf{them to} \end{cases} \textbf{leave.}$$

and with meaning: **We forced them to leave** is much stronger, for example, than **We had them leave.**[3] Yet there is another type of meaning contrast, connected to whether what happens is *intended* or an *accident* and whether something intended involves the participation of another person. Compare:

$$\begin{matrix} \textbf{Strong winds} \\ \textbf{He accidentally} \end{matrix} \Bigg\} \begin{cases} \textit{caused } \textbf{the car to} \\ \textit{made } \textbf{the car} \\ \textit{*had } \textbf{the car} \\ \textit{*got } \textbf{the car to} \\ \textit{forced } \textbf{the car to} \end{cases} \textbf{go off the road.}$$

She gave me driving lessons and soon *had* **me** $\begin{cases} \textit{*drive} \\ \textit{driving} \end{cases}$ **quite well.**
(e.g. **everyday**)

Since she wasn't feeling well, she *had* **me** $\begin{cases} \textit{drive} \\ \textit{*driving} \end{cases}$ **her to the doctor's.** (i.e. **one time**)

18-F • (See page 94.)

---

[3]**Have, make,** and a few other verbs take complements without **to**. For a discussion of this see 22-12.

18-21 ■ All the causal verbs presented above are followed by complements (see 22-10, 12) that imply that the activity of the complement was accomplished. The complements of other verbs like **prohibit, stop,** and so on, imply that the activity was not accomplished. With the complements of still other verbs, such as **order, allow, ask,** and so on, we don't know whether the activity was accomplished or not. (See also Volume I, 14-9.) For each of the following say whether or not Mary left or whether we don't know.

1. They caused Mary to leave.
   Mary left.
2. They stopped Mary from leaving.
   Mary didn't leave.
3. They told Mary to leave.
   We don't know if Mary left.
4. They had Mary leave.
5. They allowed Mary to leave.
6. They got Mary to leave.
7. They prevented Mary from leaving.
8. They enabled Mary to leave.
9. They ordered Mary to leave.
10. They discouraged Mary from leaving.
11. They forced Mary to leave.
12. They persuaded Mary to leave.
13. They begged Mary to leave.
14. They permitted Mary to leave.
15. They prohibited Mary from leaving.
16. They made Mary leave.
17. They asked Mary to leave.
18. They helped Mary to leave.
19. They warned Mary to leave.

18-G • **COMPOUNDS** (See page 95.)

18-H • **RESTATEMENT** (See page 96.)

18-22 PUNCTUATION

. . . Those unnecessary deaths are attributable in part to the woman's choice of a large automobile⊙   A lighter and smaller car probably wouldn't have gone through the fence.

The *period* is the basic mark of sentence punctuation in English. The comma can punctuate sentences only when they occur in series (e.g. S⊙ S⊙ **and** S) or when they are joined by a sentence connector (S⊙ **and/but/ or/yet/so/for** S).

18-I • (See page 97.)

Section C

18-23 ■ READING IMPROVISATION

(Complete each of the following sentences with what you remember from the Reading.)

1. There is increasing evidence that large cars cause . . .
2. In the news recently was the story of a woman who . . .
3. The car was moving so fast that . . .
4. A lighter and smaller car probably . . .
5. Furthermore, even if the lighter car had broken through the fence, . . .
6. The present design of the oversized automobile is largely responsible for . . .

Assignment of Cause

—The station wagon couldn't stop, so he hit me.
—It's obvious he was *to blame* . . . .
—. . . He claims it was *due to* faulty brakes.

18-24 In English causes of all kinds can be assigned in ways that range over the whole grammar, as we've already seen. The reading passage in Section C contains some further examples:

preposition	. . . a woman who died *of* a heart attack
adjective phrase	Those deaths are *attributable to* the choice of a large automobile.
verb	. . . large cars *cause* more highway deaths than small cars
adverbial	The car was moving *so* fast *that* it went through the fence . . .
comparative	. . . the heavi*er* the car, the great*er* the force

One of the ways in English of giving prominence to something is to put it at the end of the sentence. (See Volume I, 15-7, 8.) Statements about causes often occur in this position, especially if the "effect" is already understood or presupposed. A small number of verbs allow this:

They *blamed* the accident on the weather. (~ They *blamed* the weather for the accident.)
We *credited* our rescue to the police. (~ We *credited* the police with our rescue.)
She *attributed* his death to cancer.

> Prepositions typically allow this kind of positioning with causatives. Another example of this occurred in the Dialog:
>
> —**What do you think he'd say that for?**
> —**Why?** *Out of fear*, **or to avoid admitting that he wasn't driving the right way.**
>
> In this context **out of fear** = **He'd say that out of fear.** Placing **fear** at the beginning of the sentence (**Fear would make him say that.**) would violate the general requirement that new information be put last in the sentence.

18-25 ■ Answer the questions according to the models.

1. Why did he do it? Was he angry?
   Yes. He did it out of anger.
2. Why did he do it? Was he afraid?
   Yes. He did it out of fear.
3. Why did he do it? Was he hungry?
4. Why did he do it? Was he curious?
5. Why did he do it? Was he greedy?
6. Why did he do it? Was he confused?
7. Why did he do it? Was he concerned?
8. Why did he do it? Was he just careless?
9. Why did he do it? Does he hate us?
10. Why did he do it? Does he need something?
11. Why did he do it? Is it because it was necessary?
12. Why did he do it? Is it because he's hopeful?
13. Why did he do it? Is it because he loves us?
14. Why did he do it? Is it just because he's kind?

18-26 ■ Although more than one preposition can indicate a causal relationship, with some verbs the choice is somewhat systematic, for example, **die.** A person dies *of* a malfunction in the body but *from* something inflicted from outside. If the location is a factor, then **in, on,** and so on, are often used. For example, all three of the following "causes" of a person's death could apply simultaneously and truthfully:

John died { *of* a heart attack.
from too much exertion.
in a fight. }

The constructions below are intended to suggest causes of death. Read them all as sentences beginning "(name) died . . ." The prepositional phrase for number 17 is **at the hands of.**

1. old age → [Frank died]
   Frank died of old age.
2. overwork → [Sally died]
   Sally died from overwork.
3. an accident → [Jim died]
4. cancer → [Betty died]
5. burns → [Jerry died]
6. a fire → [Margaret died]
7. fright → [Fred died]
8. a blow on the head → [Susan died]
9. an airplane crash → [Sam died]
10. a broken heart → [Brenda died]
11. a fall → [Myrna died]
12. the surgeon's knife → [Max died]
13. starvation → [Lois died]
14. loss of blood → [Joe died]
15. a firing squad → [Paul died]
16. the electric chair → [Bob died]
17. the police → [Abe died]

18-27 ■ After each of the following reply with a comment restating cause, using the frame **You're saying that . . . [be] attributable to . . .**

1. Faulty brakes caused the accident.
   You're saying that the accident was attributable to faulty brakes.
2. The use of large cars produces more highway accidents.
3. The large number of cars on the road creates pressure for more highway construction.
4. The automobile industry puts out the propaganda.
5. The use of the wrong kind of fuel may lead to engine failure.
6. The automobile manufacturers released that price information.
7. Demand for higher wages usually triggers a price increase.
8. The *New York Times* published the story.
9. Mutual cooperation brought about a settlement of the dispute.
10. Recent government policies have given rise to new charges.

18-28 ■ In language not all causation need be stated directly or involve causative constructions. It is possible to get someone to do something in very indirect fashion. In casual conversation we often do this almost unconsciously. For example:

A **I'm hungry.**
B **How about a sandwich?**
A **Just a small one.**

The event need not even involve conversational exchange:

CUSTOMER [pointing to automobile in showroom] **That one looks nice.**
SALESMAN [opens car door]

Try to get the person sitting next to you to do something without asking him or her directly. Then let a third person describe what happened. Here are some possible goals: opening/closing a window; opening/closing a door; turning on/off the lights; picking up an object from the floor; borrowing a pencil/pen/piece of paper/cigarette/car/and so on. For example:

A **I can't find my cigarettes.**
B **Here. Have one of mine.**
A **Thanks. I will.**
C **A led B to offer him/her a cigarette.**

18-J • (See page 97.)

18-K • (See page 98.)

18-L • (See page 99.)

18-M • **CLOZE** (See page 99.)

> Reason and Purpose
>
> —*What* do you think he'd say that *for*?
> —*Why*? ... *To avoid* admitting that he wasn't driving the right way.
> —*In order to fool* the insurance company, probably.

18-29 *Reason* and *purpose* are very similar concepts. The grammar has a number of words that refer to either one:

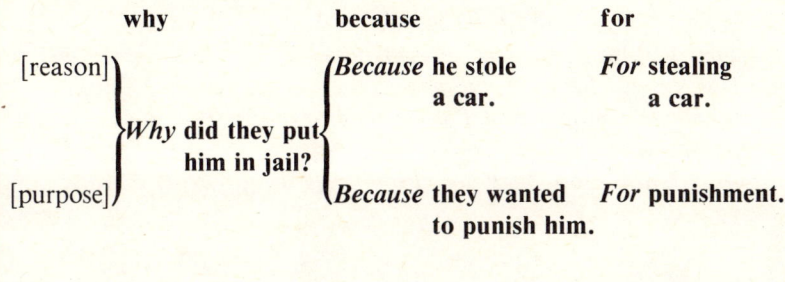

18-30 Other grammatical forms distinguish reason and purpose clearly. The forms referring to reason (or cause) were studied in Sections B and D. For purpose we also have **(in order) to** + verb or **in order that** + sentence:

The police stopped his car $\begin{cases} \textit{(in order) to question him.} \\ \textit{in order that they might question him.} \\ \textit{for questioning.} \end{cases}$

18-31 ■ Answer the following questions with full sentences.

1. What do you go to the post office for, stamps or newspapers?
   You go to the post office for stamps.
2. What do you go to the bank for, to deposit money or to buy tickets?
   You go to the bank to deposit money.
3. Why do you go to school, to study or to have a good time?
   $\begin{cases} \textbf{You go to school to study.} \\ \textbf{Neither one. You go to school to (get an education).} \end{cases}$
4. What do you go to school for, an education or a good time?
5. What do you study English for, to get a better job or to be able to communicate?
6. Why do you use a dictionary, to study English or to look up words?
7. What do you go to the barber shop for, a haircut or a shoeshine?
8. What do you use a can opener for, to open boxes or to open bottles?
9. Why do you need a passport, to register for courses or to be able to travel?

18-32 ■ Say whether you think the **for** phrases below tell the reason or the purpose.

1. He went to the hospital *for an operation*.
2. He was operated on *for cancer*.
3. He was released *for recuperation*.
4. He was arrested *for speeding*.
5. He was held *for questioning*.
6. He was sent to jail *for driving without a license*.
7. He was sent to jail *for punishment*.
8. They let him go *for lack of evidence*.
9. If it weren't *for his good record*, they would have kept him.
10. What's this money for? *For cleaning windows.* (I really appreciated your doing it.)
11. What's this cloth for? *For cleaning the windows.* (I'd really appreciate your doing it.)

18-33 ■ What makes the following statement humorous?

"He came to California for arthritis, and now he's finally got it."

18-34 ■ Make a note of all the examples of cause, effect, result, attribution, reason, purpose, and so on, that you can find in the Reading of Section C.

18-N • (See page 100.)

18-O • (See page 101.)

18-P • (See page 102.)

18-Q • (See page 103.)

18-R • (See page 103.)

18-S • (See page 103.)

WRITING EXERCISES

18-A • For each of the following words write the corresponding causative verb. Let the indication of stress placement be your guide to the choice between **-ize** and **-ify**.

1. húman   húman *ize*
2. húmid   humíd *ify*
3. mémory   mémor_____
4. eléctric   eléctr_____
5. módern   módern_____
6. wéstern   wéstern_____
7. idéntity   idént_____
8. préssure   préssur_____
9. inténse   inténs_____
10. ecónomy   ecónom_____
11. divérse   divérs_____
12. quálity   quál_____
13. équal   équal_____
14. cháracter   cháracter_____
15. mílitary   mílitar_____
16. exámple   exémpl_____

18-B • For each of the following words write first the corresponding causative verb in **-ize** or **-ify** and then the noun that is formed from the verb by adding **-ation**. The spelling of some of the roots changes before suffixation. Practice pronouncing each set of three corresponding forms.

1. person
2. personal
3. memory
4. beauty
5. familiar
6. real
7. solid

Writing Exercises

8. *popular* _____ _____

9. *false* _____ _____

10. *standard* _____ _____

11. *clear* _____ _____

12. *military* _____ _____

13. *electr(ic)* _____ _____

14. *terror* _____ _____

15. *equal* _____ _____

16. *glory* _____ _____

17. *peace* _____ _____

18. *uni(ty)* _____ _____

19. *character* _____ _____

20. *example* _____ _____

18-C • In each of the mini-dialogs that follow cross out one of the two responses, whichever does not seem acceptable and/or appropriate. Some of the **what . . . for** questions have the kind of sarcastic interpretation discussed in Volume I: 4-30, 11-5, 13-6, and 14-5.

1. A How can I carry this box?
   B { How come you've got two hands?
      { What have you got two hands for?
2. A I just don't know.
   B { How come you don't know?
      { What don't you know for?
3. A How will I be able to follow the lecture?
   B { How come you think you've got ears?
      { What do you think you've got ears for?
4. A I don't know what she said.
   B { How come you didn't hear?
      { What didn't you hear for?
5. A Would you translate those English sentences for me?
   B { How come you're learning English?
      { What are you learning English for?

18-D • Some of the following pairs are natural conversation sequences, some not. Make any necessary changes in the pairs that you think are not natural.

1. A Is he leaving now?

   B Yes, he is, because he has an appointment.

2. A Is he leaving now?

   B Because he has an appointment.

3. A Why is he leaving now?

   B He has an appointment.

4. A Why is he leaving now?

   B Because he has an appointment.

5. A He's leaving now.

   B He has an appointment.

6. A Is he leaving now?

   B It's because he has an appointment.

7. A I wonder why he's leaving now.

   B It's because he has an appointment.

8. A I wonder why he's leaving now.

   B He has an appointment.

9. A I wonder if he's leaving now.

   B He has an appointment.

10. A I wonder if he's leaving now.

    B Yes, he is, because he has an appointment.

11. A I wonder if he's leaving now.

    B Because he has an appointment.

18-E • Study the ways below in which the reason-result relationship of the following two sentences can be expressed. Use these as models for completing

Writing Exercises 93

the sketched out sentences later on. Supply needed punctuation and change nouns to pronouns where necessary.

The brakes   The car
were faulty.   was not safe
                    to drive.

The car was not safe to drive, {
 because *the brakes were faulty.*
 because of *faulty brakes.*
 due to the fact that *the brakes were faulty.*
 due to *faulty brakes.*
 since *the brakes were faulty.*

The brakes were faulty; {
 therefore *the car was not safe to drive.*
 as a result *the car was not safe to drive.*

Petroleum   The cost of
prices are   owning a car
rising.   is increasing.

1. _____ because

_____

2. Because of _____

_____

3. _____ therefore

_____

4. _____ as a result

_____

5. Due to _____

_____

6. _____ due to the fact that

_____

7. Since _____

_____

18-F • Cross out whatever verbs you think render the sentence unacceptable. Unacceptability can hinge on grammar and/or meaning.

"What {(1) a. made / b. had / c. got / d. forced / e. caused} your car to go off the road?" the officer asked. "It was {(2) a. made / b. had / c. got / d. forced / e. caused} by carelessness," the man replied. "Driving this large car {(3) a. makes / b. has / c. gets / d. forces / e. causes} me {(4) a. work / b. working} harder, and sometimes I just can't pay enough attention." "Maybe if I give you a ticket it will {(5) a. make / b. have / c. get / d. force / e. cause} your attention improve," said the officer. "I doubt it," replied the man. My wife has been trying to {(6) a. make / b. have / c. get / d. force / e. cause} me to drive differently for thirty years, and if she can't {(7) a. make / b. have / c. get / d. force / e. cause} me change, nothing can."

18-G • COMPOUNDS

(Rewrite the following sentences rearranging the words in *italics* into a compound.)

1. *Congestion in the city* is becoming impossible.
   <u>City congestion is becoming impossible.</u>

2. The *Department of Motor Vehicles* will propose new laws.

3. Large cars mean higher *claims for payment of insurance*.

4. Can the government do anything about *pollution of air over the city*?
   _____

5. *Depletion of reserves of petroleum* will force a search for other energy sources.
   _____

6. The responsibility for the increase in the *death toll on the highway* lies partly with the auto manufacturers.
   _____
   _____

7. The responsibility for the *increase in the death toll on the highway* lies partly with the auto manufacturers.
   _____
   _____

8. The *responsibility for the increase in the death toll on the highway* lies partly with the auto manufacturers.
   _____
   _____

18-H • RESTATEMENT

(Complete the restatement by supplying the correct form.)

1. They *classified* him as 1-A. (*give*)
   They *gave him a classification of 1-A.*

2. Why does he *limp so badly*? (*have*)
   Why does he _____

3. The police *blamed* the other driver. (*put . . . on*)
   The police _____

4. I *emphasized* that I wasn't interested. (*make . . . -ic*)
   I _____ that I wasn't interested.

5. I *emphasized* the fact that I wasn't interested. (*put . . . on*)
   I _____ that I wasn't interested.

6. The automobile industry *contributed sizably* to the political campaign. (*make*)
   The automobile industry _____
   _____

96   Unit 18

7. Better engines will *noticeably reduce* air pollution. (*bring about*)

   Better engines will _____

   _____

8. Two pairs of cars *collided simultaneously*. (*have*)

   Two pairs of cars _____

9. At this hour the city *is hopelessly congested*. (*have*)

   At this hour the city _____

10. You *are completely responsible* for our safety. (*have*)

    You _____

18-I • The following paragraph has been punctuated entirely with commas, some of which should be periods. Circle all commas that you think should be periods. Then capitalize the first words of new sentences.

Another factor which contributes to the accident rate of large cars is, simply, scale, T̲here is an upper limit to the size of machines that man can control with ease, human beings also have dimension, men can handle huge trucks, enormous ships, and great airplanes if their crews are qualified by proper training and experience, but our automobile drivers are not properly trained, furthermore, larger automobiles depreciate early, a ten-year-old Cadillac, provided it is in excellent condition, might be worth just as much as a ten-year-old Volkswagen, however, it is far less expensive to buy new tires and parts for a smaller car than for a larger car, it is likely, therefore, that old large automobiles will be in a poorer state of repair than old small ones,[4]

18-J • Rewrite the **because** clauses below as **because of** phrases.

1. They're moving to the suburbs { because the city is congested.
   because of congestion in the city .

[4]Hart, op. cit.

2. *Because it's small,* ⎱ it might have missed the other car completely.
   _____ ⎰

3. The speed limit is being reduced ⎰ *because the death toll on the highway is increasing.*
   ⎱ _____

4. *Because petroleum resources are rapidly being depleted,* ⎱ the government
   _____ ⎰
   is looking for new sources of energy.

5. It is ⎰ *largely because the American public continues to prefer large cars*
   ⎱ _____
   that Detroit still makes them.

6. If we don't buy large cars, it's not ⎰ *because they're expensive;*
   ⎱ _____
   it's ⎰ *because they're inconvenient.*
   ⎱ _____

18-K • Each of the following sentences, taken from student compositions, contains a causal construction that is incorrect. Change each sentence in such a way as to remove the error.

1. *Drinking causes to men lose control of themselves.*

2. *Nobody could give the real reason to that accident.*

3. *We don't recognize it because of the problem doesn't appear in our lives.*

4. I couldn't understand. *Because I was hearing English for the first time.*

5. *This is a good paying job, so, I can cover my expenses.*

6. *Careless currency devaluation will go back us to old habits.*

18-L • For each of the following sequences move something into subject position and write the resulting sentence. Choose any verb tense that seems appropriate.

1. blame - the accident - the weather - the police

   The police blamed the accident on the weather.
   The accident was blamed on the weather by the police.
   The weather was blamed for the accident by the police.

2. also attribute - carelessness - the accident - some people

   _____

3. contribute too - darkness - the accident

   _____

4. make - the police - traffic - [Traffic stops]

   _____

5. cause - the accident - traffic - [Traffic piles up]

   _____

6. credit - the police - the newspapers - [The police keep order]

   _____

7. result in - the accident - [The driver's license is taken away]

   _____

8. lead to - [The driver attempts to drive again] - [The driver is arrested]

   _____

18-M • **CLOZE**

(In each blank space write a word that you think fits naturally.)

The automobile industry _____(1) taken the position in the past _____(2) nothing can be done about traffic _____(3) —that the high automobile accident rate _____(4) caused by foolish drivers. There is _____(5) half-truth in this. Certainly the _____(6) driver is often responsible for beginning _____(7) chain of events that leads to _____(8) accident. Too often, however, the oversized _____(9) poorly

Writing Exercises

designed automobile contributes greatly to _____ unfortunate end of the chain.⁵

10

18-N • Cross out whichever phrases do not fit the meaning and structure of the sentence.

1. Larger automobiles have been
   {
   a. the cause of
   b. because of
   c. responsible for
   d. the result of
   e. for reasons of
   f. due to
   g. for the purpose of
   h. attributable to
   }
   more accidents.

2.
   {
   a. The cause of
   b. Because of
   c. Responsible for
   d. The result of
   e. For reasons of
   f. Due to
   g. For the purpose of
   h. Attributable to
   }
   its small size, the VW missed the station wagon completely.

3. Safety belts were installed
   {
   a. the cause of
   b. because of
   c. responsible for
   d. the result of
   e. for reasons of
   f. due to
   g. for the purpose of
   h. attributable to
   }
   protecting the driver.

4. Adoption of other safety standards is opposed by the automobile industry
   {
   a. the cause of
   b. because of
   c. responsible for
   d. the result of
   e. for reasons of
   f. due to
   g. for the purpose of
   h. attributable to
   }
   profit.

⁵Hart, op. cit.

5. $\begin{Bmatrix} a. & \text{The cause of} \\ b. & \text{Because of} \\ c. & \text{Responsible for} \\ d. & \text{The result of} \\ e. & \text{For reasons of} \\ f. & \text{Due to} \\ g. & \text{For the purpose of} \\ h. & \text{Attributable to} \end{Bmatrix}$ a general increase in the number of highway

deaths, more safety measures will be needed.

6. Urban congestion is partly $\begin{Bmatrix} a. & \text{the cause of} \\ b. & \text{because of} \\ c. & \text{responsible for} \\ d. & \text{the result of} \\ e. & \text{for reasons of} \\ f. & \text{due to} \\ g. & \text{for the purpose of} \\ h. & \text{attributable to} \end{Bmatrix}$ inadequate public

transportation.

7. Inadequate public transportation is partly $\begin{Bmatrix} a. & \text{the cause of} \\ b. & \text{because of} \\ c. & \text{responsible for} \\ d. & \text{the result of} \\ e. & \text{for reasons of} \\ f. & \text{due to} \\ g. & \text{for the purpose of} \\ h. & \text{attributable to} \end{Bmatrix}$

urban congestion.

18-0 • Just as written paragraphs have structure, so do conversations. Talk serves not only to convey information, express feelings, and so on, but also to get other people to do things. Study the structure of the following dialog and paraphrase.[6]

1. { A What did she say?
    B She said she hates big cars.   "She said she hates big cars
2. { A *Why did she say that?*   because
    B She doesn't think they're safe.   she doesn't think they're safe,
3. { A *What did she mean?*   in that
    B They're too hard to control.   they're too hard to control,
4. { A *What was she trying to do?*   so
    B She wants me to buy a small one. she wants me to buy a small one."

In this conversation A elicits from B a feeling (1), a reason (2), a justification

---

[6]The model for this exercise comes from *The Context of Foreign Language Teaching*, by Leon A. Jakobovits and Barbara Gordon. (Rowley, Mass.: Newbury House, 1974), pp. 229-30.

(3), and an explanation (4), in that order. The paraphrase captures these same functions through the words **because** (2), **in that** (3), and **so** (4). Reorder the four sentences below as answers, with questions added like those above. Then write a one-sentence paraphrase of the dialog using **because**, **in that,** and **so**.

> There was an air crash in the news yesterday.
> They said they don't like airplanes.
> They want us to take the train.
> They think air travel is dangerous.

1. { A _____
   B _____

2. { A _____
   B _____

3. { A _____
   B _____

4. { A _____
   B _____

"_____ because _____

_____, in that _____

_____, so _____

18-P • Rewrite the student paragraphs below, replacing the conversational structure with that indicated, which is more appropriate for written English.

"Most of the students here live in university apartments so *they come to school by bicycle* but *in my country the students live far from school* so *they have to come to the university by bus.*"

Since _____, _____

_____. However, _____.

Therefore, _____

"A driver wears his seat belt or *he runs the risk of injury in an accident* and *I had that experience when I was young* so *now I always wear them* but *there are a lot of people who don't.*"

_____ if _____

_____. _____, with the

result that _____.
_____, *however.*

18-Q • The paraphrase of the first dialog in 18-O above can be restated in a slightly more formal style suitable for most writing:

She reported that she strongly dislikes large automobiles. She doesn't believe they're safe, in that they're too difficult to control. Therefore, she wants me to purchase a small one.

Using the paraphrase you wrote of the second dialog in 18-O, write another paraphrase in a more formal style.

18-R • Write a paragraph or two similar in development to the Reading in Section C. Begin with a statement of fact that has at least some scientific support, and then use that supporting evidence to develop the paragraph.

18-S • Write a brief account of an accident that you were once involved in (car, bus, bicycle, and so on). Tell where and when it happened, who was involved, who was at fault (if anybody), what the cause was, and whether you since have in any way changed your behavior or your thinking as a result.

Writing Exercises

Unit 19

19-1 DIALOG

A LETTER FROM DOWN UNDER[1]

(A conversation is taking place at the International Student Center.)

MONA Tell me when the mail comes. I'm expecting a letter.
SYLVIA The mail just came. Michael's getting it now.
MICHAEL [entering] The mail just came.
SYLVIA I know. I saw you getting it. It's even earlier than usual this time. My watch says 9:10.
MICHAEL Well, it's early for New York City. It wouldn't be for London, though . . . . Something here for you, Mona. Looks like a letter from Australia.
MONA Thanks . . . It's from Sydney.
MICHAEL Friend of yours?
MONA Oh, that's such an old joke, Michael. It goes back further than anybody can remember. Sydney is a city, Sylvia.
SYLVIA I know. As a matter of fact, it's the farthest city in the world from New York.
MONA No, Sylvia. You're thinking of Adelaide.
MICHAEL How old is she?
SYLVIA That's enough, Michael . . . . Anyway, we're both wrong about the farthest city from here. I remember now. It's Perth.
MICHAEL Perth who?
MONA Michael, I think you're more persistent than you are funny.

---

[1] "Down Under" is a popular name for Australia and New Zealand. It derives from the position of these countries on a conventional globe.

VOCABULARY

take place   mail (mail)   early
look like   watch   further (far)
                                        farther (far)
                                        wrong
                                        persistent (persist, persistence)
                                        funny

                                        as a matter of fact

19-2 ■ DIALOG VARIATION

1. *Looks like a letter from Australia.*
   It looks like a letter from Australia.
   It appears to be a letter from Australia.
2. *It goes back further than anybody can remember.*
   It goes further back than anybody can remember.
3. *It's the farthest city in the world from New York.*
   It's the farthest city from New York in the world.
   It's farther from New York than any other city in the world.
4. *We're both wrong . . . .*
   Both of us are wrong. . . .
   You're wrong and I'm wrong . . . .
   Neither one of us is right . . . .
   Neither of us is right . . . .

19-3 ■ QUESTIONS

1. Where does the conversation take place?
2. Why is Mona interested in the mail?
3. What time does the mail usually come?
4. Which city has earlier mail service, New York or London?
5. What Australian cities are mentioned in the conversation?
6. What *is* the farthest city from New York?
7. What do you think of Michael's humor?

19-4 SOUND PATTERNS

A Tell me when the mail comes.
B The mail just *came.*
C [entering] The *mail* just came.

The sentences of B and C in the above sequence appear to be identical. Yet, they are spoken with different stress patterns. The pattern of C is what occurs in the absence of a context, where **mail** is the most important word.

The pattern of B is what occurs when "mail" has already been introduced as a topic of conversation. Interchanging B and C would produce a sequence that a native speaker of English would recognize as very unnatural.

19-A • (See page 121.)

19-5 PHRASAL VERBS

—A conversation is *taking place* at the International Student Center.

Some verbs can occur with many different particles or prepositions. **Take** is such a verb, as revealed by items in previous vocabulary lists: **take off, take out, take over, take up, take part,** and so on. Again, it is important to remember that the meanings of the separate words contribute little, if anything, to the meaning of the phrasal verb.

19-B • (See page 121.)

19-6 SPEECH ACT

A The mail is *even earlier than usual* this time.
B Well, it's *early for New York City*.
C It *would*n't *be for London*, though.

Not all meaning can be explained in terms of properties of words and phrases. Some of it takes the form of what is believed or *presupposed* by the speaker to be true in what he is saying. (See also Volume I: 9-4, 13-4, 14-20, 14-29, and 15-C.) For example, in the above dialog the use of **even** in A implies that "the mail is usually early." The use of the present tense and the prepositional phrase with **for** in B implies that the speakers are in New York City and that "in New York City one wouldn't expect the mail to be that early" and that "the mail arrives earlier in other places." The use of **would** and **for** in C implies that the speakers are not in London and that "the mail arrives earlier in London."

19-C • (See page 122.)

19-7 ■ DIALOG IMPROVISATION

(Try to re-create or even improvise a variation of the Dialog at the beginning of this unit, as you remember it.)

A Tell me when . . .
B The mail . . .
C [entering] The mail . . .
B I know. I saw you getting it. It's even earlier . . .
C Well, it's early for New York City. Something here . . .
A Thanks. It's . . .

Other Uses of Comparatives; Comparison with Other Forms

—Friend of yours?
—Oh, that's such an old joke. It goes back *further than anybody can remember.*

19-8 The comparative form can serve purposes other than that of conventional comparison. One of the commonest uses of the comparative is as an *intensifier*, stronger even than **very**.

That joke goes back *further than you have any idea of.* (= *very far*)

If the comparative form marks negated ability, a paraphrase with **too** or **so** is usually possible:

That joke goes back { *further than anybody can remember.*
too far for anybody (to be able) to remember.
so far that nobody can remember. }

19-9 ■ Finish each of the following phrases with something that comes naturally to mind.

1. [a shelf] higher than I could . . .
   higher than I could (reach)
2. [coffee] hotter than I could . . .
3. [a meeting] earlier than I could . . .
4. [a price] higher than I could . . .
5. [a store] farther than I could . . .
6. [a package] larger than I could . . .
7. [music] louder than I could . . .
8. [a table] heavier than I could . . .
9. [a cat] faster than I could . . .
10. [a film] longer than I could . . .

19-10 ■ Redo exercise 19-9 with responses in the **so** form. Notice that the object of the final verb cannot be dropped in the **so** form.

1. so high that I couldn't (reach) it
2. so hot that I couldn't . . .
3. and so on.

19-11 ■ Australian humor often uses exaggeration and leg-pulling, as in the example below using a **so . . . that** construction. Can you think of any jokes or stories from your own experience that also use a **so . . . that** construction for exaggeration?

A *It was so cold in our town that the candlelight froze, and we couldn't blow it out.*
B *That's nothing. Where we were it was so cold that the words came out of our mouths in pieces of ice, and we had to fry them to see what we were talking about.*[2]

19-12 ■ Comparison involving commonly held traits can be expressed with **both** and **neither**. For example, **John and Bill** *both* **want cars, although** *neither* **one can drive**. With this in mind, mention the characteristics that various members of the class have in common.

A **Do (name) and (name) have anything in common?**
B **Yes. They both have black hair.**
C **And neither one likes coffee.**
D **What about (name) and (name)?**
and so on.

19-13 ■ Redo exercise 19-9 with responses in the **too** form.

1. too high for me to (reach)
2. too hot for me to . . .
3. and so on.

19-14 ■ **Too** indicates an excess (**too much**) or an insufficiency (**too little**). Sufficiency is indicated by **enough**. Notice, however, that **too** precedes the word it modifies, whereas **enough** follows: **too big, big enough**. Participate in the following little dialogs by making comment-paraphrases with **too** and **enough**, as if you were repeating what was said for the benefit of a third person.

1. A **This coffee's too hot. I can't drink it.**
   B **What did he say?**
   C **He said the coffee's too hot (for him) to drink.**

[2]From *Encyclopedia of Humor,* copyright © 1968 by Joey Adams. Reprinted by permission of the publisher, The Bobbs-Merrill Company, Inc.

2. A **Is it cool outside? Should I wear a coat?**
   B What did she say?
   C **She asked if it's cool enough outside (for her) to wear a coat.**
3. A **That's too far back. I can't remember.**
   B What did he say?
   C and so on.
4. A Is it early enough? Can we hear the news?
5. A It's too late. We can't hear the news.
6. A Is the shelf big enough? Will the books fit on it?
7. A The books are too big. They won't fit on the shelf.
8. A Is there enough room in here? Can we bring in some more people?
9. A It's too crowded in here. No more people can come in.
10. A Is Monday early enough? Can we get together then?
11. A Monday's too late. We can't get together then.

19-D • (See page 122.)

19-E • (See page 124.)

19-F • (See page 125.)

19-G • (See page 126.)

19-15 READING (296 words)

AUSTRALIA AND THE UNITED STATES: A COMPARISON

Australia, the last continent to be "discovered," was sighted by Dutch, Portuguese, and Spanish ships in the seventeenth century. No colonies followed at the time, however, as these nations were less interested in colonizing than in exploring. As in the early history of the United States,
5 it was the English who established the permanent settlements in Australia. This history and the geography of these two former British colonies have some other things in common as well.

Australia and the United States are about equal in size, and barren western portions of the two bear a close physical resemblance. It was
10 the eastern coast of Australia and America that the English first settled, and both colonies soon began to expand to the west. However, this west-

ward expansion occurred more because the colonists were searching for better land than because the population was increasing. Settlement of the western part of both countries quickened after gold was discovered
15 in America in 1849 and in Australia two years later.

Although the parallels in the development of these two countries are striking, there are some sharp contrasts as well. The United States gained its independence from England by revolution, whereas Australia was granted its independence without having to go to war. Australia, unlike
20 the United States, was originally colonized by English convicts, and its economy was rooted in wheat growing and sheep raising. By 1922, for example, Australia had fifteen times more sheep than it had people, or almost half as many sheep as there are people today in the United States. Yet, in spite of these and other major differences, Australia and the
25 United States have more in common with each other than either one has with most of the rest of the world.

VOCABULARY

sight (sight)	settlement (settle)	permanent
bear/bore/borne	portion	former
settle (settlement)	resemblance (resemble)	barren (barrenness)
expand (expansion)	west (western, westward)	western (west)
occur (occurrence)	expansion (expand)	physical
search (search)	gold (golden)	eastern (east)
grant (grant)	parallel (parallel)	westward (west)
	revolution (revolt)	striking (strike)
	convict (convict, conviction)	sharp
	wheat	originally
	sheep/sheep	
		go to war

19-16 ■ INCLUDED MEANING

(For each of the following passages pick the one statement whose meaning is part of the meaning of the passage.)

1. *No colonies followed at the time, however, as these nations were less interested in colonizing than in exploring.*
    a. These nations were interested in exploring.
    b. These nations were interested in colonizing.
    c. No colonies were interested in exploring.
2. *It was the eastern coast of Australia and America that the English first settled, and both colonies soon began to expand to the west.*
    a. The eastern coast of Australia settled both colonies.
    b. Americans first settled in England.
    c. Australia and America had western expansion.

Section C

3. *By 1922, for example, Australia had fifteen times more sheep than it had people, or almost half as many sheep as there are people today in the United States.*
   a. The United States has twice as many people as sheep.
   b. The sheep-to-people ratio was fifteen to one.
   c. There are a lot of sheep in the United States.
4. *In spite of these and other major differences, Australia and the United States have more in common with each other than either one has with most of the rest of the world.*
   a. The United States and Australia do not have any major differences.
   b. The United States and Australia have something in common.
   c. The United States and Australia have nothing in common with the rest of the world.

19-17 ■ QUESTIONS

1. Why didn't the Dutch, Portuguese, and Spanish establish colonies in Australia?
2. What did the English do?
3. How do Australia and the United States compare in size?
4. What was the direction of expansion in both colonies?
5. What started the expansion?
6. How did the discovery of gold affect expansion?
7. What are some of the ways in which the two countries contrast?
8. Which country gained independence first, the United States or Australia?
9. What does the Australian economy depend on?

19-18 VOCABULARY RELATIONS

Comparison can be accomplished with single words as well as with comparative constructions. For example, in "other *major* differences," taken from the Reading, "major" implies that there are *minor* differences as well, and that the former are *bigger* than the latter. Many other opposites also have built-in comparison: **first/last, high/low**, and so on.

19-H • (See page 127.)

19-I • **COMPOUNDS** (See page 127.)

19-J • **RESTATEMENT** (See page 128.)

19-19 PUNCTUATION

The comma (,) is the most frequently used of all the punctuation marks. It is also the only sign that marks separation within a sentence. Yet it is difficult to state comprehensive rules for comma use, partly because not everyone uses commas in the same way. We will therefore focus on areas of the language in which comma usage shows the greatest uniformity and in which learners of the language err most frequently. One such area concerns how closely certain parts of a sentence are related. In general, the closer the relationship the less the need for a comma. Compare:

Australia has a lot of sheep, for example.
Australia has a lot of sheep for sale.

19-K • (See page 129.)

19-20 ■ READING IMPROVISATION

(Complete each of the following sentences with what you remember from the Reading.)

1. Australia and the United States are about . . .
2. . . . and barren western portions of the two bear . . .
3. It was the eastern coast of Australia and America that . . .
4. . . . and both colonies soon began . . .
5. However, this westward expansion occurred more because . . .
6. Settlement of the western part of both countries quickened after . . .

> Complex Comparison
>
> —Australia and the United States have *more* in common with each other *than* either one has with most of the rest of the world.

19-21 Just as it is possible to compare relatively "simple" elements,

> **This westward expansion occurred more** *in the United States* **than** *in Australia.*

so is it possible to compare elements of greater abstractness and complexity:

> **This westward expansion occurred more** *because the colonist were searching for better land* **than** *because the population was increasing.*

Another example of such complexity is the intensifier-comparative of Section B:

Australia had [X+ many] sheep ⌒ [you imagined [X many] sheep)
Australia had   more   sheep *than* **you imagined.**

Complexity is evident in "double" comparison as well:

Australia had [X+ many] sheep ⌒ [England had [X many] people]
Australia had   more   sheep *than* **England had   people.**
(England had *fewer* people *than* Australia had sheep.)

19-22 ■ Study the table below.[3] Offer comments of any kind on what you see there. For example:
Australia has more sheep than I ever realized.
Japan catches more fish than I would know what to do with.
and so on.

	Population	Area sq. miles	Sheep	Rice*	Fish*	Cotton*	Oil*	Telephones
Argentina	23,362,204	1,072,157	41,000,000	407,000	302,100	125,000	21,476,000	2,065,000
Australia	12,755,638	2,967,909	140,109,000	247,000	123,500	32,000	16,550,000	4,659,000
China	590,194,715	3,691,502	72,000,000	105,226,000	7,600,000	1,540,000	50,000,000	
Egypt	30,075,858	386,900	1,994,000	2,605,000	79,700	490,000	8,479,000	472,000
England/UK	55,506,131	94,559	27,943,000		1,144,400		88,000	19,095,000
France	49,778,540	212,918	10,191,000	91,000	796,800		1,254,000	11,337,000
India	547,949,809	1,261,810	43,300,000	63,338,000	1,958,000	1,160,000	7,197,000	1,600,000
Iran	25,785,210	635,932	37,000,000	1,350,000		201,000	292,843,000	552,000
Japan	104,665,171	143,818	19,000	16,490,000	10,701,900		700,000	38,698,000
USA	203,235,298	3,540,939	17,724,000	3,801,000	2,669,900	2,821,000	454,190,000	138,286,000
USSR	241,720,134	8,600,340	139,086,000	1,279,000	8,619,000	2,538,000	429,037,000	14,261,000

*In metric tons. All figures are for the year 1973.

[3]United Nations Department of Economic and Social Affairs, *Statistical Yearbook 1974*. Copyright, United Nations 1975. Reproduced by permission.

Section D

19-23 ■ Advertisements are a common source of comparative constructions. Usually, however, these are the so-called "incomplete comparative": **Look *younger* in thirty days; Choose from our *larger* selections; Your money buys *more* at . . . .**

1. What do you think is supposed to be understood in the missing parts of the above comparisons: Younger than who? Larger selections than whose? Buys more what than what?
2. Complete the following comparatives with whatever comes to mind.
   a. At Bankrupt Savings we give higher interest rates . . .
      . . . than they do elsewhere.
      . . . than we did last year.
      . . . than you might think.
      and so on.
   b. You feel more important on Nosedive Airways . . .
   c. A Coffin Nail cigarette has less tar and nicotine . . .
   d. Dubious Investments has a way to make you richer quicker . . .
3. What is being compared in the following tire advertisement?
   "Can a man buy tires better than a woman?"
4. Do you notice anything unusual in the following three advertisements?
   a. "We still fly more big planes East than any other airline."
   b. "Suddenly the fastest way to Europe is also the comfortablest."
   c. "*Mark of the Devil: Part II,* more horrifying than original." (film ad)
5. Thumb through a copy of any daily newspaper, and make a note of the advertisements that utilize comparative constructions. How many of them are "incomplete"?

19-L • (See page 129.)

19-M • (See page 130.)

19-N • (See page 130.)

19-O • **CLOZE** (See page 131.)

Comparison and Contrast

—The United States gained its independence from England by revolution, *whereas* Australia was granted its independence without having to go to war.

19-24 There are a number of different words and phrases in English that can signal *contrast*: **but, yet, while, whereas, instead, in contrast, on the contrary, on the other hand, conversely, however, although**, and so on. They are not freely interchangeable, however, as they mark different kinds of contrasts and have varying grammatical and punctuation restrictions. Contrasts that are "contrary to expectation," for example, are marked by **yet**, though not by **while** and **whereas**. The use of **but** is less restricted:

New Zealand is only an island, { *while / *whereas / yet / but } it supports a population of three million.

New Zealand is only an island, { while / whereas / *yet / but } Australia is a whole continent.

19-25 **While, whereas**, and **although** are subordinators; the clauses they introduce cannot take sentence punctuation. For example:

New Zealand supports a population of three million. { *Although it is only an island. / Yet it is only an island. / However, it is only an island. }

New Zealand supports a population of three million { , although it is only an island. / , yet it is only an island. / *, however, it is only an island. }

19-26 ■ In which of the following sentences can **while/whereas** substitute for **but**?

1. She's just moved to Melbourne, *but* her friends have lived there two years already.
2. She's just moved to Melbourne, *but* she likes it already.
3. Everybody says she's in Melbourne now, *but* she never left Sydney.

4. John's an Australian, *but* most of his friends are New Zealanders.
5. John's an Australian, *but* he talks like a New Zealander.
6. There's a general belief that John's an Australian, *but* he's really a New Zealander.
7. The American colonies revolted, *but* the Australian colonies didn't have to go to war to gain their independence.
8. The American colonies revolted, *but* they had to go to war again in 1812.
9. Many people assume that Australia had a revolution, *but* of course they never had to go to war to gain their independence.

19-27 ■ In which of the above sentences can **on the contrary** substitute for **but**? (Recall that **on the contrary** requires sentence punctuation.)

19-28 ■ The use of **but** often gives the hearer information that is not stated explicitly by the speaker. For example, someone who says "He's a politician, but I like him" implies, or presupposes, that that person generally dislikes politicians. **But** is used (instead of **and**) because the fact that the person knows a politician who pleases him runs contrary to his expectations. Some of the bits of conversation below contain presuppositions that may not match with your own or with what you know about the world. If this is so, respond in such a way as to show your objection to what is implied.

1. A friend of mine just took an examination. He's a very good student, he studied very hard, *but* he passed.
   (Wait a minute!) (What do you mean "but"?) (If you study hard, you *should* pass.) (You'd *expect* him to pass.) and so on.
2. I was just introduced to a man named Locke. He's from New Zealand, *but* English is his native language.
3. We were invited out to dinner last night. They served us American food, *but* we enjoyed it.
4. We interviewed some new teachers for a job here. They've all had long experience, *but* they're pleasant enough.
5. We're going to hire two of the teachers, a man and a woman, *but* they'll be paid the same.
6. There are a lot more women driving cars these days, *but* many of them drive quite well.
7. My new neighbors are Fred and Anne Wilson. Fred's a very typical sort of husband, *but* he cooks dinner now and then and sometimes cleans the house.

19-29 ■ **On the other hand** and **on the contrary** both introduce an assertion in contrast with a preceding one. The difference between the two expressions is that with **on the contrary** the truth of the two assertions is in conflict:

[Everybody thinks he's an Australian.]
       He's not an Australian.
On the contrary, ⎫
~~On the other hand,~~ ⎬ he's a New Zealander.

       He's not an Australian.
~~On the contrary,~~ ⎫
On the other hand, ⎬ he's not a New Zealander either.

Read each of the sequences below with either **on the contrary** or **on the other hand**, whichever is correct.

1. Australia doesn't import wheat. On the . . . , they export it.
2. Australia doesn't import wheat. On the . . . , it may have to if the population suddenly increases.
3. Australia is as big as the United States. On the . . . , its population is less than that of Holland.
4. The Spanish and Dutch established no colonies in Australia. On the . . . , it was the British who first settled there.
5. Many people claim that Australia grew rapidly. On the . . . , the population in 1850, for example, was still only 5000.
6. Australia doesn't have a large population. On the . . . , it doesn't have a large pollution problem either.
7. Australia doesn't have a large population. On the . . . , it does have enough space for a large population.
8. Australia doesn't have a large population. On the . . . , the number of people per square mile is among the world's lowest.

19-P • (See page 131.)

19-Q • (See page 132.)

19-R • (See page 132.)

19-S • (See page 133.)

19-T • (See page 134.)

Section E

WRITING EXERCISES

19-A • In each of the following conversational sequences, exchanges B and C appear as identical. Their stress patterns are different, however. Draw a line under the word in each pair that you think should receive the heaviest stress. Then act out the sequences.

1. A *I wish someone would write to me.*
   B *There's a letter for you in the mailbox.*
   C [entering] *There's a letter for you in the mailbox.*
2. A *When are we going to eat?*
   B *Dinner's ready now.*
   C [entering] *Dinner's ready now!*
3. A *I've been having trouble getting an appointment.*
   B *Dr. Carter will see you.*
   C [entering] *Dr. Carter will see you now.*
4. A *We've had to start without you.*
   B *I'm sorry to be late.*
   C [entering] *I'm sorry to be late!*
5. A *What time does the news come on?*
   B *The news is on.*
   C [entering] *The news is on.*

19-B • For each of the *italicized* verbs below substitute a phrasal verb with **take**. Look up the meanings in the dictionary whenever you need to.

1. A Crime seems to be { *occupying* / *taking* __up__ } more and more of our time. When did this one happen?

2. B It { *occurred* / *took* _____ } just before noon.

3. A How many { *participated,* / *took* _____, } do you think?

4. B I don't know, but the victim { *obtained* / *took* _____ } an insurance policy two days before.

5. A It looks like the murderer { *left* / *took* _____ } in a hurry.

6. B Yes. He even left his coat. He must have { *removed* it / *taken* it _____ } for some reason.

7. A Probably to try to $\begin{cases} remove \\ take \_\_\_\_\_ \end{cases}$ those blood stains.

8. B The state will $\begin{cases} assume\ control \\ take \_\_\_\_\_ \end{cases}$ from here on.

19-C • Parts of the meaning of the dialog below are indicated between the lines, in brackets. These parts are in the form of presuppositions, some of which are true for the dialog, some not. Cross out the ones that you think are not true.

A *It's rather warm for May, don't you think?*
   [May is not usually this warm] [It is not May]
B *Yes. This would even be warm for September.*
   [It is not September] [May is warmer than September]
C *Even I feel the heat and I'm from Darwin.*
   [Darwin has cooler temperatures] [I wouldn't expect to be this warm here]
D *I'm also a little thirsty. How about a drink?*
   [I'm warm] [Someone else is thirsty]
E *Just water for me. I'm on a strict diet.*
   [Water is out of the ordinary] [Water is part of the diet]
F *That's unusual for a person your age.*
   [People E's age don't usually diet]
G *That would even be unusual for a person my age.*
   [G is younger than E] [G is also on a diet] [G's dieting would be less unexpected than E's]

19-D • Negative sufficiency can be expressed with either **too** or **enough**: **too little = not enough, too short = not long enough, too young = not old enough**, and so on. Notice the pairing of opposites here: **short/long, young/old**. With descriptive adjectives such as these one of each pair is taken to be "basic." That is, we customarily ask **How old are you?** not **How young are you?** or **How long is the table?** not **How short is the table?** Choose the "basic" adjective of the paired opposites below by crossing out the other. Then write an answer to each question in the form of **too** Adj **to** . . . or Adj **enough to** . . . .

1. How $\begin{cases} young \\ old \end{cases}$ is he?

   Old enough to talk like an adult.
   Too old to talk to like a child.
   Young enough to still talk to like a child.
   Too young to talk like an adult.

2. How {small / big} are the rooms?

_____

3. How {long / short} was the movie?

_____

4. How {slow / fast} does she drive?

_____

5. How {hard / easy} was the test?

_____

6. How {near / far} is the next town?

_____

7. How {heavy / light} is that letter?

_____

8. How {short / tall} are you?

_____

9. How {high / low} is that table?

_____

10. How {shallow / deep} is that water?

_____

11. How {thick / thin} are these walls?

_____

12. How {narrow / wide} is that doorway?

_____

Writing Exercises

13. How $\begin{Bmatrix} \text{much} \\ \text{little} \end{Bmatrix}$ money do you have?

_____

14. How $\begin{Bmatrix} \text{many} \\ \text{few} \end{Bmatrix}$ people are here?

_____

19-E • Rewrite the sentences below using the words supplied. The construction in numbers 4 and 6 is **not so ... as ....**

1. Sydney is farther away from Adelaide than you can drive in a day.

   Sydney is too _____

2. There is more land in Australia than the government knows what to do with.

   There is so much _____
   _____

3. Australia on this map occupies a bigger space than you can cover with your hand.

   Australia on this map occupies too _____
   _____

4. Australia and New Zealand are less tied to each other economically than some people think.

   Australia and New Zealand are not so _____
   _____ *as* _____

5. New Zealand is made up of more islands than it is able to exercise effective control over.

   New Zealand is made up of too _____
   _____

6. Australian agricultural production is sometimes less than the government would always like to have us believe.

   Australian agricultural production is sometimes not so _____
   as _____

19-F • Comparison can be expressed in degrees of formality, just as with other parts of the language. Generally more formal (and usually more economical) than the comparative *construction* is the single comparative *word*: **Our exports now *equal* our imports** (We now export *as much as* we import); **Our exports now *exceed* our imports** (We now export *more than* we import); **Our exports are now at their all-time *maximum*** (We now export *the most* that we ever have). Rewrite the following more formally, replacing the comparative construction with the word supplied.

1. He's more persistent than funny. (*exceed*)

    His persistence exceeds his humor.

2. Economic considerations are more important than political ones. (*outweigh*)

    _____

3. Australia and Sri Lanka have roughly the same number of people. (*equal*)

    _____

4. Australia and New Zealand have had the smallest amount of conflict over the years. (*minimum*)

    _____

5. The eastern part of Australia has a better climate than the western part. (*superior*)

    _____

6. The Australian "Outback" looks somewhat like the American West. (*resemble*)

    _____

7. The Australian "Outback" looks somewhat like the American West. (*bear a resemblance to*)

    _____

Writing Exercises

19-G • Statements in the superlative (**The Sydney opera house is the most famous**) are often supported by circumstantial evidence (**Singers come there from all over the world**). Such sequences can usually be restated in the **so/such** form: **The Sydney opera house is so famous that singers come there from all over the world.** Rewrite the following paragraph, substituting **so/such** forms for the *italicized* superlatives and supporting evidence.

The men of the Australian mining city of Mt. Isa talk mostly in superlatives, for it is *the most unusual city. An accurate description would be difficult.* Mt. Isa is *the most prosperous city (average weekly wage $200).* It is *the most remote city (1200 road miles to the nearest state capital).* It is the *best integrated city (forty-seven nationalities).* It is the *smoothest running city (no major industrial problems in ten years).* And it is the *heaviest drinking city (you can't begin to describe it).* It is a city that works.[4]

The men of the Australian mining city of Mt. Isa talk mostly in superlatives. It is such

---

[4]Adapted from "Aussie Mining City an Oasis of Superlatives," by David Lamb in *The Los Angeles Times*, July 7, 1974. Copyright, 1974, *The Los Angeles Times*. Reprinted by permission.

19-H • The list below is made up of words each of which has an opposite. These opposites can be paraphrased in the sense of "more" or "less." Rewrite the entire list as paired opposites arranged under the vague categories of "more" and "less."

	more	less
1.	*top*	*bottom*
2.	_____	_____
3.	_____	_____
4.	_____	_____
5.	_____	_____
6.	_____	_____
7.	_____	_____
8.	_____	_____
9.	_____	_____
10.	_____	_____
11.	_____	_____
12.	_____	_____
13.	_____	_____

a. bottom
b. command
c. decrease
d. deficiency
e. excess
f. follow
g. increase
h. inferior
i. junior
j. lack
k. lead
l. least
m. lower
n. maximum
o. minimum
p. most
q. nadir
r. obey
s. over
t. senior
u. superior
v. surplus
w. top
x. under
y. upper
z. zenith

19-I • **COMPOUNDS**

(Rewrite the following sentences rearranging the words in *italics* into a compound. Do not include **based** in the compound for number 4.)

1. Australia had a *rush for gold* in 1851.

   Australia had a gold rush in 1851.

2. The conversation took place at the *Center for International Students*.

   _____

3. The *occupation of sheep raising* is less common today than in the past.

   _____

Writing Exercises   127

4. Australia used to have an *economy based on wheat growing and sheep raising*.

   _____

5. The early *history of the United States* parallels somewhat that of Australia.

   _____

6. For Australia there are some *parallels in the early history of the United States*.

   _____

19-J • RESTATEMENT

(Complete the restatement by supplying the correct form. Leave out **each other** in the restatement of number 6.)

1. Dutch, Spanish, and Portuguese ships *sighted* Australia in the seventeenth century. (*catch*)

   Dutch, Spanish, and Portuguese ships *caught sight of Australia in the seventeenth century*.

2. The colonies *revolted*. (*start*)

   The colonies _____

3. This westward expansion *occurred* early in the nineteenth century. (*have*)

   This westward expansion _____ its _____

   _____

4. They're *searching quickly* to find a replacement for him. (*conduct*)

   They're _____

5. The government *generously granted* the settlers a large piece of land. (*give*)

   The government _____

   _____

6. Barren western portions of the two countries *closely resemble each other physically*. (*bear*)

   Barren western portions of the two countries _____

   _____

19-K • Decide where comma punctuation is needed in the following sentences and write it in. Not all sentences will need commas, however.

1. They were angry frankly.
2. They were angry probably.
3. They were angry immediately.
4. On the table I've laid out some plans.
5. On the advice of my friends I've laid out some plans.
6. On the contrary I've laid out some plans.
7. They wanted us to tell you the truth.
8. They understand us to tell you the truth.
9. They contacted you to tell you the truth.

19-L • Write the constructions below as full sentences in the comparative form. **X+** is **more/-er**; **X–** is **less**; **X** is **than**.

1. Sydney is [X+ far] away from Adelaide [You can drive [X far] in a day]

   Sydney is farther away from Adelaide than you can drive in a day.

2. There is [X+ much] land in Australia [The government knows what to do with [X much] land]

3. Australia on this map occupies a [X+ big] space [You can cover a [X big] space with your hand]

4. Australia and New Zealand are [X– tied] to each other economically [Some people think that Australia and New Zealand are [X tied] to each other economically]

5. New Zealand is made up of [X+ many] islands [New Zealand is able to exercise effective control over [X many] islands]

Writing Exercises

6. Australian agricultural production is sometimes [X-] [The government would always like to have us believe that Australian agricultural production is [X]]

_____

_____

(Check the sentences you have written against the sentences given in exercise 19-E.)

19-M • Each of the following sentences, taken from student compositions, contains a comparative construction that is incorrect. Change each sentence in such a way as to remove the error.

1. *Some of the students here look like busier than other students.

2. *I think this school is more well equipped than the other.

3. *I spent my school years mainly in a student activity like an athlete than in an academic one.

4. *I was always on the practice field than in the library.

5. *Mexico doesn't need as much oil as the United States needs it.

6. *For most people a television set is still too expensive to buy it.

19-N • Refer again to the table in 19-22. Using the information you see there, write observations in the form of double comparisons. For example:

Japan has more telephones than Argentina has people.
The U.S. produces less coal than Egypt does cotton.

19-O • CLOZE

(In each blank space write a word that you think fits naturally.)

The Venetian traveler, Marco Polo (1254-1324), _____ to a land now
                                                       1
generally believed _____ be Australia, though the name originated
                    2
_____ the Spanish explorer, De Quiros, about 1605. _____ Dutch-
   3   4
man, Abel Tasman, discovered New Zealand _____ 1642 and visited
                                           5
the island south _____ Australia which now bears his name.
                   6
_____ than a hundred years later, the _____, Captain Cook with
   7   8
the members of _____ astronomical expedition, landed at Poverty Bay,
                 9
_____ Zealand, in 1769. After sailing around _____ islands, he
   10   11
proceeded to Australia, explored _____ southwestern coast, and gave
                                    12
it the _____ of New South Wales. [5]
         13

19-P

• The paragraph below, containing many constructions of contrast and comparison, has as yet been given no punctuation. Write in commas (,) or periods (.) or semi-colons (;) wherever you think they should be. Change small letters to capitals where necessary.

New Zealand unlike Australia was settled by free English citizens not convicts yet much of the history of the two countries is quite similar both had to conquer native populations for example both adopted a form of state socialism and both have always had strong ties with England

5 *yet New Zealand led the way in progressive government while Australia gave women the right to vote just before the turn of the century New Zealand did so even a few years earlier although both countries pursue independent policies by being members of the British Commonwealth they have retained loose economic ties with England.*

[5] Adapted from *A Shorter History of England and Greater Britain,* rev. ed., by Arthur L. Cross. (New York: Macmillan, 1929).

Writing Exercises

19-Q • Each of the following sentences, taken from student compositions, contains a contrast construction that is incorrect. Change each sentence in such a way as to remove the error.

1. *Although I was educated in the Far East. I am familiar with many western customs.

2. *This country is very expensive when compare with mine.

3. *Although they live a long way from school, but there are buses they can take.

4. *Newspapers should be free, on the contrary, they should also be responsible for what they write.

5. *If I did badly at my former university I would only fail, although here I would be kicked out.

19-R • Write out the contrasts indicated below using the supplied terms but otherwise with constructions of your own choice. Incorporate facts from the Reading if you wish.

1. Australia/England (size)

    Australia is about the size of the U.S., whereas *England is much smaller*.

2. Australia/the United States (independence)

    _____. However, _____

    _____

3. size/population (Australia)

    _____; yet _____

    _____

4. exploration/colonization (Dutch and Spanish)

    _____, but _____

    _____

Unit 19

5. people in Australia/sheep in Australia (number)

   _____. On the other hand, _____

6. Dutch, Spanish, and Portuguese/English (discovery, settlement)

   Although _____, _____

   _____

19-S • In the paragraph below cross out whichever items do not fit the meaning and structure of the sentence.

Both Australia and Great Britain are islands; (1) { a. yet / b. conversely, / c. in contrast, / d. on the contrary, / e. instead, / f. while } the former colony is vastly bigger than the mother country. Britain could have held on to her Australian colony longer. (2) { a. Yet / b. Conversely, / c. In contrast, / d. On the contrary, / e. Instead, / f. While } however, the Australians were granted their independence before the turn of the century. One might well imagine that two nations as far apart geographically as England and Australia would have little contact with each other. (3) { a. Yet / b. Conversely, / c. In contrast, / d. On the contrary, / e. Instead, / f. While } this is not so. (4) { a. Yet / b. Conversely, / c. In contrast, / d. On the contrary, / e. Instead, / f. While } the two have close economic ties. For example, Australia exports wool and imports textiles. (5) { a. Yet / b. Conversely, / c. In contrast, / d. On the contrary, / e. Instead, / f. While } Great Britain imports wool and exports

Writing Exercises

textiles. (6) {
a. Yet
b. Conversely,
c. In contrast,
d. On the contrary,
e. Instead,
f. While
} thousands of miles of ocean separate them, membership in the Commonwealth draws them together.

19-T • Using the Reading from Section C as a model, write a short composition of three paragraphs in which you compare and contrast. Let the first paragraph justify the basis for making a comparison; let the second paragraph compare similarities; and let the third contrast differences. Possible topics might be comparison of two countries, such as China and Japan, Egypt and Saudi Arabia, Argentina and Brazil, India and Pakistan, and so on. Or you might choose to compare two fields of study (e.g. geology and geography), two historical figures, two religions, and so on.

Unit 20

20-1 DIALOG

THE NEW YORK TIMES

RAY The paper's rather small this week.
RAMÓN Small! You call that small? There must be a couple of hundred pages there.
RAY I expected there to be more. The *Times* is always much bigger on Sunday.
RAMÓN Well, I thought I'd already seen big newspapers, but this is insane. It should be illegal to use that much paper. What makes it so large, anyway?
RAY A lot of advertising, for one thing. And it also puts out a lot of news that you don't see anywhere else.
RAMÓN But it's impossible to read it all. Has it always been this big?
RAY Oh no. This is fairly recent. . . . Since the war. Until then the *Times* had been about the size of most other papers.
RAMÓN The war! You call that recent? I guess we have different ideas about time.
RAY It's recent if you consider that the *Times* began publishing in 1851. Back then it had just a few pages and only cost a penny.
RAMÓN What do you think it'll cost in the year 2000?
RAY I'm sure by then the price will have gone over a dollar. But the *Times* is irreplaceable, and I still say that'll be fairly cheap for what you get.
RAMÓN Cheap! You call that cheap?

VOCABULARY

advertise (advertisement)   penny   insane (insanity)
put out   dollar   illegal (illegality)
consider (consideration)   impossible (impossibility)
                                     irreplaceable
                                     cheap

                                     rather
                                     fairly

20-2 ■ DIALOG VARIATION

1. *It should be illegal to use that much paper.*
   To use that much paper should be illegal.
   Using that much paper should be illegal.
   It shouldn't be legal to use that much paper.
2. *Has it always been this big?*
   Has it always been as big as this?
   Has it always been so big?
3. . . . *the* Times *had been about the size of most other papers.*
   . . . the *Times* had been about as big as most other papers.
   . . . the *Times* had been no bigger than most other papers.
4. . . . *the* Times *began publishing in 1851.*
   . . . the *Times* began to publish in 1851.
   . . . the *Times* began its publishing in 1851.
   . . . Publication of the *Times* began in 1851.
5. *Back then it had only a few pages.*
   Back then it consisted of only a few pages.
   Back then there were only a few pages in it.

20-3 ■ QUESTIONS

1. What disagreements do Ray and Ramón have?
2. How do you explain them?
3. What disadvantage does Ramón find with the size of the newspaper?
4. What day is it in the Dialog?
5. What war is mentioned?
6. What does "recent" mean for each of the two men?
7. Does Ray think the *Times* would be worth a dollar?
8. What kind of newspaper do you think Ramón has been most familiar with?

20-4 SOUND PATTERNS

Appearing in the Dialog are four adjectives with a prefix: *in*sane, *il*legal, *im*possible, and *ir*replaceable. However, these four seemingly different prefixes (**in-, il-, im-,** and **ir-**) are actually the same: basically **in-**, meaning "not." The form **in-** occurs before words beginning with vowels and most consonants (**in***a*ccurate, **in***c*orrect); **im-** occurs before words beginning with **m, b,** and **p** (im*m*ovable, im*b*alance, im*p*ossible); **il-** and **ir-** occur before words beginning with **l** and **r**, respectively (il*l*egal, ir*r*eplaceable). Prefixes generally do not change the stress patterns of words in English.

20-A • (See page 151.)

20-5 ■ Not all instances of initial **in-/im-/il-/ir-** are negative prefixes. For example, the initial syllables of the words *in*terest, *im*portant, *Il*linois, and *ir*ritate are not negative, and some are not even prefixes. From the list of words below, most of which have appeared in previous units, identify those that you think contain a negative prefix.

1. indecision
2. introduce
3. imprint
4. impractical
5. illustrate
6. immoral
7. inattention
8. irrational
9. insurance
10. inequality
11. improbable
12. irrigate
13. inspect
14. illusion
15. impulse
16. inexact
17. imprecise
18. illiterate
19. instruct
20. imperial
21. inability
22. irrelevant
23. impress
24. irresistable
25. information
26. illegitimate
27. include
28. immigrate
29. irreversible
30. involuntary

20-6 PHRASAL VERBS

—And it also *puts out* a lot of news that you don't see anywhere else.

In Unit 17 it was pointed out that verb + particle constructions that take direct objects allow them in either of two positions, before or after the particle:

It puts out *a lot of news.* ~ **It puts** *a lot of news* **out.**

If the object is long, however, it can come only *after* the particle:

It puts out *a lot of news that you don't see anywhere else.*
⊬ *It puts *a lot of news that you don't see anywhere else* **out.**

These restrictions are similar to those relating to the position of direct and indirect objects, as practiced in Volume I, exercise 9-D.

Section A

20-B • (See page 151.)

SPEECH ACT

—The paper's *rather* small this week.
　　　　　　　　　• • •
—I still say that'll be *fairly* cheap for what you get.

20-7 The modifiers **fairly** and **rather** reflect attitudes of the person speaking. **Fairly** suggests movement toward an ideal of some kind; **rather** suggests movement away from that ideal. Compare:

　　We won, although it was a $\begin{Bmatrix} rather \\ ?fairly \end{Bmatrix}$ close game.
　　　　(I wish it hadn't been so close.)

　　We lost, although it was a $\begin{Bmatrix} ?rather \\ fairly \end{Bmatrix}$ close game.
　　　　(I wish it had been even closer.)

In addition, **rather**, but not **fairly**, can often suggest lack of expectation:

　　I thought the book was $\begin{Bmatrix} rather \\ ?fairly \end{Bmatrix}$ good (, which surprised me).

20-8 ■ Read the following sentences with either **fairly** or **rather**, whichever seems more natural. For practice purposes, do not use **rather** in its sense of surprise.

1. This coffee is _____ hot; I can't drink it yet.
2. This coffee is _____ hot; I can still drink it.
3. He's _____ young; he needs more time to learn.
4. He's _____ young; he has a lot of time to learn.
5. You speak _____ slowly; it's easy to understand you.
6. You speak _____ fast; it's hard to understand you.
7. You speak _____ slowly; you ought to go a little faster.
8. You speak _____ fast; have you been practicing?
9. I made a _____ large deposit.
10. I made a _____ large withdrawal.
11. Wages are _____ high, but so are prices.
12. Prices are _____ high, but so are wages.
13. The city is _____ far away, but we don't mind it.

14. The city is _____ far away, so we don't mind it.
15. They're _____ likely to help us.
16. They're _____ likely to hurt us.

B

20-9 ■ DIALOG IMPROVISATION

(Try to re-create or even improvise a variation of the Dialog at the beginning of this unit, as you remember it.)

A The paper's rather . . .
B You call that small? There must . . .
A I expected there . . .
B What makes it . . .
A A lot of advertising, for one thing, and . . .
B Was it always . . .
A Oh no. This is fairly . . .
B You call that . . .

More on Modals

—You call that small? There *must be* a couple of hundred pages there.
 . . .
—I'm sure by then the price *will have gone* over a dollar.

20-10 Most modals can have more than one meaning, as first suggested in Unit 4, Section B:

He *won't* be here. (He refuses.)   He *won't* be here. (He's sick.)
He *must* be here. (It's an order.)   He *must* be here. (There's his hat.)
He *should* be here. (He has an obligation.)   He *should* be here. (He doesn't live far.)
He *can't* be here. (He's busy.)   He *can't* be here. (I don't believe it.)
He *may* be here. (He has permission.)   He *may* be here. (That's my guess.)
He *could* be here. (Nothing prevents him.)   He *could* be here. (It's very possible.)
He *wouldn't* be here (even if you paid him).   He *wouldn't* be here (if he were sick).

20-11 The modals in the left-hand column generally switch to other forms for past time (see Volume I, 4-10); (will) He *was going to* be here; (must) He *had to* be here; (should) He *was supposed to* be here; (can) He *was able to* be here; (may) He *was allowed to* be here.

The verb following all the modals in the right-hand column assumes the *perfect* form for past-time reference:

He *will have been* here (and gone before we arrive).
He *must have been* here. (There's his hat.)
He *should have been* here (hours ago).
He *can't have been* here. (It's just not possible.)
He *may have been* here. (There's no way of telling.)
He *could have been* here. (It's entirely possible.)
He *would have been* here (if he hadn't been sick).

The modal-like forms **happen, seem, supposed,** and **likely** (See Volume I, 4-10) interact with past events according to how the speaker feels himself related to the event he is talking about. They therefore have past-time forms corresponding to those of either of the above columns. Compare:

He *seemed to be* confused. (= It *seemed* to me *then* that he was confused.)
He *seems to have been* confused. (= It *seems* to me *now* that he was confused.)

20-12 **Will** and **would** are not generally used in subordinate clauses:

Will you call us before you ~~will~~ arrive?
When you ~~will~~ see him, say "hello" for me.

20-13 ■ Imagine that a party is about to take place at this location. Decide on the probability of each of the guests' being already here on the basis of the evidence supplied.

1. I hear Frank's car outside.
   Then he must be here.
2. I saw Sally down the street.
   Then she may/should be here.
3. Fred doesn't like parties.
   Then he won't be here.
4. Suzie wasn't sure if she'd be free.
5. I hear Jack's voice in the other room.
6. Mary said she'd tell us as soon as she arrived.
7. I don't see Harry anywhere around.
8. Barbara says she'd arrive at 8:00. My watch says 7:58.

9. Max said he was coming, and you can always believe him.
10. There's Nancy's coat.
11. Steve's sick. I know that for a fact.
12. It takes Karen a half hour to get here, and she left home a half hour ago.

20-14 ■ Harvey's daily life is one disaster after another, and on top of that he's not very bright. Here's what happened to him last week.

1. He failed his exam.
   He should have (studied harder).
2. No, he failed because he was too tired.
   He should have (gotten more sleep).
3. That was hard. Some of his neighbors played loud music all night.
4. He asked them to stop, but they refused.
5. He called the police and then went out for a drive.
6. He fell asleep at the wheel and had a little accident.
7. The first thing he did was try to call his mother-in-law.
8. The line was busy, but he had to break open the telephone to get his money back.
9. He left the scene of the accident and took a bus back home.
10. When he got home he discovered that a fire had destroyed a thousand dollars that he had been keeping under his mattress.

20-15 ■ The expressions **would rather, would just as soon,** and **might as well** indicate varying degrees of preference and desire. Compare:

A **Will you order now?**
B I*'d rather* wait until we're all here. [strong]
C I*'d just as soon* not be the only one. [less strong]
D I *might as well.* I have to leave first anyway. [weak]

With this in mind, respond to each of the following as alternatives to choose between:

1. a subscription to the *New York Times* or the *Times* of London?
   A **Do you want a subscription to the *New York Times* or the *Times* of London?**
   B **I'd just as soon subscribe to the London *Times*. (It's cheaper.)**
   C **I might as well subscribe to the *New York Times* (since I'm in New York).**
   D **I'd rather not subscribe to either. (I don't have time to read them.)**
2. tea or coffee?
3. milk or lemon in your tea?
4. conversation in English or (your native language)?
5. talk about school or something else?
6. listen to music or not listen to music?
7. go on to the writing exercises now or later?

Section B

20-C • (See page 152.)

20-D • (See page 153.)

20-E • (See page 153.)

20-16   READING (326 words)

A GREAT NEWS STORY

Carr Van Anda, managing editor of the *New York Times*, believed in "hard" news, thoroughly and accurately presented. A tireless worker, he often stayed at the office all night. He was there at 1:20 A.M. on April 15, 1912, when a distress signal came in from Newfoundland that the
5   pride of Britain's passenger fleet, the *Titanic*, was in trouble. The new ship, believed unsinkable, had hit an iceberg and was in some kind of danger. But was it really serious or just a narrow escape? Had the passengers needed to abandon ship? Van Anda could not tell from the short and confusing message. Although he was generally considered a conser-
10 vative and cautious man, Van Anda gambled on the unthinkable: that the *Titanic* was sinking.

He threw his staff into action; the story was approached from all angles. Some reporters put together lists of famous persons on board; others turned out features about the ship and other important passenger
15 liners; still others did stories on similar sea disasters. In other words, Van Anda and the *Times* went all the way with the story; they played it big. At other newspapers, editors were more cautious, inserting such words as "rumored" here and there. Van Anda's three-column headline reflected the sureness that has marked the *Times* throughout its history:

20   NEW LINER HITS ICEBERG;
                    SINKING BY THE BOW AT MIDNIGHT;
                    WOMEN PUT OFF IN LIFEBOATS;
                    LAST WIRELESS 12:27 A.M.

Officials of the White Star Line, which owned the *Titanic*, had been
25 releasing optimistic statements all during the day of April 15, and did not confirm Van Anda's story until the evening of April 16. Van Anda's final edition, which went to press about three hours after the *Times* had received the first brief wireless report, stated flatly that the *Titanic* had sunk. This was perhaps a great risk on Van Anda's part and his "deduc-

30 tive journalism" may have shocked many, but it remains as one of the great against-a-deadline news-coverage feats in all journalism.[1]

VOCABULARY

abandon (abandonment)	editor (edit, edition)	tireless
gamble (gamble)	distress (distress)	unsinkable
sink/sank/sunk	signal (signal)	narrow
throw/threw/thrown (throw)	pride (proud)	conservative (conserve, conservation)
approach (approach)	fleet	
turn out	iceberg	cautious (caution)
insert (insertion)	danger (dangerous)	unthinkable
rumor (rumor)	escape (escape)	optimistic (optimism)
reflect (reflection)	message	brief (brevity)
mark (mark)	staff	deductive (deduce, deduction)
own (ownership)	action (act)	
release (release)	angle	
confirm (confirmation)	feature	thoroughly (thoroughness)
shock (shock)	liner	
	disaster (disastrous)	accurately (accuracy)
	headline	flatly
	bow	
	lifeboat	
	wireless	
	press	
	risk (risk)	
	journalism	
	deadline	
	feat	

20-17 ■ INCLUDED MEANING

(For each of the following passages pick the one statement whose meaning is part of the meaning of the passage.)

1. *Carr Van Anda, managing editor of the* New York Times, *believed in "hard" news, thoroughly and accurately presented.*
    a. The *New York Times* believed in "hard" news.
    b. The managing editor was accurate.
    c. Van Anda was managing editor.
2. *He was there at 1:20 A.M. on April 15, 1912, when a distress signal came in from Newfoundland that the pride of Britain's passenger fleet, the* Titanic, *was in trouble.*

[1]Adapted from *The Elite Press*, by John C. Merrill. Copyright 1968 by the Pitman Publishing Corporation. Reprinted by permission.

Section C

a. Newfoundland was the pride of Britain's passenger fleet.
   b. The *Titanic* was part of Britain's passenger fleet.
   c. Britain's passenger fleet was in trouble.
3. *Although he was generally considered a conservative and cautious man, Van Anda gambled on the unthinkable: that the* Titanic *was sinking.*
   a. Van Anda didn't think the *Titanic* was sinking.
   b. Van Anda took a chance.
   c. Van Anda gambled on the *Titanic.*
4. *Van Anda's three-column headline reflected the sureness that has marked the* Times *throughout its history.*
   a. The *Times* has been sure.
   b. The *Times* is thorough.
   c. The history of the *Times* is reflected in its headlines.
5. *Officials of the White Star Line, which owned the* Titanic, *had been releasing optimistic statements all during the day of April 15, and did not confirm Van Anda's story until the evening of April 16.*
   a. The owners of the *Titanic* did not at first send out accurate reports.
   b. The owners of the *Titanic* quickly admitted it was sinking.
   c. The owners of the *Titanic* did not confirm Van Anda's story.

20-18 ▪ QUESTIONS

1. What did the White Star Line think of the *Titanic*?
2. Why was the sinking so hard to believe?
3. How did Van Anda know the *Titanic* was sinking?
4. What part of the *Times*'s story could have been written before the *Titanic* set sail?
5. What three sources of information about the sinking are mentioned?
6. About how much time elapsed between the first distress signal and the confirmation of Van Anda's story?
7. What was the "risk" that Van Anda took?

20-F • VOCABULARY RELATIONS (See page 154.)

20-19 COMPOUNDS

A newspaper headline tries to compress a large amount of information into a small space, as in the headline sample in the Reading. One of the ways of achieving such compression (for other ways see 20-Q) is through the frequent use of noun compounds. If later in 1912, for example, the government had *investigated* the *sinking* of the *Titanic*, the corresponding newspaper story might have been headlined TITANIC SINKING INVESTIGATED. If the *investigation* had been *renewed* at a later date, the corresponding headline might have read TITANIC SINKING INVESTIGATION RENEWED, or

RENEWAL OF TITANIC SINKING INVESTIGATION, or RENEWED INVESTIGATION OF TITANIC SINKING, and so on.

20-G • (See page 155.)

20-H • **RESTATEMENT** (See page 156.)

20-20 PUNCTUATION

The *semicolon* (;) usually functions in place of the period or full stop as a mark of punctuation between sentences that are closely related. Generally, the semicolon is equivalent in this regard to a comma plus **and**. Thus, in the Reading we have, for example:

He threw his staff into action; the story was approached from all angles.
. . . into action, *and* **the story was . . .**

Notice that, contrary to sentences following periods, the first letter of the sentence following a semicolon is not capitalized. Find the other three semicolons in the second paragraph of the Reading and note their function.

20-I • (See page 156.)

20-21 ■ **READING IMPROVISATION**

(Complete each of the following sentences with what you remember from the Reading.)

1. Carr Van Anda believed in . . .
2. He often stayed . . .
3. He was there when . . .
4. The new ship had . . .
5. Van Anda could not tell . . .
6. He gambled . . .
7. Van Anda threw . . .
8. Some reporters put together . . .
9. Van Anda's three-column headline . . .

Section D

The Past in the Past

—Until the war the newspaper *had been* about the size of most other papers.

20-22 The "basic" time sequence for citing series of events is from earlier to later. The simple tenses suffice for this:

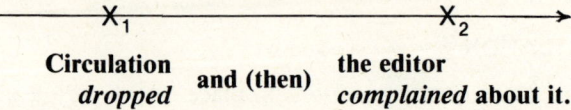

Circulation   **the editor**
dropped and (then) *complained* about it.

If in the citing of the events the earlier-to-later sequence is reversed, a *perfect* form is often required for the earlier event. For the above example this would be the *past perfect*, a "past within a past," so to speak:

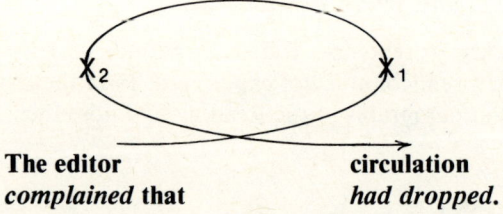

The editor   **circulation**
complained that   *had dropped*.

For earlier past events that had duration, the *past perfect continuous* can be used:

The editor complained that circulation *had been dropping*.

With adverbials that already make the time relationships explicit, such as **before, after,** and **when,** both events can be expressed in the simple past:[2]

After } circulation { *dropped* } the editor complained.
When   { *had dropped* }

---

[2]For an outline/summary of all the tenses in English, see Appendix C.

20-23 ■ Using information supplied in the table below,[3] comment on the comparative ages and circulations of the various newspapers. For example:

> When *Asahi Shimbun* began in 1879, *La Prensa* had already been publishing for ten years.
> By the time *Excelsior* reached a circulation of 120,000, it had been in existence for 43 years.

and so on.

name	city	founded	present circulation	circulation in 1960
Al Ahram	Cairo	1876	280,000	150,000
Asahi Shimbun	Tokyo	1879	6,000,000	4,000,000
Excelsior	Mexico City	1917	130,000	120,000
The Hindu	Madras	1878	140,000	90,000
Le Monde	Paris	1944	310,000	156,000
La Prensa	Buenos Aires	1869	290,000	250,000
The New York Times	New York	1851	900,000	700,000
Pravda	Moscow	1912	7,000,000	6,000,000
The Times	London	1785	360,000	255,000
Die Welt	Hamburg	1946	300,000	230,000

20-24 ■ Both **had** and **would** contract to **'d** after vowels. This means that sometimes the only clue to the identity of **'d** is the verb form following it: **They said they'd called the police** (*had called*); **They said they'd call the police** (*would call*). Listen to the following constructions and say whether **'d** is **would** or **had**.

1. She said she'd studied English.
   had
2. She said she'd study English.
   would
3. (The rest of the statements are supplied in the Instructor's Manual.)

---

[3] From *The Europa Yearbook 1975*. Published by Europa Publications Ltd., London.

20-25 ▪ Mark a recent year in terms of some previous event in your life.
1. **By 1970 (I had finished high school).**
2. **By 1972 (I had been living in _____ for _____ years).**
3. **By 1971 (I had my degree).**
4. and so on.

20-J • (See page 157.)

20-K • (See page 158.)

20-L • (See page 158.)

20-M • (See page 158.)

E

20-N • **CLOZE** (See page 159.)

> The Past for the Present
>
> —But *was* it really serious or just a narrow escape? *Had* the passengers *needed* to abandon ship?

20-26 The use of tenses in present time reporting of past events is largely dependent on style and point of view, both of which are matters of choice. Although the two sentences above are in the form of questions, they are not questions addressed to the reader of the story. Rather, they represent the thoughts of the person being written about. Typically serving such a function in a story are sentences having any or all of the following characteristics:

- direct-speech word order (**"*Is it* really serious . . . ?"**)
- omission of the reporting verb (**He wondered if . . .**)
- tense shift backward (**Did . . . need→Had . . . needed**)

Alternatively then, lines 5-8 of the Reading could have been written using quotation marks:

> *The new ship, believed unsinkable, had hit an iceberg and was in some kind of danger. "But is it really serious or just a narrow escape?" he wondered. "Have the passengers needed to abandon ship?" Van Anda could not tell . . .*

or they could have been written purely as a report:

> *The new ship, believed unsinkable, had hit an iceberg and was in some kind of danger. But he wondered if it was really serious or just a narrow escape, and whether the passengers needed to abandon ship. Van Anda could not tell . . .*

20-27 ■ The following newspaper description of a commune in China contains observations of the author as well as of a person mentioned in the article. Identify each sentence according to whose viewpoint you think is being represented, the author's or the party secretary's. In a couple of sentences it could be either.

> *1 One student had made the general statement that in the commune pay for men and women was already equal. 2 This provoked discussion among teachers and students during the question period. 3 It was settled by the third commune member present, the party secretary. 4 Hadn't equal pay for equal work long been party policy? 5 And of course it has constantly been called for by Chairman Mao. 6 But it had not yet been fully put into practice. 7 You had to work hard to achieve this. 8 He said that in their own brigade much progress had been made. 9 But pay rates still slightly favored the men, and the struggle for equality had to be carried through to the end. 10 It appeared that this was being done.*[4]

20-28 ■ Each of you will be given a slip of paper containing a different sentence from a brief newspaper story. Don't show your sentence to anyone else in the class, but memorize it and then destroy the piece of paper. Everyone will then compare sentences and together try to determine through discussion the order in which they should occur so as to reconstruct the story.[5]

---

[4]Adapted from "Class Exams in China," by David Crook. *The Los Angeles Times,* August 17, 1975, Part IV. Reprinted by permission.
[5]The story is provided in the Instructor's Manual.

20-O • (See page 160.)

20-P • (See page 161.)

20-Q • (See page 161.)

20-R • (See page 161.)

WRITING EXERCISES

20-A • Before each of the words listed below write the negative prefix **in-** or one of its variants (**im-/il-/ir-**), whichever is required.

1. _in_complete
2. _____perfect
3. _____logical
4. _____regular
5. _____mature
6. _____expensive
7. _____formal
8. _____religious
9. _____human
10. _____personal
11. _____definite
12. _____legible
13. _____active
14. _____measurable
15. _____visible
16. _____responsible
17. _____polite
18. _____sensitive

20-B • Rewrite the following sentences substituting the verb+particle in parentheses for the *italicized* verb. Change **to** to **on** in number 4.

1. It *prints* all the news it can. (*put out*)
   It puts out all the news it can.

2. It *prints* it. (*put out*)
   It puts it out.

3. The newspaper *provided* the money for the scholarship. (*put up*)

4. When you're finished, *return* the newspaper to the shelf. (*put back*)

5. The paper's circulation *covers* a wide area outside the city. (*take in*)

6. The newspaper *dispatched* a reporter to the scene of the accident. (*send out*)

7. The government *removed* the newspaper's freedom to publish. (*take away*)

8. The police *took* the reporter to jail. (*carry off*)

20-C • Complete the following sentences by writing in the main clauses corresponding to the constructions in brackets.

1. *They must have spoken Spanish*, because they were Spaniards.
   must - [They spoke Spanish]

2. *They had to speak Spanish*, because that was the rule.
   must - [They spoke Spanish]

3. _____
   must - [There were enough students to fill a classroom]

   _____, and all we needed were two.

4. _____
   must - [There were enough students to fill a classroom]

   _____, otherwise we couldn't have a class.

5. _____
   can [Neg] - [The papers have printed the story]

   because it just happened.

6. _____ until
   can [Neg] - [The papers printed the story]

   they had all the facts.

7. _____
   may - [There were no more than two visitors in the room]

   Two is all I saw.

8. _____
   may - [There were no more than two visitors in the room]

   That's a hospital regulation.

9. She _____, because her eyes were closed.
   seem - [She wasn't paying attention]

10. She _____, because
    seem - [She hasn't been paying attention]

    her eyes are closed.

11. He _____ if he didn't study.
    be likely - [He would fail]

12. He _____ if he hasn't studied.
     be likely – [He has failed]

20-D • A newspaper reporter (A) is interviewing the police (B) at the scene of a murder. In the blank spaces write **must, may, can, should,** and so on and a form of the verb supplied that seems natural. Some of the constructions should be negative.

A Did you say that I _____?
                      (1) come in

B Yes, you _____. You _____ here an hour ago though.
             (2)   (3)   be

A I _____. I _____ in another part of town. Why?
     (4)   (5) be

B We arrested a suspect, somebody who _____ here at the time
                                        (6)   be

   the murder _____ committed.
               (7) be

A The murderer _____ very strong, since it looks like the victim
                 (8) be

   _____ 200 pounds, easily.
   (9) weigh

B No. The murderer _____ strong. Death was by shooting, not by
                     (10) be

   strangulation, as first announced. Even a child _____ this
                                                    (11) commit

   murder.

A Well, the motive certainly _____ robbery. Those paintings on
                               (12) be

   the wall _____ worth several thousand, at least.
            (13) be

20-E • Each of the following sentences, taken from student compositions, contains an error concerning the description of future events. Change each sentence in such a way as to remove the error.

1. *I wish to apply to your company for a job when I graduated from college.

2. *After I will obtain my bachelor degree, I will work toward a masters.

3. *After four or five years I have a chance to transfer to another job.

4. *I left my country five years ago, and when I would return I want to have some money.

5. *In the future there are many opportunities.

20-F • VOCABULARY RELATIONS

The verbs **keep, possess, own, belong to,** and **have,** all of which have appeared in previous vocabulary lists, share elements of grammar and meaning. Yet they are often not interchangeable:

The Times began publishing in 1851. Back then it
{
~~a. kept~~
~~b. possessed~~
~~c. owned~~
~~d. belonged to~~
e. had
}
just a few pages.

The White Star Line
{
~~a. kept~~
~~b. possessed~~
c. owned
~~d. belonged to~~
~~e. had~~
}
the *Titanic*.

In the sentences below cross out whatever verbs you think render the sentence unacceptable.

A I can't find my book. Who
(1)
{
a. keeps
b. possesses
c. owns
d. belongs to
e. has
}
it?

B I do. But how can you call it yours when it really
(2)
{
a. keeps
b. possesses
c. owns
d. belongs to
e. has
}
me?

A No it doesn't; it
(3)
{
a. keeps
b. possesses
c. owns
d. belongs to
e. has
}
my name inside. See? Just because it's

in your
(4)
{
a. keep
b. possession
c. ownership
d. belonging
e. having
}
doesn't mean you
(5)
{
a. keep
b. possess
c. own
d. belong to
e. have
}
it, you know.

B It was mine long before you wrote your name inside. I've
(6) ⎧ a. kept
⎨ b. possessed
⎪ c. owned ⎬ it on my shelf over a year. I discovered it among
⎪ d. belonged to
⎩ e. had ⎭

my father's (7) ⎧ a. keep.
⎨ b. possessions.
⎪ c. ownership.
⎪ d. belongings.
⎩ e. having.

A You're (8) ⎧ a. kept
⎨ b. possessed
⎪ c. owned ⎬ of a bit of obstinacy, I must say.
⎪ d. belonged to
⎩ e. had ⎭

20-G • For the *italicized* compounds within each of the headlines below write a paraphrase using prepositional phrases.

1. *FORD '74 SMALL CAR MILEAGE CLAIMS* UNSUPPORTED

   the claims of Ford about the mileage of its small cars produced in 1974

2. NEW *BUILDING SERVICE EMPLOYEES UNION*

3. *FOOD PROCESSING PLANT MANAGER* FIRED

4. *'75 AUTO FIRE DANGER DEBATE* RENEWED

5. *WARREN COMMISSION REPORT CONTROVERSY* CONTINUES

6. *SUEZ UNITED NATIONS PEACE KEEPING FORCE* WITHDRAWN

20-H • RESTATEMENT

(Complete the restatement by supplying the correct form.)

1. The White Star Line did not *immediately confirm* Van Anda's story. (*give*)

   The White Star Line did not _give immediate confirmation to Van Anda's story._

2. Some of the passengers *narrowly escaped* drowning. (*have*)

   Some of the passengers _____ from drowning.

3. At other newspapers, editors were *more cautious*. (*show*)

   At other newspapers, editors _____

4. The liner *urgently signaled* that it was in trouble. (*send*)

   The liner _____

5. Britain was *very proud* of its passenger fleet. (*take*)

   Britain _____ in its passenger fleet.

6. The managing editor believed in "hard" news, *thoroughly and accurately presented*. (---)

   The managing editor believed in "hard" news, presented with _____

   _____

20-I
• The following paragraph contains only periods for sentence punctuation. After reading it over, change a period into a semicolon whenever you think it would make the meaning and organization of the paragraph clearer. After any punctuation changes, be sure also to change capitals to small letters where necessary.

One of the best ways to improve both the appearance and the content of newspapers is to improve their use of photography. Effective pictures can pull readers into the newspaper. They also help it compete with television and other activities for the consumer's time. Improvements
5 *are being made to produce clearer and more effective pictures. Yet most of the nation's newspapers were not realizing their photographic potential in the early 1970s. Many still had an excess of self-serving pictures.*

Many were still using trivial pictures that lacked both news and human interest values. Some were expressing bias in reporting controversy.
10 *Some were failing to reproduce pictures effectively. But perhaps most distressing, many were not using photojournalism to supplement and complement their verbal reporting. Numerous opportunities for reaching people through pictures were being overlooked.*[6]

20-J • Write in the correct verb forms for the following paragraph.

By the middle 1970s an electronic revolution _____(1) be_____ already under way for several years in the American newspaper industry. It _____(2) be_____ based on new technology that _____(3) be_____ made possible over the years by the development of computers and their adaptation to newspaper functions. During this time computer operation _____(4) become_____ faster and their size and cost _____(5) get_____ smaller, and this _____(6) open_____ the way for exciting changes. In the decades prior to the introduction of computers, there _____(7) be_____ no great changes in newspaper technology. But now the application of computers to newspapers _____(8) be_____ called the fourth fundamental step in the development of written communication. The first breakthrough _____(9) be_____ the translation of a spoken language into symbols or letters. That _____(10) be_____ followed after a long period of time by the invention of movable type and after several more centuries by the development of the linecasting machine. Then _____(11) come_____ the computer with its potential for changing virtually all newspaper operations.[7]

[6]From *American Newspapers in the 1970's,* by Ernest C. Hynds. Copyright © 1975 by Ernest C. Hynds. Permission by Hastings House, Publishers.
[7]Ibid.

Writing Exercises

20-K • Rewrite the last three sentences of exercise 20-J in reverse order. In other words, start with the most recent breakthrough, the computer, and move backwards to the invention of writing. Reword the sentences freely, but fit them into the following frame.

The most recent breakthrough in newspaper technology _____

_____

Until the use of computers _____

_____

Prior to the development of the linecaster _____

_____

But the very first breakthrough, even long before the appearance of movable type, _____

_____

20-L • Each of the following sentences, taken from student compositions, contains an error in time reference. Change each sentence in such a way as to remove the error.

1. *My father's company is making much progress these recent years.

2. *Recently the social studies fields find an absolute need for mathematics.

3. *When I come here, the Immigration Department already gave me permission to stay for two years.

4. *I had a long trip during these ten days vacation.

5. *A couple of hours ago I had received a telephone call.

20-M • We often need to describe events as they are actually happening. Radio and television commentators do this when they relate the details of a sporting event to a distant waiting audience. The verb constructions used in such reporting are those of present time, even though a few seconds elapse between the occurrence of an event on the playing field and its immediate verbal description. Stories are often told also as though the event and the telling of it are simultaneous. Below is a sample of this kind of writing, a passage from a book about what goes into printing a single issue of the *New York Times*. Read over the passage carefully and then change it into a conventional description of something that in fact happened on February 28, 1969.

In Nairobi, Kenya, it ~~has~~ *had* rained for three nights. It ~~is~~ *was* 11 o'clock on a heavily overcast morning, and the reporter is arguing with an immigration officer over extension of the re-entry permit on his passport. He may have to go on short notice to any country in Black Africa, and the
5 permit will let him come and go at will. Without it, he will have difficulty leaving Kenya and even more difficulty getting back in. The permit must be renewed each year, and in his four years in the country this reporter has never had trouble with it before. But the Immigration Department has been "modernized," and the person who formerly did the job in
10 minutes has been replaced by seven or eight people. Efficiency seems to have suffered in the process.[8]

20-N • CLOZE

(In each blank space write a word that you think fits naturally.)

MILWAUKEE (AP)—Anthony Arvan is not the type _____(1) take his own death lying down.

_____(2) when Arvan, 65, learned that the _____(3) Social Security office had classified him _____(4) and qualified his wife for widow's _____(5), he started out to prove he _____(6) alive.

First "I called the people up _____(7) the Social Security office and told _____(8) I wasn't dead," he said.

A _____(9) looked up his

---

[8]Adapted from *A Day in the Life of the New York Times*, by Ruth Adler (Philadelphia: J. B. Lippincott Co., 1971).

Writing Exercises 159

name, found the _____(10)____ "D" for deceased after it and _____(11)____ the record showed he was indeed _____(12)____. Was Arvan sure he was alive?

_____(13)____, a furniture salesman who retired July _____(14)____, then put in an appearance at _____(15)____ Security to convince officials he was _____(16)____ dead.

"I became concerned, not about whether _____(17)____ was alive, but how such a _____(18)____ could happen," Arvan said.[9]

20-O • Write in what you think should be the verb forms in the following paragraph, which concerns a British newspaper called the *Manchester Guardian*. Which of the sentences represent the viewpoint of Scott, the person being written about?

A young Oxford graduate _____(1) join____ The Guardian *in 1871, a person* who _____(2) be____ *going to give the paper a worldwide reputation. He* _____(3) be____ *Charles Prestwich Scott. Before he* _____(4) come____ *to The Guardian, he* _____(5) work____ *briefly as a journalist in Edinburg. Scott* _____(6) be____ *with The Guardian only a year when he* _____(7) be____ *appointed editor. At the time he* _____(8) be____ *only twenty-one years old.* Scott _____(9) be____ *determined to improve the quality of the paper and immediately* _____(10) attack____ *its careless writing. People* _____(11) talk____ *of "journalese" as though a journalist* _____(12) have____ *to be a careless writer;* he might _____(13) be____, *on the contrary, and very often* _____(14) be____, *one of the best writers in the world. At least, he should not* _____(15) be____ *cut out to be much less. Scott* _____(16) gather____ *an outstanding group of journalists around him.*[10]

---

[9]*The Los Angeles Times,* August 20, 1975, Part II, p. 8. Reprinted by permission of The Associated Press.
[10]Merrill, op. cit.

20-P • Take all the information supplied in the first paragraph of the Reading in Section C and write a brief news announcement such as Van Anda might have written for the *New York Times* on the morning of April 15, 1912. The sentences in lines 7 and 8 need to be changed into the style of straight news reporting. Do not make reference to the reporter himself, either as "Van Anda" or "I." Open the news item with **A distress signal** . . .

20-Q • Newspaper headlines follow a slightly different set of grammar rules for the reporting of past events, as you can see from the headlines in the Reading of Section C. Where a normal sentence would use the simple past or the present perfect (**The Titanic *has hit* an iceberg**), the headline uses the simple present (**TITANIC *HITS* ICEBERG**). Furthermore, forms of **be** are simply dropped. (**The women *have been* put off in lifeboats** →**WOMEN PUT OFF IN LIFEBOATS**). As can be seen also, articles are omitted. With these principles in mind, rewrite the following headlines as normal sentences. Do you notice anything unusual about numbers 5 and 7?

1. BLACK LEADER ASKED TO BE PRESIDENTIAL ADVISOR

    _____

2. RUBENS AND OWNER MISSING IN DENMARK

    _____

3. BUENOS AIRES BARS PROTEST BY STUDENTS

    _____

4. EX-REP. MARTIN DIES OF TEXAS, 72, SUCCUMBS

    _____

5. SLAIN CONSUL SENT PLEA TO U.S. ENVOY

    _____

6. LABOR, MANAGEMENT REPORTED NEAR AGREEMENT

    _____

7. BANDITS RUN OUT OF NORTHERN TOWN

    _____

20-R • Retell in writing a brief story that you know, or make up one of your own. Use a mixture of the styles you have seen, and pay close attention to the representation of time sequences. Refer to any of the sample paragraphs of this unit for ideas in possible means of expression.

Writing Exercises

Unit 21

21-1 DIALOG

THE PERSONAL LETTER

LAURA Allan! It's a letter from Terry!
ALLAN Great! Can you read it to me? My hands are all greasy from working on the car.
LAURA Yes. Now where did I put my glasses?
ALLAN I think they're on the table.
LAURA No. Here they are . . . .

Tuesday, Sept. 27

Dear Mom and Dad,
   Your letter dated the 24th reached me yesterday, which is really fast. Thanks so much for sending the extra cash. There are a lot of things here to spend money on, but prices on the continent are so much higher now, which amazes me. It's impossible for Americans to vacation here the way they used to.
   Though Europe is expensive, there are a lot of conveniences here that I've never seen

anywhere else. Every subway station in Paris has an electrified map of the city that you can light up and see your route on, just with the push of a button. And when I was in Amsterdam I noticed that there are mailboxes on the backs of all the buses, which certainly saves time when you can't find a regular mailbox. A passenger sitting in my compartment on the train to Munich — more about that trip in another letter — told me that in all the large railroad terminals in Italy there's a place where you can get a haircut, a shoeshine, a manicure, even a shower, and all this without ever leaving the station.

My train to Edinburgh leaves in about an hour, which makes time a little short right now. I'll write you a longer letter in a few days. Say "hello" to everybody for me. And thanks again for sending the money.

Love,
Terry

P.S. I'll pay you back the money as soon as I can.

ALLAN   Wasn't that interesting! About those European conveniences, I mean.
LAURA   Yes. I wonder how much it costs to take a shower in the Rome railroad station.

VOCABULARY

amaze (amazement)
vacation (vacation)
electrify (electrification)
light up
pay back

subway[1]
route
push (push)
button
compartment
terminal
haircut
shoeshine
manicure
shower

greasy (grease)

21-2 ■ DIALOG VARIATION

1. *Your letter . . . reached me yesterday.*
   I received your letter yesterday.
   Your letter arrived here yesterday.
2. *It's impossible for Americans to vacation here the way they used to.*
   Americans can't possibly vacation here the way they used to.
   For Americans to vacation here the way they used to isn't possible.
3. *. . . there are mailboxes on the backs of all the buses.*
   On the backs of all the buses are mailboxes.
   The backs of all the buses have mailboxes on them.
   Mailboxes are on the backs of all the buses.
4. *A passenger sitting in my compartment on the train to Munich . . . told me that . . .*
   Sitting in my compartment on the train to Munich was a passenger who told me that . . .
   There was a passenger sitting in my compartment on the train to Munich who told me that . . .
   On the train to Munich there was a passenger sitting in my compartment who told me that . . .
5. *I wonder how much it costs to take a shower in the Rome railroad station.*
   How much does it cost to take a shower in the Rome railroad station, I wonder?
   How much does it cost, I wonder, to take a shower in the Rome railroad station?

21-3 ■ QUESTIONS

1. Were Allan and Laura happy to receive a letter from Terry?
2. What relationship is Terry to Allan and Laura?
3. Why can't Allan read the letter himself?
4. How many days did it take the letter to reach Terry?

---

[1] In British English **subway** = **underground** or **tube**.

Section A

5. What was Terry grateful for?
6. Are there any compensations for the high prices in Europe, according to Terry?
7. What cities were mentioned in the letter, and in what connection?
8. What is so unusual about taking a shower in Italy?
9. Where do you think Terry was when he wrote the letter? What are your reasons?

21-4 SOUND PATTERNS

—Now where did I put my glasses?
—I think *they're* on the table.
—No. Here *they are* . . . .

There is a general rule in English that present tense forms of **be**, **have**, and a few modals can "contract" with most preceding words, especially in conversation:

—*Who's* got an extra pencil?	(Who has . . .)
—*There's* one on my desk.	(There is . . .)
—*I'll* just be using it for a second.	(I will . . .)

Contraction cannot take place, however, if any words have been moved from the position following the contractable elements, or if anything is "understood" in that position:

—**Has anybody got an extra pencil?**	
—Yes. *I have*	(Yes. *I've.)
—But don't forget to give it back.	
—*I will* . . . ; I promise.	(*I'll; I promise.)

21-A • (See page 183.)

21-5 ■ PHRASAL VERBS

—P.S. I'll pay you *back* the money as soon as I can.

Sometimes it is possible to isolate the meaning of an element in a phrasal verb. **Back** is such an element. Read the following dialog out loud inserting **back** in each blank space; then think about the possible meanings that **back** can have.

1. SECRETARY   Do you want me to read the letter _____ to you, Mrs. McDonald?

2. EXECUTIVE   Yes. But read it _____ to me slowly, Miss Perry, and pull _____ the curtains a little. It's getting dark in here.

3. SECRETARY No wonder. It's later than you think. We changed _____ to standard time last night. You forgot to set the clock _____. Here, I'll just do it now and put it _____ on the shelf . . . . Wait, there's something wrong with it; I can't move the hands _____.

4. EXECUTIVE I've been having trouble with that clock. I'll have to send it _____ to the store where I bought it. Sometimes I look _____ at the good old days of mechanical clocks—you know, the kind that tick, with a pendulum that swings _____ and forth.

5. SECRETARY Well, I guess we can't go _____ in time, can we?

6. EXECUTIVE No. So let's get _____ to the rereading of that letter. Don't bother going _____ to the very beginning, Miss Perry. Just pick up about two paragraphs _____.

21-6 SPEECH ACT

—*Wasn't that interesting!* About those European conveniences, I mean.

Exclamations like the above superficially resemble yes-no questions. One major difference, however, between questions and exclamations of this kind is intonation. Compare:

[question] **Does that taste good?** (Let me have some.)

[exclamation] **Does that taste good!** (Let me have some more.)

21-7 ■ Take the part of speaker B in the following little dialogs and read the part as an exclamation, with proper intonation.

1. A Dinner's ready!
   B Am I hungry!
2. A Look at those puppies in the window.
   B Aren't they cute!
3. A There's a new girl in class. That's her over there.
   B Is she beautiful!
4. A Let's open a window.
   B Yes. Isn't it hot in here!

Section A

5. A After that what did you do?
   B I stepped out to see what the weather was like, and was it cold!
6. A Who did you hear?
   B Cliburn, and can he play!
7. A How do you like my new suit?
   B Boy, does that look good on you!

21-B • (See page 183.)

21-8 ■ DIALOG IMPROVISATION

(Try to re-create or even improvise a variation of the Dialog at the beginning of this unit, as you remember it.)

A It's a . . .
B Can you read . . .
A Yes. Now where did . . .
B I think they're . . .
A No. Here . . .
    [letter]
A Wasn't that . . .
B Yes. I wonder . . .

> Relatives with verb-**ing** and **to** verb
>
> —A passenger *sitting* in my compartment on the train to Munich . . . told me that . . .
> —There are a lot of things here *to spend* money on.

21-9 There is a very common relative clause version that uses the **-ing** form of the verb, as first mentioned in Volume I, 12-8. Only subject relative clauses have this version. Often such a verb-**ing** construction is a reduction of the continuous form:

> **A passenger (who was) sitting in my compartment . . .**

Reduction, however, cannot explain other clauses, especially those with verbs that do not ordinarily occur in the continuous, such as **like, have, want, know, need,** and so on. The **-ing** form for such verbs corresponds to the simple present or past:

> The students $\begin{Bmatrix} \text{wanting} \\ \text{who wanted} \end{Bmatrix}$ extra help were assigned to a special class.

21-10 Many object relative clauses, especially those expressing obligation, intention, or ability, have another version using the form **to** verb:

> **There are a lot of things here** *(for a person) to spend money on.*
> (There are a lot of things here *that/which a person can spend money on.*)

In more formal English, a preposition can be moved along with the relative marker:

> **There are a lot of things here** *on which to spend money.*
> (There are a lot of things here *on which a person can spend money.*)

21-11 ■ Respond to each of the following with a sentence beginning **Anybody** verb-**ing** . . .

1. I know somebody who weighs three hundred pounds.
   Anybody weighing three hundred pounds (should see a doctor).
2. I know somebody who speaks ten languages.
   Anybody speaking ten languages (must be a genius).
3. I know somebody who makes $100,000 a year.
4. I know somebody who writes twenty letters a week.
5. I know somebody who spends more than he earns.
6. I know somebody who admires Adolf Hitler.
7. I know somebody who smokes three packs of cigarettes a day.
8. I know somebody who owns seven cats.

9. I know somebody who needs only two hours of sleep a night.
10. I know somebody who doesn't make enough money to live on.

21-12 ▪ Take part in the following little dialogs by responding with a **to** verb construction.

1. A I want to arrange a trip to Europe. Who should I contact?
   B **The person to contact is (your travel agent).**
2. A I want to find the name of a nearby florist. Where should I look?
   B **The place . . .**
3. A I want to hear the news. When should I tune in?
   B **The time . . .**
4. A I've accepted two different dinner invitations for Friday evening. What should I do?
   B **The thing . . .**
5. A I want to know what the weather will be like tomorrow. How can I find out?
   B **The way . . .**
6. A I need some advice on starting a business. Who should I talk to?
   B **The person . . .**

21-13 ▪ In changing expressions like **the money to be paid** into relative clauses, different modals are often usable in the clause: **the money that will/should/must be paid**. The choice is usually determined by what fits the larger context of the surrounding sentences. Change the following expressions into natural sounding relative clauses.

1. a man to be remembered
   a man that will/is going to/should be remembered
2. a letter to be mailed
3. money to be spent
4. work to be done
5. a person to be watched
6. children to be cared for
7. deadlines to be met
8. risks to be taken
9. sights to be seen
10. a force to be reckoned with
11. problems to be avoided
12. wild animals to be found there

21-14 ■ Restate each of the following sentences with full relative clauses.

1. Is there anybody here driving to school every day?
   Is there anybody here who drives to school every day?
2. Is there anybody here driving to school today?
   Is there anybody here who is driving to school today?
3. Is there anybody here having school today?
   Is there anybody here who has school today?
4. Here's a photo showing the front of the church.
5. Do you see that man standing on the corner?
6. Students needing extra paper can get it here.
7. I think there are a lot of people vacationing in Europe every summer.
8. I got a card from a friend vacationing in the South.
9. I need a dictionary containing a list of irregular verbs.
10. Are there any stores offering discounts?
11. Are there any stores offering discounts right now?
12. There are a lot of verbs consisting of two words.

21-C • (See page 184.)

21-D • (See page 184.)

21-E • (See page 185.)

21-15 READING (293 words)

THE FORMAL LETTER

6021 Gower Street
Los Angeles, CA 90068
October 5, 1975

Social Security Administration
Department of Health, Education, and Welfare
Washington, D.C. 20201

Dear Sirs:

    I am writing to your office to attempt to determine why I have encountered so many obstacles to receiving my proper monthly social security allotment. The trouble started ten months ago and has actually gotten worse, making it extremely difficult for me to meet normal financial obligations.

    The first problem with which I had to deal was simply getting a monthly check from you, without having to wait four or five extra weeks for it. Then two of the checks arrived made out for the wrong amount, giving me fifty dollars less than I should have received. Another check was mailed to me at an address from which I moved more than two years ago. My letter of inquiry, which I sent to the Los Angeles office of the Social Security Administration, never brought an answer, and when I finally telephoned them I was able to talk only with an arrogant clerk from the tone of whose voice I could tell that he didn't want to be bothered with me. The final blow is a letter received from your office just yesterday in which you state that my allotment is being discontinued, your records indicating that I am legally dead.

    Beyond this letter of protest I have at least one other recourse: filing suit against the Social Security Administration, which I would prefer not to have to do. Therefore I am asking you to please take whatever steps are necessary to ensure that from now on I receive my social security benefits without further obstacles. This letter is mute testimony to the fact that I am indeed not dead, legally or otherwise.

                                                  Sincerely yours,

                                                  Thelma Spencer

                                                  (Mrs.) Thelma Spencer

CULTURAL NOTES

"Dear Sirs" or "Gentlemen" is a fixed convention in letter writing and not necessarily sexist.

Social Security is economic assistance provided by the U.S. Government to persons faced with unemployment, disability, or old age. The money for this assistance is paid in by employers and employees.

VOCABULARY

attempt (attempt)
encounter (encounter)
deal with/dealt/dealt
make out
discontinue
indicate (indication)
file suit
ensure

obstacle
allotment (allot)
obligation (obligate, obligatory)
inquiry (inquire)
blow
protest (protest)
recourse
benefit (benefit)
testimony (testify)

proper
financial (finance)
arrogant (arrogance)
mute

legally

21-16 ■ INCLUDED MEANING

(For each of the following passages pick the one statement whose meaning is part of the meaning of the passage.)

1. *The trouble started ten months ago and has actually gotten worse, making it extremely difficult for me to meet normal financial obligations.*
   a. My financial obligations are worse.
   b. My financial obligations are hard to meet.
   c. My financial obligations are hard to make.
2. *The first problem with which I had to deal was simply getting a monthly check from you . . .*
   a. To get a monthly check was a problem.
   b. The problem got a monthly check.
   c. Getting a monthly check was simple.
3. *My letter of inquiry, which I sent to the Los Angeles office of the Social Security Administration, never brought an answer . . .*
   a. An answer was never brought by the Social Security Administration.
   b. The Social Security Administration never answered the letter.
   c. The answer never brought a letter of inquiry.
4. *. . . I have at least one other recourse: filing suit against the Social Security Administration, which I would prefer not to have to do.*
   a. I would prefer not to have to file suit.
   b. I would prefer not to have one other recourse.
   c. I would prefer not to have to do the Social Security Administration.

Section C

5. ... *I was able to talk only with an arrogant clerk from the tone of whose voice I could tell that he didn't want to be bothered with me.*
   a. I was bothered by his voice.
   b. His voice could tell that he didn't want to be bothered.
   c. The tone of his voice told me something.

21-17 ■ QUESTIONS

1. What mood was the writer of the letter in?
2. How long had she been having trouble?
3. Were all the things that happened to her of equal seriousness? Which do you think is the least serious? Which is the most serious?
4. What happens if Mrs. Spencer's letter gets no results?
5. How would you describe the tone of the letter? Is it firm, threatening, insulting, polite, impolite, strong, weak, conciliatory, aggressive, justified, unjustified, and so on?

21-18 VOCABULARY RELATIONS

The verb **ask** has occurred frequently throughout these units. It appeared again in the Reading: "Therefore, I am *ask*ing you to please take whatever steps . . ." Although we often think of **ask** as a verb of questioning, in the example just cited **ask** has the meaning not of questioning but of requesting. In some contexts **ask** can also be a verb of invitation. Compare:

We *ask*ed them if they had a party.   [question]
We *ask*ed them to have a party.   [request]
We *ask*ed them to the party.   [invitation]

21-19 ■
All of the sentences below contain the verb **ask**. For each occurrence of **ask** say whether you think it represents a question, a request, or an invitation.

1. I *ask*ed my secretary if there were any messages for me.
2. She said there was one *ask*ing me to dinner.
3. I *ask*ed her to let me see it.
4. It was from the Millers, and this wasn't the first time I had been *ask*ed.
5. I *ask*ed her when the message was delivered.
6. "Around four," she said, and then *ask*ed me a favor.
7. She *ask*ed if she could leave early that day.
8. She had put her car up for sale, and a buyer, had already *ask*ed about it.
9. She was *ask*ing for time off because the potential buyer was free to see the car only in the late afternoon.
10. "How much are you *ask*ing for it?," I said.
11. "A thousand," she replied. After a pause she *ask*ed me whether to make up the lost time the next day.
12. I *ask*ed her not to worry about it.

21-F • **COMPOUNDS** (See page 185.)

21-G • **RESTATEMENT** (See page 186.)

21-20 PUNCTUATION

Dashes (—), along with commas and parentheses, are commonly used as *correlative* punctuation marks. They mark the beginning and end of a construction that is not properly part of the clause in which it has been inserted:

A passenger sitting in my compartment on the train to Munich—*more about that trip in another letter*—**told me that in all the large railroad terminals in Italy there's . . .**

The dash used in this way is more typical of informal writing, such as a personal letter, in which the writer is more likely to make impromptu insertions. Dashes and parentheses are chosen over commas where commas are already in use elsewhere in the sentence and where confusion might otherwise result.

21-H • (See page 186.)

21-21 ■ READING IMPROVISATION

(Complete each of the following sentences with what you remember from the Reading.)

1. I am writing to your office to . . .
2. The first problem with which . . .
3. Then two of the checks arrived made out for . . .
4. Another check was mailed to me at an address from which . . .
5. My letter of inquiry, which I sent . . .
6. When I finally telephoned them I was able to . . .
7. The final blow is a letter . . .
8. I have at least one other . . .
9. I am asking you to please . . .

Section D

References for **which**; Relatives within Units

—My train to Edinburgh leaves in about an hour, *which* makes time a little short right now.

—. . . I was able to talk only with an arrogant clerk *from the tone of whose voice* I could tell that he didn't want to be bothered with me.

21-22 It is often necessary for the speaker or writer to make reference to an entire preceding sentence or sentences, sometimes for the purpose of making a comment about the content of a previous statement:

Prices on the continent are so much higher now, *which amazes me.*

Most subject relative clauses of this kind also have a version in the **-ing** form, as discussed in 21-9. Since both versions will always be nonrestrictive, with commas (see Volume I, 12-23), we can express each of them as well with two separate sentences or two sentences joined by **and**. Compare the following:

The trouble . . . has actually gotten worse {
, **which makes it difficult . . .**
, **making it difficult . . .**
. **This makes it difficult . . .**
, **and this makes it difficult . . .**
}

21-23 In 21-10 and in Volume I, 12-24, it was pointed out that in more formal English movement of the relative marker often includes a larger unit, usually a prepositional phrase, of which the marker is a part:

    ... **an arrogant** *clerk* [I could tell *from* ~~*the clerk's*~~ *voice* **that** ...]
    ... **an arrogant** *clerk from whose voice* I could tell   **that** ...

Relative markers can also be buried even deeper within prepositional phrases:

    ... **an arrogant** *clerk* [I could tell *from the tone of* ~~*the clerk's*~~ *voice* **that** ...]
    ... **an arrogant** *clerk from the tone of whose voice* I could tell   **that** ...

Section D

21·24 ■ Add a comment of your own to each of the following.

1. In Amsterdam the buses carry mailboxes,

    which { is a great idea.
    amazes me.
    I find funny.
    I think is rather silly.
    . . .

2. In Los Angeles a few of the supermarkets are open all night, which . . .
3. In Paris every subway station has an electrified map of the city that you can light up and see your route on, which . . .
4. In Japan some of the trains go as fast as 250 km an hour, which . . .
5. In Italy a lot of railroad stations have a place where you can get a haircut, a shoeshine, a manicure, and even a shower, which . . .
6. In Mexico City there are taxis that operate on a certain route, like buses, for a fixed fare, which . . .
7. In Germany there are a lot of public restrooms where you can drop a coin into a machine and get some "cologne water" blown in your face, which . . .
8. In Vienna you can dial a certain telephone number and get a musical pitch for tuning up your string quartet, which . . .

21·25 ■ Each of the sentences below contains a relative clause in *italics*. For each such clause give the full sentence that it represents.

1. The first problem *with which I had to deal* was simply getting a monthly check from you.
   I had to deal with the problem.
2. Another check was mailed to me at an address *from which I moved more than two years ago.*
3. The teacher *from whom we received the most encouragement* was Mrs. Wilson.
4. There are so many things here *on which a person can spend money.*
5. Here's the dictionary, *in the back of which you'll find a list of proper names.*
6. There are different kinds of populations *among whom advertisers try to sell their products.*
7. I was able to talk only with an arrogant clerk *from the tone of whose voice I could tell that he didn't want to be bothered with me.*
8. Politics fascinates the candidate, *some of whose "friends" now refuse to have anything to do with him.*
9. Politics fascinates the candidate, *some of whose "friends" he now refuses to have anything to do with.*

21-26 ■ Relative clauses attached to proper nouns are almost always nonrestrictive, since a proper noun usually denotes something that is already unique **(Cairo, which is in Egypt)**. The clause will be restrictive, however, if it is needed to distinguish between two or more things having the same name **(the Cairo that's in Illinois)**. Notice also the presence of **the** in this kind of relative clause, as first pointed out in 17-9. Act out the following little dialogs on the order of the model.

1. A Did you hear about the flood in Cairo? [Illinois]
   B No. Did the Nile overflow?
   A Oh, I'm not talking about Cairo, Egypt; **I'm talking about the Cairo that's in Illinois.**
2. A Did you hear about the plane crash near Córdoba? [Argentina]
   B No. Was it a Spanish airliner?
   A Oh, I'm not talking about Córdoba, Spain; I'm . . .
3. A Did you hear about the bombing in London? [Ontario]
   B No. Was it on the BBC?
   A Oh, I'm not talking about London, England; I'm . . .
4. A Did you hear about the shipwreck near La Paz? [Mexico]
   B No. But Bolivia doesn't have a seacoast.
   A Oh, I'm not talking about La Paz, Bolivia; I'm . . .
5. A Did you hear about the riot in Rome? [New York]
   B No. Was it related to the Italian elections?
   A Oh, I'm not talking about Rome, Italy; I'm . . .
6. A Did you hear about the big fire in Alexandria? [Virginia]
   B No. But I bet it must have been visible far out in the Mediterranean.
   A Oh, I'm not talking about Alexandria, Egypt; I'm . . .

21-I • (See page 187.)

21-J • (See page 187.)

21-K • (See page 188.)

21-L ■ **CLOZE** (See page 189.)

> Other **-ing** Clauses; the Use of Nonrestrictives
>
> —The final blow is a letter . . . in which you state that my allotment is being discontinued, *your records indicating that I am legally dead.*

21-27 Nonrestrictive relative clause versions with **-ing** (as in 21-9) are movable, usually to the front of the sentence:

> The students, (wanting extra help,) were given a special class.
>
> *Wanting extra help,* **the students were given a special class.**

It is possible, however, to have **-ing** versions, without relative clause counterparts, that bear only a loose explanatory relationship to the rest of the sentence:

> **The students wanting extra help,** *a special class was arranged.*
> (Since the students wanted extra help, a special class was arranged.)
>
> **The students wanted extra help,** *exams being only a week away.*
> (The students wanted extra help, since exams were only a week away.)

Notice that the **-ing** half by itself cannot be a sentence.

21-28 The meaning of a sentence containing a nonrestrictive relative clause (see Volume I, 12-23) can usually be expressed as two sentences joined together:

> (1) **Paris, which offers convenient bus service, also has a good subway system.**
> (2) **Paris offers convenient bus service, and it also has a good subway system.**

Although the general meaning of (1) and (2) is the same, the relative clause in (1) contains parenthetical information. That is, the clause in (1) would not be offered as any part of the answer to a question about transportation in Paris:

> A What's public transportation like in Paris?
> B { **Paris offers convenient bus service, and it also has a good subway sytem.**
>   ~~Paris, which offers convenient bus service, also has a good subway system.~~ }

21-29 ▪ Recall a time when you lost your way in a strange city or town, or imagine that you did. Describe what happened, or might have happened, by finishing the sentences started for you below.

1. Not knowing exactly what to do, I . . .
2. Not having much money with me, I . . .
3. Not being able to understand the language very well, I . . .
4. Not wanting to appear rude, I . . .
5. Not saying much, I . . .
6. Not wishing to spend my time wandering around, I . . .
7. Not being the kind of person who goes around looking for trouble, I . . .

21-30 ▪ As explained in 21-28, if the answer to a question is given entirely in the form of a relative clause, it sounds peculiar. In the little dialogs below, say whether or not the answer to each question is appropriate. Restate the inappropriate answers in more acceptable form.

1. A What did you think of the movie?
   B That movie, which I've wanted to see for a long time, actually disappointed me.
   Appropriate.
2. A What did you think of the movie?
   B That movie, which I found disappointing, has nevertheless gotten good reviews.
   Inappropriate. [The real answer to the question is contained in the relative clause.] **I found it disappointing, although it's gotten good reviews.**
3. A What do you think of the postal service?
   B I don't think the postal service, which needs to be improved here and there, can be run for profit.
4. A What's your impression of the New York subway?
   B That subway, which began operating in 1904, by the way, is just about the noisiest one I've ever seen.
5. A Where can you eat dinner in a restaurant these days for under five dollars?
   B Cheap restaurant dinners that are also good, which is the subject of a book I'm putting together, are not easy to find.
6. A Who do you think should be the next Secretary General of the U.N.?
   B Echeverria of Mexico, who would be my choice, has a lot of things in his favor.

Section E

21-31 ■ In the following paragraphs the *italicized* relative clauses should be main sentences, and the *italicized* sentences should be relative clauses, according to the principles discussed in 21-28. Restate the sentences with these changes.

1. It is necessary first to mention the cost. The installation, *which cost fifty-five dollars*, took three hours.
   It is necessary first to mention the cost. The installation cost fifty-five dollars, and it took three hours.
2. She wanted to change the color of her phone. *The phone was black*. The phone company didn't think this was important, however, and made her wait three weeks.
   She wanted to change the color of her phone, which was black. The phone company . . .
3. There is one other advantage to buying now. This course of action, *which will afford us the opportunity of paying a lower interest rate,* will turn out later to have been a wise move.
4. There is one other advantage to buying now. *I'm in favor of buying now*. This is that it will afford us the opportunity of paying a lower interest rate.
5. Mark was no longer satisfied with the field of study he had chosen. *The field of study was economics*, and he decided that he would rather be a mathematician.
6. When they asked Mark what field he would rather be in, he replied that mathematics, *which he much preferred*, has seldom been more highly respected.

21-32 ■ Look again at the sample letters in Sections A and C, the one a personal letter and the other a formal letter. Compare the two and mention all the ways in which they appear to differ. Consider the content as well as the form.

21-M • (See page 189.)

21-N • (See page 191.)

21-O • (See page 192.)

21-P • (See page 192.)

21-Q • (See page 193.)

WRITING EXERCISES

21-A • In the following dialog cross out whatever *italicized* contractions are not possible, and write in the full form. Then act out the corrected dialog.

1. A *It's* more fun to get letters than ~~*it's*~~ *it is* to send them.

2. B *That's* not true, at least for me. *You're* not a letter writer, but *I'm*.

3. A *It's* obvious *you're*, but *I'm* too. *It's* just that *writing's* hard. *It's* not for some people but *it's* for me.

4. B Then *you've* got to do it more. Maybe *it's* that you think *you've* got no ability. *You've*, you know. I've seen how *you're* behind a typewriter.

5. A I can't get over how insistent *you're* today. I appreciate your encouragement. But I really wonder if *you're* aware of how much fun *it's* for me to get letters.

6. B If I weren't *you'd* really know it. And *I'd* too.

21-B • In the following little dialogs each response for speaker B is either a question or an exclamation. Write in ! for what you think is an exclamation, ? for a question. Then act out the dialogs.

1. A I can't drink this coffee.
   B Why? Is it hot *?*

2. A Here, have some coffee.
   B Mmmm; is it hot *!*

3. A The hall was packed.
   B Yes, and didn't he sing well

4. A The hall was half full after intermission.
   B Didn't he sing well

5. A They weren't expecting a real party.
   B Were they surprised

6. A Who gave the party for them?
   B Who do you think, and were they surprised

7. A She's beautiful, intelligent, and kind.
   B Yes, and can she cook

8. A She's beautiful, intelligent, and kind.

   B Yes, but can she cook

9. A She's not very kind, intelligent, or beautiful.

   B No, but can she cook

21-C • The form that a particular relative clause takes can vary, according to degree of formality (see Volume I, 12-24). The following sentences all have **to** verb relative clauses that are informal. Put them into more formal style by moving the preposition back to the position before the relative marker. **Who** will then become **whom**.

1. There isn't enough evidence ^*on which* to base those opinions ~~on~~.

2. It must be certain that there is enough equipment to perform the experiment with.

3. Does the court believe there is enough of an argument to build a case around?

4. The law defines the area to conduct the investigation within.

5. The person to place your trust in is your advisor.

6. Where is the evidence to draw these conclusions from?

7. Advertisers identify different populations to try to sell their products among.

8. The government has a number of agencies to obtain that kind of information from.

9. The container to pour the solution into should be very clean.

21-D • Occasionally, the relationship expressed in a **to** verb relative clause is subject-verb instead of object verb. Compare:

the first book to arrive / the first book to read

Within the **to** verb constructions of the sentences to follow, draw an arrow from subject to verb or from verb to object, whichever you think expresses the meaning of the sentence.

1. In *the sentences to follow*, look for relationships.

2. In *the sentences to write*, look for relationships.

3. *The first person to talk* should be me.

4. *The first person to talk to* should be me.

5. Get off at the corner, and *the next bus to take* will be number 70.

6. Get off at the corner, and *the next bus to arrive* will be number 70.

7. Call me in *the days to come*.

8. *The days to come* are Tuesdays and Thursdays.

9. Call me for *the days to come on*.

10. That was *a terrible thing to do*.

11. That was *a terrible thing to happen*.

12. See if you can find *somebody to help*.

21-E • All relative clauses in the following letter have been represented as full sentences, within brackets. (See also exercises D, H, J, and L in Unit 12.) Rewrite the letter in usable English by changing the bracketed sentences into relative clauses. You may want further to reduce some of the clauses to a verb-**ing** or **to** verb form.

November 1, 1975

Dear Ken and Kathy,

We just received *the note* [You sent us *the note* two days ago [*The note* mentions the transporation problem]]. There probably isn't *much* [We can do *much* about it], since we have only *one car* [We would have to fit seven people into *one car*]. Maybe *the thing* [We should do *the thing*] is delay your arrival a few days, at least until we can make *a decision* [*The decision* gives us more freedom]. Let us hear any *further suggestions* [You might have *further suggestions*].

As always,
Barb and Dave

21-F • **COMPOUNDS**

(Rewrite the following sentences rearranging the words in *italics* into a compound.)

1. Why can't I receive my proper *allotment of social security?*

   Why can't I receive my proper social security allotment?

2. I sent a letter to the *office of the Social Security Administration in Los Angeles.*

3. I sent a letter to the *office in Los Angeles of The Social Security Administration.*

4. They're starting an investigation of problems with *payment of checks from social security.*

   _____

5. They're starting an investigation of *problems with payment of checks from social security.*

   _____

6. They're starting *an investigation of problems with payment of checks from social security.*

   _____

21-G • RESTATEMENT

(Complete the restatement by supplying the correct form.)

1. They *quickly attempted* to find a solution. *(make)*

   They *made a quick attempt to find a solution.*

2. He's *financially obligated* to us. *(have)*

   He _____

3. The bank *quietly inquired* into their financial status. *(make)*

   The bank _____

4. I heard that somebody *loudly protested. (make)*

   I heard that somebody _____

5. Did he *testify honestly? (give)*

   Did he _____

6. We plan to *vacation briefly* in the mountains. *(take/have)*

   We plan to _____

21-H • Refer again to the personal letter within the dialog of Section A. Decide where each of the incidental comments below can plausibly be inserted and rewrite the sentence with the insertion separated by dashes. If the comment is added to the beginning or end of the sentence, only one dash is required.

—the British refer to the rest of Europe as the "continent"—

—some of our subways don't have maps of any kind—

—*can you imagine!*—

—*did I tell you I was including Scotland?*—

21-I • Each of the following sentences, taken from student compositions, has a faulty relative clause construction. Change each sentence in such a way as to remove the error.

1. *I live in Algiers which I will compare it with Athens.*

2. *I went to a movie in which was played by Robert Redford.*

3. *I tried to pass the truck on the left, but the truck driver who was quite drunk moved over to the left too.*

4. *I decided to turn left, but the car, that was in front, was flashing to turn right.*

5. *I read a lot of stories which some of them are concerned with religion.*

6. *These are laws for everybody to obey them.*

21-J • Rewrite the following combinations by changing the sentences within brackets to nonrestrictive relative clauses. Do not use AND or BUT in the clause.

1. He showed me *a book* [AND I could tell from the cover of *the book* that it was pretty old] *He showed me a book, from the cover of which I could tell that it was pretty old.*

2. Open *the bag* [AND you'll find a small package in the bottom of *the bag*]

Writing Exercises 187

3. More and more interest is now being directed toward *medical knowledge* [AND advances in *medical knowledge* will hopefully benefit mankind]

_____

_____

4. One of the worst hazards of nuclear warfare is *atomic radiation* [BUT public awareness of the effects of *atomic radiation* is constantly spreading, however. _____

_____

5. In the election of 1968 the Democratic presidential candidate turned out not to be *Johnson* [AND most of the people were tired of the Viet Nam war by the end of *Johnson's* administration] _____

_____

6. Many diplomats criticized both *the United States and the Soviet Union* [BUT the United Nations mission wouldn't have been able to succeed, however, without the cooperation of *the United States and the Soviet Union*] _____

_____

_____

21-K • The following letter is made up of short sentences, all of which are grammatical. Rewrite the letter, combining pairs of these sentences into longer sentences according to the directions below.

Nov. 1, 1975

Dear Kathleen,

1 Thank you so much for the book that you sent. 2 It arrived three days ago. 3 Jim has already read three chapters of it. 4 This is unusual because he hardly ever takes time to read more than the newspaper. 5 The book has been admired also by one of our neighbors, Mr. Cummings. 6 You once played volleyball with his children. Remember? 7 Why don't you think about paying us a visit over the holidays? 8 You know it would please us immensely. Give your mother our best, and thank you again for the book.

As always,
Ruth

(Put sentences 1 and 2 together as . . . **sent, which** . . . Put 3 and 4 together as . . . **it, which** . . . Put 5 and 6 together as . . . **Cummings, with whose.** . . Put 7 and 8 together as . . . **holidays, which** . . .)

21-L • CLOZE

(In the blank spaces of the "open letter" below, write **which**, **who**, **whom**, or **whose**, whichever is correct.)

An Open Letter to Teachers

We are shocked by the recent action wh*ich*___ was taken against
                                        1
two members of the faculty at Simpson College. These are teachers
wh_____ only "crime" is membership in a political party many of
   2
wh_____ views are disliked by the people wh_____ support the
   3   4
college. We are greatly concerned by the attack on academic freedom
wh_____ this action implies. Freedom to teach without interference is
   5
the foundation upon wh_____ our schools and colleges have always
                         6
stood. Those from wh_____ these attacks have come must be made
                      7
aware that the academic community in wh_____ we serve stands united.
                                         8
against the use of such tactics. We therefore urge (1) that the two teachers
against wh_____ the accusations have been made be assured that they
            9
will be judged only by the quality of their teaching and (2) that any future
efforts to discredit a faculty member with wh_____ opinions some
                                               10
people are not in sympathy be strongly resisted.

UNITED TEACHERS ASSOCIATION

21-M • In 21-27 it was pointed out that verb-**ing** phrases can occur in a loose relationship with main sentences. This applies as well to verb-**ed** phrases and adjective phrases:

The writer, { fired from his job, / without a job, / jobless, } needed money.

{ Fired from his job, / Without a job, / Jobless, } the writer needed money.

In the sentences that follow, choose between verb-**ed** and verb-**ing** by crossing out the one that is incorrect.

1. { Needing money, / ~~Needed money,~~ } Howard decided to write home to his parents.

2. ~~Needing at home,~~ / Needed at home, } Howard decided to return to his parents.

3. Making out for the wrong amount, / Made out for the wrong amount, } the check was quickly returned.

4. The check was quickly returned, { having been made out for the wrong amount. / had been made out for the wrong amount.

5. Carl gave his testimony, { still believing that he was innocent. / still believed that he was innocent.

6. Carl gave his testimony, { believing by nobody. / believed by nobody.

7. The teacher gave a very easy test, { amazing everybody. / amazed everybody.

8. The teacher recorded the test scores, { amazing at how well everybody did. / amazed at how well everybody did.

9. I sent an angry letter to the mayor's office, { bringing an immediate reply. / brought an immediate reply.

10. Sending an angry letter, / Sent an angry letter, } the mayor's office replied immediately.

11. The mayor's office replied immediately, { sending an angry letter. / sent an angry letter.

21-N • The following business letter has as yet been given no comma punctuation. Write in commas wherever you think they are needed.

Thomas Hudson & Son
Instrument Makers
63 Gloucester Road
London W2V 4BF

2nd May 1976

TSH/rdb

Mr. E. M. Bender

2016 N. Beverly Glen Blvd.

Los Angeles CA 90024

U.S.A.

<u>AR/25/76</u>

Dear Mr. Bender

Thank you very much for your letter of the 26th April placing an order for a guitar which has today been entered against the above number. Please quote this order number in all future correspondence.

Our manufacturer of carrying cases has ceased production and having been unable to find another supplier we regret that we are unlikely to be able to furnish you with one.

We will write to you again nearer the time that the guitar is due for shipment which due to the very long waiting list for these instruments will not we regret be for about eighteen months or so.

Yours sincerely

T. S. Hudson

T. S. Hudson

21-O • Sketched out below is a letter of application in which clauses have been represented as full sentences, within brackets. Rewrite the letter in usable English by changing the bracketed sentences into clauses, some of them relative clauses, a few of which are further reducible to verb-**ing** or **to** verb.

                                                        2605 Azalea Drive
                                                        Tampa, Florida 33601
                                                        May 18, 1976

Mr. Timothy B. Carr, Director of Personnel
Applied Data Systems, Inc.
6750 Olympic Blvd.
Chicago, Illinois 60621

Dear Mr. Carr:

    I am writing in response to *your company's announcement* [AND *your company's announcement* appeared in last Sunday's edition of the Tampa Herald] of an opening for a systems analyst. [I assume that the position has not already been filled] I enclose herewith *my resume* [AND one more piece of information should now be added to *my resume*]. [I have been given a further opportunity to study by my present employers] I have just completed *a graduate course* in systems design at the University of South Florida [Credit for *the graduate course* will be applied toward the Ph.D.]. [I trust that you will feel free to contact me for any further information [You might need *further information*] and I hope to hear from you soon] I am

                                                              Yours sincerely,

                                                              Joseph Bergman
                                                              Joseph Bergman

21-P • Messages on post cards are usually very personal and very short. Words are often left out, due to limitations of time and space. Study the sample post card below and then compose one of your own. Write it to anyone you choose and describe briefly where you are and what you are doing, closing with a wish that you and that person were not so far apart.

21-Q • Models of four formal letters, three personal letters, and a post card have appeared in this unit. The letters were (a) a letter home, (b) a letter of complaint, (c) a short note, (d) a thank-you letter, (e) an open letter, (f) a business letter, and (g) a letter of application. Choose one of these as a model for writing a letter of your own. Be sure to observe all the details of form.

Unit 22

22-1 DIALOG

OTHER "AMERICANS"

BRENDA You Americans just don't know what it's like for a Canadian.
CLYDE Don't know what *what*'s like, Brenda?
BRENDA To live next door to a superpower, with your big banks and corporations interfering in our affairs.
CLYDE But the U.S. and Canada are practically one country. I mean we speak the same language, and we can visit each other without a passport.
BRENDA Well, *I* don't consider us one country.
PIERRE Neither do I. As a matter of fact, in Quebec it's even hard for some of us French speakers to think of ourselves as Canadians.
BRENDA Now Pierre . . . Just because English is spoken throughout most of Canada, you can't . . .
PIERRE Except in Quebec, that is. We work hard at keeping our French culture.
MARINA I'm with *you*, Pierre. I know what you're feeling. Or rather, I think I know. In Mexico we have to protect ourselves against "Yankee imperialism."
CLYDE Now just a minute, Marina! That's not fair. I'll have you know that Americans have done something to . . . , er, for . . . most of the countries in this hemisphere, if not all of them.
MARINA You hear that! That's typical! "Americans," he says, as if "Americans" lived only in the United States.
CLYDE Well, call yourself "American" too, Marina, if that'll make you happier. No law can keep you from doing that.

VOCABULARY

interfere (interference)

superpower
affairs
passport
imperialism (empire)
hemisphere

fair
typical (type)

next door
practically
throughout

22-2 ■ DIALOG VARIATION

1. *. . . we can visit each other without a passport.*
   We don't need a passport to visit each other.
   We don't have to have a passport to visit each other.
2. *I don't consider us one country.*
   I don't consider us as one country.
   I don't consider us to be one country.
3. *We work hard at keeping our French culture.*
   We work hard to keep our French culture.
   Keeping our French culture is something we work hard at.
   Our French culture is something we work hard at keeping.
4. *. . . we have to protect ourselves against "Yankee imperialism."*
   We have to be protected against "Yankee imperialism."
   We have to have protection against "Yankee imperialism."
5. *. . . as if "Americans" lived only in the United States.*
   "Americans" don't live only in the United States.
   Not all "Americans" live in the United States.

22-3 ■ QUESTIONS

1. How many people does the conversation involve?
2. What different countries do they represent?
3. What "superpower" is Brenda talking about?
4. What is her criticism?
5. Does anybody in the conversation take sides? Who? In what way?
6. Which speaker is least inclined to consider the U.S. and Canada one country?
7. What slip of the tongue does Clyde make?
8. What does the word "American" mean for Marina?
9. Would Marina be likely to consider Brenda and Pierre as "Americans" also?

22-4 SOUND PATTERNS

Some of the ways in which written vowels and consonants are related to actual sounds have been discussed in earlier units. For example, suffixation (with **-ing, -ed,** and so on) to a word-final lax syllable requires the doubling of the final consonant if laxness is to be preserved (Volume I, Exercise 6-B):

lax: **pref*er* + ing = pref*err*ing**
tense: **interf*ere* + ing = interf*er*ing**

Final consonants in weak-stressed syllables, however, are not doubled before such suffixes: **cons*íd*er + ing = cons*íd*ering.**

22-A • (See page 213.)

22-5 PHRASAL VERBS

—We *work* hard *at* keeping our French culture.
• • •
—No law can *keep* you *from* doing that.

A number of phrasal verbs consisting of verb + preposition (see 17-6) can be followed by sentence constructions. Sentences occurring as objects of prepositions[1] always assume the **-ing** form:

No law can keep you *from* [You do that]
↳ ~~your~~ *doing that.*

22-6 ■ Act out the following dialog, changing all bracketed sentences into usable English.

1. A I *feel like* [I take a break]. Let's go have a cup of coffee.
2. B Fine. Anything to *get out of* [I sit at this desk for hours on end].
3. A Some compliment! Doesn't sound like you *care* very much *about* [You have coffee with me].
4. B Oh, I didn't mean it that way. But I *object to* [I have to put in such long hours].
5. A I know what you mean. It *prevents* us *from* [We have a decent social life].
6. B I'm always too tired by the end of the day. But my wife and I still *believe in* [We enjoy life while we can].
7. A You should practice what you preach. Why don't you *think about* [You shorten your hours]?
8. B Then I'd make less money. And that would *keep* me *from* [I have a decent social life] too.
9. A You can't win either way. *Plan on* [You be here for awhile].

[1] A list of verb-prepositions taking sentence complements will be found in Appendix D.

22-7 SPEECH ACT

—Just because English is spoken throughout most of Canada, you can't. . .
—Except in Quebec, *that is*.

• • •

—Americans have done something . . . for most of the countries in this hemisphere, *if not* all of them.

• • •

—I know what you're feeling. *Or rather*, I think I know.

That is, **if (not)**, and **or (rather)** allow extensions, clarifications, or changes within previous sentences, much in the way that we have seen for **in other words** (Volume I, exercise 12-B), **for example**, and **namely** (Volume I, 10-5).

22-8 ■ Match up the expressions listed below with the appropriate sentence endings. Say the resulting sentences.

Parliament has been meeting only two days a week
{
. *Namely,*   since last week.
. *That is,*   they've met at all.
. *For example,*   they're taking it easy.
, *if*   Tuesdays and Thursdays.
. *In other words,*   last week it was Tuesday and Thursday
. *Or rather*   three days a week.
}

B

22-9 ■ DIALOG IMPROVISATION

(Try to re-create or even improvise a variation of the Dialog at the beginning of this unit, as you remember it.)

A You Americans just don't . . .
B Don't know . . .
A To live next . . .
B But the U.S. and . . .
A Well, *I* don't . . .
C Neither do I. As a matter of fact, it's even hard . . .
A Just because English . . .
C Not in . . .
D I know what . . .

More on Complementation

—It's hard *for us to think of ourselves as Canadians.*

. . .

—We work hard at *keeping our French culture.*

. . .

—I think *(that) I know.*

. . .

—I know *what you're feeling.*

22-10 The above examples from the Dialog illustrate four basic ways of putting sentences inside other sentences in English. (See also Units 9 and 14.) The four (*italicized*) inside sentences are in the form of verb complements, and each of the four is marked by a different *complementizer*: **for . . .to**, **('s) . . . -ing**, **that**, and **wh-**. A complement can be marked by only one complementizer at a time. We can therefore say

          I think *that* **I know.**
and   **I know** *what* **you're feeling.**
and even **I think** *that* **I know** *what* **you're feeling.**
but not   ***I know** *that what* **you're feeling.**

22-11 Where verbs or adjectives have corresponding nouns we can have noun complementation (Volume I, 14-25).[2] For example:

(They *requested us to sit.*)	their *request* ~~of~~ *for us to sit*
(He *risked losing.*)	his *risk of losing*
(We *know that she sings.*)	our *knowledge* ~~of~~ *that she sings*
(I *discovered who he was.*)	my *discovery of who he was*

22-12 There is a small class of verbs in English that take a complement without a complementizer. For example, **I'll have you know that Americans have done . . .** The rest of the verbs in this class, which have been scattered throughout earlier units, are **hear, see, feel, listen (to), watch, help, make,** and **let**. It is important to avoid mistakes like ***We let him** *to* **go,** ***She made us** *to* **stop,** and so on. (Rather, **We let him go, She made us stop.**)

---

[2]For lists of verbs and nouns and the types of complement that they take, see Volume I, Appendixes C-E.

22-13 ■ Divide the class into two equal teams and have this exercise be a game to see which team can produce the most correct responses. Let the sentence **She helps us** be the complement in each of the following.

1. say
   I said that she would help us.
2. intend
   I intended for her to help us.
3. count on
   I counted on her helping us.
4. make
   I made her help us.

5. mention
6. want
7. object to
8. have
9. assume
10. doubt
11. favor
12. ask
13. insist on
14. think
15. think about
16. let

17. pray
18. know
19. postpone
20. request
21. watch
22. argue against
23. imagine
24. appreciate
25. mean
26. look forward to
27. dislike
28. expect

29. dream
30. arrange
31. regret
32. approve of
33. see
34. hate
35. realize
36. resist
37. prefer
38. feel
39. stop . . . from
40. make
41. believe

22-14 ■ Give the noun phrase forms corresponding to the sentences.

1. I intended for him to help us.
   my intention for him to help us
2. I appreciated his helping us.
   my appreciation of his helping us
3. I believed that he would help us.
   my belief that he would help us
4. I discovered who helped us.
   my discovery of who helped us
5. I prayed for him to help us.
6. I disliked his helping us.
7. I realized that he had helped us.
8. I knew who had helped us.
9. I requested for him to help us.
10. I insisted on his helping us.
11. I anticipated that he would help us.
12. I decided who should help us.
13. I arranged for him to help us.
14. I suggested his helping us.
15. I assumed that he would help us.

16. I considered who might help us.
17. I desired for him to help us.
18. I argued against his helping us.
19. I felt that he should help us.
20. I discussed who should help us.

22-15 ■ State the following sketched-out sentences after the models.

1. He has *an idea* [*We don't like him*]

    He has an idea that we don't like him.
2. He has *an idea* [We don't like *the idea*]

    He has an idea that we don't like.
3. He has *information* [We need *the information*]
4. But we have *the impression* [*He won't give it to us*]
5. We think it's for *the reason* [*He's in the pay of someone else*]
6. It's *a problem* [We'll have to deal with *the problem*]
7. It used to be *a problem* [*We had to deal with his secretary*]
8. There is *another possibility* [We're investigating *the other possibility* at the moment]
9. There is some *possibility* [*We can obtain the information elsewhere*]
10. This is *a fact* [We hadn't considered *the fact* before]

22-16 ■ Tell about your own desires, experiences, preferences, intentions, and so on by matching the complement structures on the left with appropriate verbs on the right. Or you can supply your own complements.

1. go to school
2. get up early in the morning
3. have a good time
4. be fluent in English
5. travel
6. speak several languages
7. visit England/the U.S./Canada/Australia
8. have a large/small family
9. gain/lose weight
10. drink beer
11. sing
12. be around other people
13. be by myself
14. entertain

a. look forward to
b. know
c. intend
d. think
e. prefer
f. dislike
g. like
h. feel
i. believe in
j. approve of
k. want
l. object to
m. refuse
n. can't stand
o. expect
p. hope
q. hate
r. doubt
s. love

Section B

22-B • (See page 213.)

22-C • (See page 214.)

22-D • (See page 214.)

22-E • (See page 215.)

22-17 READING (312 words)

FRENCH CANADA

Although the British conquered French Canada in 1759, the Province of Quebec has resisted efforts to deprive it of its distinct French-speaking identity. At the same time there have been increasing cultural, economic, and political pressures from English-speaking North Americans for
5 conformity to *their* linguistic norms. Nationalistic activities within Quebec in recent years have led to a tense period of confrontation, together with the threat of Quebec's secession from the rest of Canada.

In 1974 the provincial government passed a bill making French the official language of Quebec. The bill respects fully the right of speakers
10 of English to an education in English. However, non-English speakers (both French and immigrant) must henceforth attend schools where the language of instruction is French. The passing of this bill has given rise to further bitterness among the various linguistic communities in the province. In one corner is the French-speaking majority (65 percent in
15 Montreal, but 80 percent in Quebec as a whole), some of whom label the bill as too moderate and would like to prohibit the use of English entirely. Other French Canadians find it important to learn English because it is a virtual necessity in the upper echelons of business and the professsions. In another corner is the English-speaking minority, mostly
20 living in or near Montreal, some of whom enjoy considerable wealth and power. Lastly, in a third corner is the rapidly increasing minority of immigrants whose more mobile members want to learn English in order to be able to work in any part of North America. Some immigrants have started private schools, where it is hoped that enough English will

25 be learned for the children to be accepted by the English-speaking schools. Only time will tell how the different communities will adapt to the fact that the Quebec government takes it for granted that French is to be given priority over English in this province.[3]

VOCABULARY

conquer (conquest)
resist (resistance)
deprive (deprivation)
respect (respect)
attend (attendance)
give rise to
label (label)
prohibit (prohibition)
accept (acceptance)
adapt (adaptation)
take for granted

conformity (conform)
norm (normal)
activity (active)
confrontation (confront)
secession (secede)
right (rightful)
immigrant
instruction (instruct)
bitterness (bitter)
echelon
priority (prior)

tense (tenseness)
moderate (moderation)
virtual
considerable (consider, consideration)
mobile (mobility)

henceforth

22-18 ■ **INCLUDED MEANING**

(For each of the following passages pick the one statement whose meaning is part of the meaning of the passage.)

1. *At the same time there have been increasing cultural, economic, and political pressures from English-speaking North Americans for conformity to their linguistic norms.*
   a. There has been pressure to conform to English-language norms.
   b. English-speaking North Americans are increasingly political.
   c. Political pressures conform to linguistic norms.
2. *Nationalistic activities within Quebec in recent years have led to a tense period of confrontation, together with the threat of Quebec's secession from the rest of Canada.*
   a. Nationalistic activities threaten Quebec.
   b. Quebec threatens to secede.
   c. The rest of Canada threatens to secede.
3. *The passing of this bill has given rise to further bitterness among the various linguistic communities in the province.*
   a. The various linguistic communities are bitter.
   b. Bitterness caused the bill to be passed.
   c. The province is bitter at the linguistic community.

---

[3]Adapted from a letter from Palmer Acheson to the Editor, *English Around the World*, November, 1975, Number 13. Reprinted by permission of *English Around the World*, a publication of The English-Speaking Union of the United States.

Section C

4. *In one corner is the French-speaking majority . . . , some of whom label the bill as too moderate and would like to prohibit the use of English entirely.*
   a. The French-speaking majority is too moderate.
   b. The bill will prohibit the use of English.
   c. Some of the French speakers would like to prevent the use of English.
5. *Lastly, in a third corner is the rapidly increasing minority of immigrants whose more mobile members want to learn English in order to be able to work in any part of North America.*
   a. Mobile immigrants are in the minority.
   b. Minorities want to work in any part of North America.
   c. The purpose of learning English is to be able to work in North America.
6. *Only time will tell how the different communities will adapt to the fact that the Quebec government takes it for granted that French is to be given priority over English in this province.*
   a. Time will tell how the community adapts to the Quebec government.
   b. The Quebec government wants English to be subordinate to French.
   c. It is taken for granted that the province speaks English.

22-19 ■ QUESTIONS

1. Did Quebec lose its French-speaking identity?
2. Is Quebec still part of Canada?
3. Is it illegal to speak English in Canada?
4. What three linguistic communities are found in Quebec?
5. What language is most useful for a high-paying job in business?
6. In Canada do all immigrants want to learn English?
7. If you were living in Quebec which language would you want to study, English or French?

22-F • VOCABULARY RELATIONS (See page 216.)

22-20 COMPOUNDS

In the Reading there occurred four compounds of the form Noun-Verb**ing** Noun. Compare the meanings of these compounds as defined by the context in which they appeared:

French-speaking identity   (= identity as a place where French is spoken)
French-speaking majority   (= the majority, who speak French)
English-speaking minority   (= the minority, who speak English)
English-speaking schools   (= schools where English is spoken)

Notice that in all the compounds the relationship between the first two elements is that of object-verb, whereas the third elements can be related to the rest of the compound in a variety of ways.

22-21 ■ For each of the compounds listed below give what you think is a plausible paraphrase, using whatever context comes to mind.

1. the English-speaking world
2. a French-speaking official
3. Spanish-speaking homes
4. Chinese speaking problems
5. a Russian-speaking interpreter
6. Arabic-speaking countries
7. Farsi speaking experience
8. German speaking preparation

22-G • **RESTATEMENT** (See page 217.)

22-22 PUNCTUATION

Parentheses, ( ), are correlative punctuation marks, as are commas (19-19) and dashes (21-20). As markers of inclusion, explanation, and clarification, parentheses are more frequently used than either commas or dashes. For an idea of why this is so, compare the three punctuation samples below:

French Canada (312 words)
French Canada—312 words
French Canada, 312 words

Notice that parentheses, not commas or dashes, can indicate relationships of subordination for elements that come last (or first), since neither a dash nor a comma can serve as final punctuation.

22-23 ■ Look back through some previous units, find ten examples of parenthetical material, and decide whether or not dashes or commas could be substituted. Where you think substitution is not possible, give your reasons.

22-24 ■ **READING IMPROVISATION**

(Complete each of the following sentences with what you remember from the Reading.)

1. The Province of Quebec has resisted . . .
2. At the same time there have been increased cultural . . .
3. Nationalistic activities within Quebec . . .

4. In 1974 the provincial government . . .
5. The passing of this bill has . . .
6. In one corner is the . . .
7. In another corner is the . . .
8. Lastly, in a third corner is the . . .
9. Only time will tell how . . .

Simple Complements; Object Movement

—But the U.S. and Canada are practically one country.
—Well, I don't *consider us (to be) one country*.

22-25 Simple complementation involves classes of verbs all of which can be represented by **consider**:[4]

$$\text{I don't} \left\{ \begin{array}{c} \text{consider} \\ \text{feel} \\ \text{believe} \\ \ldots \end{array} \right\} us\ to\ be \left\{ \begin{array}{l} one\ country. \\ bound\ together. \end{array} \right.$$

$$\text{I don't} \left\{ \begin{array}{c} \text{consider} \\ \text{regard} \\ \text{think of} \\ \ldots \end{array} \right\} us\quad as \left\{ \begin{array}{l} one\ country. \\ bound\ together. \end{array} \right.$$

$$\text{I don't} \left\{ \begin{array}{c} \text{consider} \\ \text{call} \\ \text{find} \\ \ldots \end{array} \right\} us \left\{ \begin{array}{l} one\ country. \\ bound\ together. \end{array} \right.$$

22-26 It was pointed out in Volume I, 13-18 and 13-19 that a sentence whose subject is itself derived from a sentence

~~For us~~ *to think of ourselves as Canadians* **is hard.**

is more likely to move that subject to the end of the sentence, leaving **it** in its place:

It **is hard** *for us to think of ourselves as Canadians*.

When the object of a verb-complement construction derives from a sentence, **it** replacement *must* take place:

(*We find *to think of ourselves as Canadians* hard.)
    We find   *it*   **hard** *to think of ourselves as Canadians.*

---

[4]For lists of such verbs see **Appendix E**.

22-27 ■ Answer each of the following in the form **I Verb NP Adjective**.

1. How do you like your tea, iced or hot?
   I like it (hot).
2. What color did they paint the walls here, (green) or (gray)?
   They painted them (green).
3. How does (name) wear her hair, long or short?
4. How do you like your coffee, strong or weak?
5. How do you find English, easy or hard?
6. How do you like your steak, rare, medium, or well done?
7. How do they drink coffee in (Brazil), with sugar or without?
8. How do they serve fruit in (Mali), peeled or unpeeled?
9. How do you prefer your vegetables, cooked or raw?

22-28 ■ Sentences like **She made him a good husband** (= She made a good husband out of him) are superficially similar to ones like **She made him a good wife** (= She made a good wife for him). (See Volume I, 9-9.) In each of the following sentences express the relationship between **him** and the noun phrase in *italics*.

1. They found *him a sick man*.
   He (was) a sick man.
2. They found *him a job*.
   He (got) a job.
3. They made *him a member*.
4. They made *him an offer*.
5. They called *him a taxi*.
6. They called *him a liar*.
7. They left *him a millionaire*.
8. They left *him a million dollars*.
9. They found *him an audience*.
10. They found *him a bore*.
11. They made *him a promise*.
12. They made *him a success*.
13. They called *him a comedian*.
14. They called *him a cab*.

22-29 ■ The preposition in noun complement constructions is difficult to predict. In the Reading we saw the expressions **pressure** *for* **conformity**, **threat** *of* **secession**, and **right** *to* **an education**. Listed below are noun complement constructions with their prepositions missing, all of them taken from earlier units in this volume. See if you can recall those prepositions.

1. obstacles _____ receiving an allotment
2. opportunities _____ reaching people

3. adaptation _____ newspaper functions
4. changes _____ newspaper technology
5. potential _____ changing newspaper operations
6. responsibility _____ higher death tolls
7. the process _____ continental drift
8. answers _____ important geological questions
9. insistence _____ moving to more spacious quarters
10. conflict _____ each other

22-30 ■ Complete the following sentences with whatever comes naturally to mind.

1. I make it a rule never to . . . **(smoke in bed)**.
2. I made it clear that . . . **(I never smoke in bed)**.
3. Some people hold it a crime to . . .
4. Some people regard it as an insult that . . .
5. I feel it my duty to . . .
6. I find it hard to believe that . . .
7. We're leaving it up to you whether . . .
8. We know it for a fact that . . .
9. We consider it important to . . .
10. We consider it important that . . .
11. We consider it unimportant whether . . .
12. I take it for granted that . . .

22-H • (See page 218.)

22-I • (See page 219.)

22-J • (See page 219.)

22-K • **CLOZE** (See page 220.)

Weight and Focus

—... *it* is hoped that enough English will be learned ...
—... *there* have been increasing ... pressures ... for conformity ...

22-31 It has been pointed out in a number of places (Volume I: 13-18, 13-19, 15-18) that **it** replacement allows complex phrases and clauses to be shifted to the end of their sentences. This is an application of the general principle that in English "heavier" or more "complex" material tends to occur last in a sentence: the *weight* principle. Several grammatical devices that allow such positioning are shown in the right hand column:

Unnatural	Natural
That he helped **pleased me.**	**It pleased me** *that he helped.* [it replacement]
	I was pleased ~~by~~ *that he helped.* [passive]
... *the pleasure that he helped* **for me**	... *the pleasure* **for me** *that he helped* [split]

In this last example the "heavy" complement (**that he helped**), in order to occur last in the sentence, splits from the noun to which it is attached.

22-32 If the shifting to the right of heavy material leaves the subject position vacant, it is usually filled by the "empty" word **it**, since almost all English sentences must have grammatical subjects. But **it** is not the only empty word in English. Subject position is sometimes filled instead by the empty word **there**. **There** is often needed with application of the *focus* principle (Volume I, 15-7), that, generally speaking, new information occurs last in the sentence. This is especially true if the new material establishes the existence of a state or event:

Pressure has been increasing. ⟶ *There* **has been increasing pressure.**

The principles of weight and focus both require that certain elements be put last in the sentence. Since complex material is usually new information as well, the two principles work together rather than against each other.

22-33 ■ The word **it** is sometimes meaningless or "empty" (**It seems that you're right**) and sometimes meaningful, that is, a pronoun (**It says that you're right**). Determine whether **it** in the following sentences is meaningful or not by replacing it wherever possible with an appropriate noun phrase.

1. It teaches them to be able to speak English.
   (The book) teaches them to be able to speak English. (It is meaningful.)
2. It pleases them to be able to speak English.
   (**It** is not meaningful.)
3. It warned him that he was driving too fast.
4. It alarmed her that he was driving so fast.
5. It turns out that taxes will have to rise again.
6. It points out that taxes will have to rise again.
7. It allows us to see what they're doing.
8. It annoys us to see what they're doing.
9. It surprised them that they owed five thousand dollars in back taxes.
10. It advised them that they owed five thousand dollars in back taxes.
11. It has been notified that its products do not meet federal standards.
12. It has been noticed that its products do not meet federal standards.

22-34 ■ Complete the following sentences with whatever comes to mind.

1. There's news in the paper that . . .
2. There's no word yet of wh-. . .
3. There's still a possibility, we think, of . . .-ing . . .
4. There's not much desire among the people for . . . to . . .
5. There's a feeling going around that . . .
6. There's a decision to be made on wh-. . .
7. There's no evidence of . . .'s . . .-ing . . .
8. There's no need at all for . . . to . . .
9. There's a rumor circulating that . . .
10. There's a question of wh-. . .
11. There's the problem of . . .'s . . .-ing . . .
12. There's a request going to be made for . . . to . . .

22-35 ■ Read the following dialog putting **it** or **there** into the blanks, whichever fits.

1. A   It's cold enough outside for _____ to be snowing.
2. B   It's even cold enough for _____ to be ice on the ground.
3. A   The paper says _____'s a fifty percent chance of rain.
4. B   Then _____'s smart to close all the windows.
5. A   _____'s a good thing we thought of it before leaving.
6. B   But _____'s always something else to do that we forget.

7. A Like what? Is _____ necessary to turn off the electricity?

8. B And spoil the food in the refrigerator? Don't be silly. _____ *is* one more necessity, though.

9. A I know. _____'s the need to stop worrying.

10. B Right. But _____ doesn't seem to be much that we can do about it.

11. A _____ doesn't seem that we can do much about anything.

22-L • (See page 221.)

22-M • (See page 221.)

22-N • (See page 222.)

22-O • (See page 223.)

22-P • (See page 223.)

Section E

WRITING EXERCISES

22-A • Listen to the pronunciation of each of the following verbs + **ing**, and cross out either the single or the double consonant, whichever is incorrect. After you have arrived at the correct spellings practice pronouncing them.

1. occu $\genfrac{}{}{0pt}{}{r}{rr}$ ing
2. secu $\genfrac{}{}{0pt}{}{r}{rr}$ ing
3. murmu $\genfrac{}{}{0pt}{}{r}{rr}$ ing
4. bu $\genfrac{}{}{0pt}{}{s}{ss}$ ing
5. focu $\genfrac{}{}{0pt}{}{s}{ss}$ ing
6. confu $\genfrac{}{}{0pt}{}{s}{ss}$ ing
7. confi $\genfrac{}{}{0pt}{}{d}{dd}$ ing
8. forbi $\genfrac{}{}{0pt}{}{d}{dd}$ ing
9. pyrami $\genfrac{}{}{0pt}{}{d}{dd}$ ing
10. profi $\genfrac{}{}{0pt}{}{t}{tt}$ ing
11. benefi $\genfrac{}{}{0pt}{}{t}{tt}$ ing
12. dynami $\genfrac{}{}{0pt}{}{t}{tt}$ ing
13. equa $\genfrac{}{}{0pt}{}{l}{ll}$ ing
14. inha $\genfrac{}{}{0pt}{}{l}{ll}$ ing
15. enthra $\genfrac{}{}{0pt}{}{l}{ll}$ ing
16. regre $\genfrac{}{}{0pt}{}{t}{tt}$ ing
17. comple $\genfrac{}{}{0pt}{}{t}{tt}$ ing
18. rocke $\genfrac{}{}{0pt}{}{t}{tt}$ ing
19. prepa $\genfrac{}{}{0pt}{}{r}{rr}$ ing
20. colla $\genfrac{}{}{0pt}{}{r}{rr}$ ing
21. wa $\genfrac{}{}{0pt}{}{r}{rr}$ ing
22. determi $\genfrac{}{}{0pt}{}{n}{nn}$ ing
23. begi $\genfrac{}{}{0pt}{}{n}{nn}$ ing
24. combi $\genfrac{}{}{0pt}{}{n}{nn}$ ing
25. mode $\genfrac{}{}{0pt}{}{l}{ll}$ ing
26. rebe $\genfrac{}{}{0pt}{}{l}{ll}$ ing

22-B • Complete the following paragraph by writing in the proper form of the complement corresponding to the underlying sentence.

The Norse explorer, Leif Ericson, succeeded in _____
(1) The Norse explorer
_____, *but it is thought* _____
reaches the shores of Canada about 1000 A.D.   (2) The history of the white man there doesn't begin until much later
_____. *In 1497, John Cabot, in the service of Henry VII, managed* _____
(3) John Cabot reaches the
_____. *The Frenchman, Jacques Cartier, in 1534 saw to it*
shores of Nova Scotia

_____, and soon after that it came
(4) Canada comes under the control of France

_____. France failed _____
(5) It is called "New France"   (6) France establishes many

_____; they were prevented from _____ by war and bad
colonies there   (7) They do this

planning. Meanwhile, the English Hudson's Bay Company had started

_____. It soon appeared _____
(8) The Hudson's Bay Company does business   (9) The

French and English will be in conflict.[5]

22-C • Each of the following sentences, taken from student compositions, contains a faulty complement construction. Change each sentence in such a way as to remove the error.

1. *There are many indications which the scientific method is being applied to public management.

2. *People wonder how could China have possibly been ignored for the last 22 years.

3. *I suggested her to drive a little slower.

4. *It is interesting that how some people learn languages very quickly.

5. *I avoid to drink anything alcoholic.

22-D • Rewrite the following sketch as usable English by changing the bracketed sentences into complements. Use the noun forms for **demand** and **state**.

In the 1960s many people wondered [Will Canada be divided?]. The Prime Minister wanted [The Prime Minister improves relations between the federal and provincial governments]. In answer to [Quebec demands [Canada

---

[5]Adapted from *Information Please Almanac 1974*, edited by Dan Golenpaul (New York: Simon and Schuster, 1973).

is reorganized as a republic]], the Prime Minister, although he had avoided [The Prime Minister states Canada's loyalty to the British Queen], declared [The monarchy will stay until the people insist on [The monarchy is abolished]].

22-E • Write each of the following as one sentence by converting the sentences within circles into complements. *Italicized* verbs suggest noun complements. Change nouns to pronouns when necessary.

1. In 1970 Canada hoped for (One *creates* an opportunity (Other nations begin dialogs with China))

    Canada hoped for the creation of an opportunity for other nations to begin dialogs with China.

2. In the 1972 elections the government was hurt by (Living costs *rise* and the public is *opposed* to bilingualism)

3. The Prime Minister felt (The Prime Minister cannot support measures for (Provincial autonomy is *increased*))

4. The Prime Minister had to answer (Quebec *demands* (Canada is reorganized as a republic))

5. The government favored (A new society is *created* for the purpose of (The new society faces the problem of (French- and English-speaking Canadians are *divided*)))

Writing Exercises   215

22-F • VOCABULARY RELATIONS

The verbs listed below have somewhat similar meanings but different grammatical restrictions. Study the sample paragraph carefully, and then in each of the exercise sentences that follow cross out whatever verbs you think render the sentence unacceptable, as in the example.

> *avoid*   *keep*
> *deny*   *prevent*
> *deprive*   *prohibit*
> *forbid*

Although the Province of Quebec has resisted efforts to *deprive* it *of* its French-speaking identity, no one cay say that he is *forbidden to* speak English. That is, in making French the official language of Quebec, the laws still do not { *keep* / *prevent* / *prohibit* } anyone *from* speaking whatever language he chooses. Some speak French and *avoid* speaking English. In Canada they don't *deny* you your rights.

(1) The army has regulations that {
 a. ~~avoid~~
 b. ~~deny~~
 c. ~~deprive~~
 d. forbid
 e. ~~keep~~
 f. ~~prevent~~
 g. ~~prohibit~~
} a person to leave camp without permission. But Corporal Smith thought this was a(n)

(2) {
 a. avoidance
 b. denial
 c. deprivation
 d. forbiddance
 e. keeping
 f. prevention
 g. prohibition
} of his basic freedom. No regulation was going to

(3) {
 a. avoid
 b. deny
 c. deprive
 d. forbid
 e. keep
 f. prevent
 g. prohibit
} him from going into town if he wanted to. Even as a

civilian he had already been
(4)
- a. avoided
- b. denied
- c. deprived
- d. forbidden
- e. kept
- f. prevented
- g. prohibited

of too many pleasures, he thought. By wearing civilian clothes, Corporal Smith managed to

(5)
- a. avoid
- b. deny
- c. deprive
- d. forbid
- e. keep
- f. prevent
- g. prohibit

detection by the military police for several hours, but it

didn't
(6)
- a. avoid
- b. deny
- c. deprive
- d. forbid
- e. keep
- f. prevent
- g. prohibit

them from capturing him and returning him to camp.

Now Corporal Smith is really
(7)
- a. avoided
- b. denied
- c. deprived
- d. forbidden
- e. kept
- f. prevented
- g. prohibited

his basic freedom.

22-G • RESTATEMENT

(Complete the restatement by supplying the correct form.)

1. The bill *respects fully* the rights of speakers of English. *(have)*

   The bill *has full respect for the rights of speakers of English.*

2. The confrontation over nationalistic activities *was very tense*. *(bring)*

   The confrontation over nationalistic activities _____

   _____

3. The province *strongly resisted* efforts to change its identity. *(offer)*

   The province _____

Writing Exercises

4. *Consider* this matter *carefully*. *(give)*

   _____ this matter your _____

5. We have to *protect* ourselves *the best we can*. *(give)*

   We have to _____

6. They were *clearly instructed* not to resist. *(give)*

   They were _____

7. Some communities *are very bitter* over the passage of the bill. *(feel)*

   Some communities _____

22-H • Rewrite the following constructions as usable sentences. The choice between **for-to** and **that-S** for the bracketed sentences will be determined in part by the meaning of the complement. (See also Volume I, 14-29.) In two of the constructions the complementizer is **whether**.

1. Many French Canadians find [They learn English] important.

2. Quebec makes [Quebec preserves its French-speaking identity] a rule.

3. Quebec takes [French is to be given priority over English] for granted.

4. The government left [Will French be the official language of Quebec?] up to the people to decide.

5. In Canada they don't consider [One smokes marijuana] a serious crime.

6. Canada saw [Other nations will soon look to China] as inevitable.

7. For a time they regarded [Will Quebec secede?] as an open question.

22-I • In the blank spaces below write **as, to be,** or **X** (for nothing), as required. In many cases you will have a choice.

Maria considered Canada _____ a place worth visiting but imagined
                                       1
it _____ very cold there all the time. She understood it _____ a
       2   3
country that was perpetually covered by snow, but she didn't picture it
_____ that way for long. On reading something about Canada, she dis-
       4
covered it _____ a country of many contrasts of climate, with a topo-
                5
graphy that is described _____ extremely diversified. Maria also found
                                 6
Canada _____ larger even than the United States, whereas previously
              7
she had thought of it _____ no larger than Australia. Some people find
                            8
it _____ surprising that much of Canada lies above the Arctic Circle.
       9
Years ago Norway claimed some of this area _____ theirs but eventu-
                                                       10
ally left it _____ under Canadian control.
              11

22-J • As already mentioned (22-26), **it** replacement applies when the object of a verb complement construction is itself a sentence, but not if that sentence is part of still another complement. Therefore, compare the following:

I find	*that he objects* **odd.**	⟶	**I find it odd** *that he objects.*
I find *the fact that he objects* **odd.**		⟶̸	~~I find it odd the fact that he objects.~~
I find	*for him to object* **odd.**	⟶	**I find it odd** *for him to object.*
I find *the idea for him to object* **odd.**		⟶̸	~~I find it odd the idea for him to object.~~

Rewrite the sketches below as usable sentences by moving something into subject position and making any other required changes.

1. find quite odd − I − that fact
   I find that fact quite odd.

2. find quite odd − I − [They had to lie]
   I find it quite odd that they had to lie.

3. find quite odd − I − the fact [= They had to lie]
   I find the fact that they had to lie quite odd.

Writing Exercises

4. consider to be serious — the Canadian government — the pollution problem

_____

5. consider a serious matter — the Canadian government — [Pollution is increasing]

_____

6. consider serious — the Canadian government — *the tendency* [= *People pollute*]

_____

7. assume to be an open question — many Canadians — English-language domination

_____

8. assume to be an open question — many Canadians — [Will English completely dominate?]

_____

9. assume to be an open question — many Canadians — *the idea* [= *Will English completely dominate?*]

_____

_____

22-K • CLOZE

(In each blank space write a word that you think fits naturally.)

    Quebec separatists kidnapped _____(1)_____ British trade official, James R. Cross, and _____(2)_____ Canadian Labor Minister, Pierre Laporte, in _____(3)_____, 1970. When their demands were refused, _____(4)_____ was strangled but Cross was released _____(5)_____ fifty-nine days. Cross's seven kidnappers _____(6)_____ given safe passage to Cuba, but _____(7)_____ three killers were captured and their _____(8)_____ was sentenced to life imprisonment. The _____(9)_____ were attended by the largest manhunts _____(10)_____ Canadian history and imposition by the _____(11)_____ Minister, for the first time in _____(12)_____ of the War Measures Act.[6]

[6]Ibid.

22-L • Each of the following sentences, taken from student compositions, contains an error involving complementation. Change each sentence in such a way as to remove the error.

1. *It is some mail for you on the table.

2. *Is nice to see you again.

3. *I think it had snow on the ground.

4. *Will be some questions for her to answer.

5. *There wasn't possible to help them.

6. *We considered important for them to be here.

22-M • Rewrite each of the following sketches as a usable sentence by moving something into subject position and making other changes such that the subject of each sentence is **it** or **there**. Choose a natural sounding verb tense. Some of the sketches represent more than one possible sentence.

1. be possible — [It will rain]
   It is possible that it will rain.
   It is possible for it to rain.

2. be — a possibility — [It will rain]
   There is a possibility that it will rain.

3. be on the window — rain

4. rain

5. [Neg] be yesterday — rain

6. [Neg] rain yesterday

Writing Exercises

7. be — a likelihood — [It will rain tomorrow]
_____

8. be likely — [It will rain tomorrow]
_____

9. be — a shame — [It's raining]
_____

22-N • Convert the sketched-out constructions below to full sentences by adding complementizers to the *italicized* sentences and making any other necessary changes. Put circles around these new constructions and move them if this is required. Decisions concerning movement and **it** replacement should be based on the principles of weight and focus.

1. Dr. Weiss is carefully considering tomorrow's experiment.

    It (That It might not work) is his opinion at the moment.

2. Several scientists are of the opinion that tomorrow's experiment may not be successful. (That It might not work) is also Dr. Weiss's opinion.

3. Although there is some doubt whether the experiment can succeed,

    Will it even take place at all? is even less sure.

4. Although there has been endless argument for and against performing the experiment, *Will it take place?* has still to be decided.

5. They wanted him to tell a lie, but *He is dishonest* would have been very uncharacteristic of him.

6. They wanted him to tell the truth, and of course *He tells a lie* would have been very uncharacteristic of him.

7. *It might not receive support* is the fear of the originator of a comprehensive plan to fight environmental pollution, Dr. Patrick Kelly, of the University of Mulcaster.

8. *The comprehensive plan to fight environmental pollution might not receive support* is the fear of its originator, Dr. Patrick Kelly.

22-O • Rewrite the following sketch as a complete paragraph by changing the sentences within brackets into complements. Make any other necessary changes. *Italicized* verbs suggest noun complements.

We will finish by [We *say* something about Canada's form of government]. Although [Canada has a Governor General appointed by the Queen of England] is true, modern laws have made [He exercises power] impossible. The laws let him [He acts] only with [The Prime Minister and the Cabinet *advise* and *consent*]. Parliament has two houses: a Senate and a House of Commons. [Elections are held every five years or whenever the majority party considers [The majority party *appeals* to the people] necessary] is required. [Bills must be passed by both houses and signed by the Governor General] is the law.

22-P • Write a composition of several paragraphs describing a situation with which you are familiar where differing languages pose a problem. This could be a geographical area where two or more languages compete for supremacy, the problem of newly arrived immigrants not knowing how to communicate in a strange language, the difficulty of governing a large territory in which a number of different languages are spoken, and so on.

Writing Exercises

Unit 23

23-1 DIALOG

THE TELEVISION STUDIO

RUDY This show comes to you live from New York. At least it *starts out* live—it sometimes dies in twenty minutes. . . . And here's lovable, laughable, Jerry Carrozza! [applause]

JERRY I'm in big trouble, Rudy. The stock market cleaned me out. I'm about to go bankrupt—unless I can raise some cash—and I haven't the slightest idea where I'm going to get it.

RUDY I'm glad to hear that—I was afraid for a minute you might have an idea that you could borrow it from me.

JERRY Thanks, pal. Just don't provoke me. You know, I wish I were living back in the Stone Age—ask me why.

RUDY Okay—why?

JERRY Because they used rocks for money—and I would like to pay off my landlord.

RUDY Well, Jerry, just remember this—money isn't everything.

JERRY I know—and if you stay in this city long enough—it's nothing.

RUDY What I mean is, money can't buy you happiness.

JERRY No? Well, at least it lets me choose my own form of misery. . . . And even if money *could* buy happiness, there would be a big luxury tax on it.

RUDY I really feel for you, Jerry. If only the bank would lend you some money.

JERRY The bank? That's where they'll let you borrow money only if you can prove you don't need it.

RUDY If you think this is sad, folks, you should see our paychecks.

JERRY I've got to be going now, Rudy. If I'm not home by midnight—my wife rents out my room.

RUDY Good night, Jerry. [applause] Next, I'd like to welcome our special guest for the evening. . .[1]

[1]From *Encyclopedia of Humor,* copyright © 1968 by Joey Adams. Reprinted by the permission of the publisher, Bobbs-Merrill Company, Inc.

VOCABULARY

clean out	stock market	live (alive)
borrow	pal	lovable
provoke (provocation, provocative)	Stone Age	laughable
	landlord	bankrupt (bankruptcy)
pay off (payoff)	misery (miserable)	slight
lend/lent/lent	luxury (luxurious)	sad (sadness)
rent out	paycheck	

23-2 ■ DIALOG VARIATION

1. *I haven't the slightest idea where I'm going to get it.*
   I have no idea where I'm going to get it.
   I haven't the faintest idea where I'm going to get it.
2. *I wish I were living back in the Stone Age.*
   I would like to be living back in the Stone Age.
   If only I were living back in the Stone Age.
3. *At least it lets me choose my own form of misery.*
   At least it allows me to choose my own form of misery.
   At least it makes it possible for me to choose my own form of misery.
4. *They'll let you borrow money only if you can prove you don't need it.*
   They'll let you borrow money provided that you can prove you don't need it.
   They'll let you borrow money as long as you can prove you don't need it.
   They'll let you borrow money on condition that you can prove you don't need it.
5. *If I'm not home by midnight, . . .*
   If I don't get home before midnight, . . .
   If I'm not home before midnight, . . .

23-3 ■ QUESTIONS

1. Who is the host on the show, Rudy or Jerry?
2. What is the cause of Jerry's money problems?
3. Does Rudy offer to lend him money?
4. How does Jerry feel about his landlord?
5. What advantage does money have for Jerry?
6. What problem does he find with borrowing money from banks?
7. Which parts of the dialog do you find funny? Why?
8. Who gets the funny lines, Rudy or Jerry?

23-4 SOUND PATTERNS

Some letters of the English alphabet can represent more than one sound, often depending upon the letters that precede or follow:

    traffi*c*   *c*ity   ci*t*y   na*t*ion
    /k/   /s/   /t/   /sh/

The representation of certain contrasting sounds by the same letter of the alphabet is especially useful in spelling pairs of related words:

    medi*c*al   medi*c*ine   defini*t*e   defini*t*ion
    /k/   /s/   /t/   /sh/

However, not all contrasting but corresponding consonants in pairs of related words will necessarily be represented by the same consonant letter. Contrasting consonant sounds cannot be written with the same letter if the wrong pronunciation would result. Compare:

    igni*t*e   igni*t*ion   divi*d*e   divi[s]ion   (*divi*d*ion)
    /t/   /sh/   /d/   /zh/   /d/

Occasionally, in pairs of related words, the *same* consonant sound will be represented by *different* letters. Again, this is done to avoid a wrong pronunciation. Compare:

    invi*t*ation   invi*t*e   provo*c*ation   provo[k]e (*provo*c*e)
    /t/   /t/   /k/   /k/   /s/

Finally, in some pairs of related words a consonant letter will be sounded in one word but "silent" in the other. The presence of the silent consonant serves to preserve the relationship:

    si*g*n   si*g*nature   bom*b*   bom*b*ard
    /-/   /g/   /-/   /b/

23-A • (See page 245.)

23-5 PHRASAL VERBS

—The stock market *cleaned* me *out*.

It is sometimes possible to assign some kind of meaning to the particle in a phrasal verb. The particles **out** and **off**, for example, have a meaning of their own when they occur with certain kinds of verbs. **Out** is used with verbs dealing with the interior of something; **off** is related to the exterior:

    The car needs to be *cleaned* { *out.* (Use a vacuum.)
                                                      { *off.* (Use a hose.)

23-6 ■ Each of the following objects needs to be cleaned. From your knowledge of their shape and form say whether you think they would normally be cleaned "out" or "off."

1. a drawer
2. a shelf
3. a closet
4. a table
5. shoes
6. a garage
7. walls
8. a pocket
9. a seat
10. a cellar
11. a sidewalk
12. a fireplace
13. the outside
14. the inside

Can you think of any objects that would normally be cleaned *either* out *or* off?

23-B • (See page 246.)

SPEECH ACT

—... and I haven't the slightest idea where I'm going to get it.
—I'm glad to hear *that*.

• • •

—Well, just remember *this*—money isn't everything.

23-7 One of the commonest uses of **this** and **that** (and **these/those**) is for distinguishing between different degrees of proximity: **Don't take** *that* **road; stay on** *this* **one.** Another, related, use is for reference back to what has just been said or written, or reference forward to something that is about to be said or written. For backward reference **that** (and often **this**) can occur; for forward reference only **this** is possible:

> **Jerry says** *he's bankrupt*. **Do you believe** *that*?
>
> **You won't believe** *this*: **Jerry says** *he's bankrupt*.

23-C • (See page 246.)

23-8 ■ What do you notice about the use of the word **this** in the following cartoon?

Used by permission of Chicago Tribune-New York News Syndicate.

23-9 ■ **DIALOG IMPROVISATION**

(Try to re-create or even improvise a variation of the Dialog at the beginning of this unit, as you remember it.)

A I'm about to go bankrupt—unless I can raise some cash—and I haven't the slightest . . .
B I was afraid for a minute you might . . .
A You know, I wish I . . .
B Okay— . . .
A Because they used . . .
B Well, just remember . . .
A I know—and if . . .
B What I mean is . . .
A No? Well, at least . . .
B If only the bank . . .
A The bank? That's where . . .

Condition: **if**

—*. . . if money could buy* happiness, *there would be* a big luxury tax on it.
—If only the bank would lend you some money.
—The bank? That's where *they'll let* you borrow money *if you can prove* you don't need it.

23-10 Generally speaking, **if** clauses that state a condition can be divided into three kinds:

$\begin{bmatrix} \text{future} \\ \text{possible} \end{bmatrix}$ **If he** *has* **any money, he** *'ll pay* **off his landlord.**

$\begin{bmatrix} \text{present} \\ \text{hypothetical} \end{bmatrix}$ **If he** *had* **any money, he** *would pay* **off his landlord.**

$\begin{bmatrix} \text{past} \\ \text{hypothetical} \end{bmatrix}$ **If he** *had had* **any money, he** *would have paid* **off his landlord.**

Notice that in the two "hypothetical" forms the **if** clause expresses an idea that is not true:

if he had any money . . . (but he doesn't have any)
if he had had any money . . . (but he didn't have any)

The verb tense in the hypothetical **if** clause is called *subjunctive*, and it is identical to the regular past forms except with the verb **be**. The past subjunctive of **be** is **were**:

if $\begin{Bmatrix} \text{I} \\ \text{you} \\ \text{he} \\ \text{she} \\ \text{we} \\ \text{they} \end{Bmatrix}$ **were** rich . . .

23-11 ■ Tell each of the following short jokes to the rest of the class. Use a form of reported speech.

1. *"If you stay overnight you'll have to make your own bed."*
   "That's okay with me."
   "Here's a hammer and saw."[2]
2. The clerk at the post office refused his package: *"It's too heavy; you'll have to put more stamps on it."*
   "And if I put more stamps on it—will that make it lighter?"[2]

[2]Ibid.

3. *"That man is going around telling lies about you."*
   "I don't mind—but I'll break his head if he begins telling the truth."[2]
4. *"Can you tell if your husband is lying or not, just by looking at his face?"*
   "No trouble at all. If his lips are moving, he's lying."[3]
5. *The mother said to her daughter, "Marriage is a matter of give and take—if he doesn't give what you want, take it!"*[2]
6. *"You can't sleep in my class!"*
   "If you didn't talk so loud, I could."[2]
7. *You can't win these days. If you pay your income tax you go to the poorhouse, and if you don't pay it you go to the jailhouse.*[2]

23-12 ■ Given below is an "old saying" in which parts of all verb phrases have been removed and listed at the right. Complete the quotation with words from the list that you think fit or add some of your own.

"If a man runs after money, he's . . . ; if he keeps it,

he's . . . ; if he spends it, he's . . . ; if he doesn't get it,   ambition
                                                                   a capitalist
he's . . . ; if he doesn't try to get it, he lacks . . . ; if he gets it   a failure
                                                                              a fool
without working for it, he's . . . ; and if he accumulates it   money-mad
                                                                   a parasite
after a lifetime of hard work, people call him . . . who got   a playboy

very little out of life."[4]

23-13 ■ Finish each of the following.

1. If I were rich, . . .
2. If I knew English perfectly, . . .
3. If I were able to have anything I wanted, . . .
4. If I knew that the world was going to end tomorrow, . . .
5. If I were able to live anywhere I wanted, . . .

---

[2]Ibid.
[3]Harry Golden, *The Golden Book of Jewish Humor,* (New York: G. P. Putnam's Sons, 1972).
[4]Adapted from *A Complete Treasury of Stories for Public Speakers,* by Morris Mandel. Reprinted by permission of Jonathan David Publishers.

23-14 ■ Participate in the following little dialogs and use the indicated forms.

1. A Did (name) pass the course last semester?
   B **(Yes, he/she did.)**
   A How do you know?
   B **(Because if he/she hadn't, he/she wouldn't have been permitted to take this course.)**
2. A Was it (name)'s birthday yesterday?
   B and so on.
3. A Was the day before yesterday a holiday?
4. A Was there by chance a big earthquake near here last week?
5. A Have they scheduled a national election in your country for next month?
6. A Has (name) had enough money to live on during the past year?
7. A Was there a big sale downtown with copies of this book selling for half price?

23-15 ■ Conditional sentences of the kind **If you do that again, (then) I'll have to punish you** have very common alternate versions in the form of two conjoined sentences without **if**: **Do that again** *and* **I'll have to punish you** / **Don't do that again** *or* **I'll have to punish you**. Restate each of the following familiar "sayings" with **if**, and say whether or not you agree with it. If you wish, change the saying to suit your own beliefs.

1. *"Give him an inch and he'll take a mile."*
2. *"Give him a free hand and he'll put it right in your pocket."*[5]
3. *"Help a man in trouble and he'll never forget you—especially the next time he's in trouble."*[5]
4. *"Marry for money and you'll probably earn it."*[5]
5. *"Laugh and the world laughs with you; cry and you cry alone."*

23-16 ■ RIDDLES[6]

1. What two coins equal 55¢—if one of the coins is not a nickel?[7]
2. If you threw a black stone into the Red Sea, what would it become?[7]
3. What is unusual about this sentence: *Pull up if I pull up.*[8]
4. If I were in the sun and you were out of it, what would it become?[9]

---

[5]Adams, op. cit.
[6]The solutions to these riddles can be found in the Instructor's Manual.
[7]Adams, op. cit.
[8]Howard W. Bergerson, *Palindromes and Anagrams*, (New York: Dover Publications, 1973).
[9]Edith B. Ordway, *Handbook of Conundrums*, (Detroit: Gale Research Co., 1915).

23-17 ■ Look at the cartoon below and tell what you think the situation is. What form would the man's question take if the game had already ended?

Men & Women by Mel Calman,
© 1976 Courtesy of Field Newspaper Syndicate

23-D • (See page 247.)

23-E • (See page 247.)

C

23-18 READING (262 words)

THE CONVERSION

A famous evangelist had come to town and the auditorium was packed. For the better part of an hour he denounced the evils of drink, his impassioned denunciations taking in the distillers and sellers, as well as the drinkers.

5   The vast audience was enthralled with the fiery speech, but no one was more fascinated than Sammy, who had come into the hall only to get out of the rain, and who was hearing him for the first time.

Now the evangelist was coming to the end of his sermon, and he went into a frenzy of excitement. "Who has the largest bank account?" he thundered. "I'll tell you who—the liquor store owner, that's who! And who lives in the finest house and in the most exclusive neighborhood? Again, the liquor store owner! Who buys his wife mink coats, Cadillacs, and jewels? The liquor store owner! And who is keeping him in all this luxury? You, the factory worker who spends his hard-earned money for all that whiskey, wine, and beer! If it weren't for you, the liquor store owner couldn't live like this!"

At the close of the sermon the audience gave him the most enthusiastic ovation he had ever received.

Sammy rushed up to the platform and grapsed the evangelist's hand. "Thank you! Oh, thank you!" he cried. "You are indeed an inspiring man!"

"Then you are saved? You're converted?" asked the good minister. "You've come to realize that drinking is sinful?"

"Well, no, not that," explained Sammy. "But I'm going right out and buy a liquor store!"[10]

VOCABULARY

pack
denounce (denunciation)
enthrall
fascinate (fascination)
thunder (thunder)
grasp (grasp)
inspire (inspiration)
convert (conversion)

conversion (convert)
evangelist (evangelical)
auditorium
evil
denunciation (denounce)
distiller
audience
sermon
frenzy
liquor
neighborhood
mink
jewel/jewelry
ovation
platform

impassioned
fiery (fire)
exclusive (exclude, exclusion)
sinful (sin)

23-19 ■ INCLUDED MEANING

(For each of the following passages pick the one statement whose meaning is part of the meaning of the passage.)

[10]Mandel, op. cit.

1. *For the better part of an hour he denounced the evils of drink, his impassioned denunciations taking in the distillers and sellers, as well as the drinkers.*
   a. Distillers and sellers are as good as drinkers.
   b. The distillers and sellers were denounced.
   c. The distillers and sellers were taken in by evil denunciations.
2. *... no one was more fascinated than Sammy, who had come into the hall only to get out of the rain, and who was hearing him for the first time.*
   a. Sammy was fascinating.
   b. Sammy didn't want to get wet.
   c. Sammy had planned to hear him.
3. *And who is keeping him in all this luxury? You, the factory worker who spends his hard-earned money for all that whiskey, wine, and beer!*
   a. A lot of liquor is bought by the factory worker.
   b. The factory worker is kept in luxury.
   c. Hard-earned money is a luxury.
4. *Sammy rushed up to the platform and grasped the evangelist's hand. "Thank you! Oh, thank you!" he cried. "You are indeed an inspiring man!"*
   a. Sammy was inspiring.
   b. The evangelist thanked Sammy.
   c. Sammy was inspired.

23-20 ■ QUESTIONS

1. Were there very many people in the audience?
2. How many times had Sammy heard the evangelist before?
3. Was the evangelist against luxury?
4. What does the liquor store owner's luxury depend on?
5. How did Sammy react to the sermon?
6. What assumption did the evangelist make about Sammy?
7. Did Sammy profit by the sermon?

23-21 VOCABULARY RELATIONS

—He *went into a frenzy* of excitement.
• • •
—You've *come to realize* that drinking is sinful?
• • •
—I'm *going* right *out* and buy a liquor store.

Section C

The use of **come** and **go** in English is influenced by several factors, most commonly direction of movement and the relative positions of speaker and hearer. **Come**, for example, is used for movement toward a center of reference, usually the speaker's present location or where the speaker intends to be at some time in the future. **Go** indicates movement away from that point of reference:

Come to my office right away.   [Speaker is in his office]
Go to my office right away.   [Speaker is not in his office]
Come to my office tomorrow.   [Speaker will be in his office tomorrow]
Go to your seat.   [Speaker is not at hearer's seat]

23-F • (See page 248.)

23-22 ■ **Come** and **go** are also used to describe changes of state. In these cases the "reference point" is not speaker-hearer location but what is considered a normal or natural state. For example, since sanity is considered normal, insanity is what a person *goes* to, sanity what he *comes* (back) to:

He temporarily *went insane*.
Then he *came back to his right mind*.

23-G • (See page 249.)

23-23 COMPOUNDS

—And who is keeping him in all this luxury? You, *the factory worker* . . .
If it weren't for you, *the liquor store owner* couldn't live like this.

There are many compounds in English that include an *agent* noun, made up of a verb + the suffix **-er**, and less commonly **-or** (e.g. **driver**, **owner**, **singer**, **actor**, and so on). The compound usually reflects a verb-object relationship:

A truck driver **drives trucks.**
A liquor store owner **owns a liquor store.**

Often, however, the relationship is not one of verb-object. For example,

A factory worker **works** *in* **a factory.**
A radio announcer **announces** *on* **the radio.**
A vacuum cleaner **cleans** *by* **(means of) vacuum.**

23-24 ■ Look at the compounds listed below. Which ones reveal a verb-object relationship? For those that don't have this relationship give a definition in the form of the examples above. For example, "A prize fighter fights for prizes," and so on.

1. stamp collector
2. English teacher
3. bus rider
4. window washer
5. can opener
6. newspaper reporter
7. house painter
8. movie actor
9. trouble maker
10. cigarette lighter
11. window shopper
12. letter opener
13. dairy farmer
14. garbage collector
15. wage earner
16. theater goer
17. baby sitter
18. record player
19. piano mover
20. water cooler
21. home owner
22. pressure cooker
23. well-wisher
24. pencil sharpener
25. baseball player
26. late comer
27. storyteller
28. tape recorder

23-25 ■ How would you say the sentence in the last frame of the cartoon below?

Reprinted by permission of Newspaper Enterprise Association.

23-26 ■ RESTATEMENT

Hypothetical **if** clauses can be restated in very formal English without **if**, simply by reversing subject and **were** or **had**, as in questions:

    If it weren't for you . . .   =   Were it not for you . . .
    If it hadn't been for you . . .   =   Had it not been for you . . .

The conditional clauses in the following sentences are very formal. Restate them less formally with **if**:

1. Had we known the rules, we wouldn't have broken them.
2. Had there been more time, it would have been possible to finish.
3. Had it not rained, the game would have been played.
4. Were I to give her the answer, I'd be cheating.
5. Were the plane on schedule, it would be arriving now.
6. Were the people not already suffering, we might talk of higher taxes.

Section C

23-27 PUNCTUATION

What someone actually says is placed in writing within *quotation marks* (" "):

"Thank you! Oh, thank you!" he cried.

If what someone says includes in turn another quote, the innermost is enclosed within *inverted commas* (' '):

"I want to say, 'Thank you,' " he cried.[11]

23-H • (See page 250.)

23-28 ■ READING IMPROVISATION

(Complete each of the following sentences with what you remember from the Reading.)

1. A famous evangelist had . . .
2. He denounced the evils of . . .
3. No one was more fascinated . . .
4. Now the evangelist was coming . . .
5. "Who has the largest . . .
6. "And who lives . . .
7. "Who buys his wife . . .
8. "And who is keeping him in . . .
9. At the close of the sermon the audience . . .
10. Sammy rushed up to . . .
11. "Thank you! . . .
12. "Then you are . . .
13. "Well, no, not that, . . .

---

[11] In British English the use of quotation marks and inverted commas is just the reverse. For example, **'I want to say, "Thank you,"' he cried.**

Condition: **only if**; Negative Condition

—... they'll let you borrow money *only if* you can prove you don't need it.

⋯

—I'm about to go bankrupt—*unless* I can raise some cash ....

23-29 The meaning of **only if** is captured as well by the subordinators **provided that, on condition that,** and **as/so long as**:

The banks will lend you money $\begin{Bmatrix} \text{only if} \\ \text{provided that} \\ \text{on condition that} \\ \text{as long as} \end{Bmatrix}$ you don't need it.

23-30 Negative conditions are commonly expressed with **unless**. The correspondence of **unless** with **if ... not** can be represented like this:

$$S_1 \text{ unless } S_2 \begin{matrix} \nearrow S_1 \text{ if neg } S_2 \\ \searrow \text{neg } S_1 \text{ if } S_2 \end{matrix}$$

He can drive *unless* he's been drinking. $\begin{matrix} \nearrow \text{He can drive } \textit{if} \text{ he has}n\textit{'t} \\ \text{been drinking.} \\ \searrow \text{He } \textit{can't} \text{ drive } \textit{if} \text{ he's} \\ \text{been drinking.} \end{matrix}$

Also expressing negative condition are the conjunctions **or else** and **otherwise**. The correspondences with **if** are less direct, however, as **or else** and **otherwise** often include the idea of causation as well as condition:

Don't let him drink $\begin{Bmatrix} \text{, because if you do,} \\ \text{.} \quad \text{Otherwise,} \\ \text{,} \quad \text{or else} \end{Bmatrix}$ he can't drive.

23-31 ■ Restate each of the following "old sayings"[12] with **unless** instead of **if ... not**.

1. *"Life begins at forty—but* if *you do*n't *start before then you'll miss a lot of fun."*
2. *"Never underestimate a woman—if you're* not *talking about her weight or her age."*
3. *"If you're right, nobody remembers;* if *you're* not *right, nobody forgets."*

---

[12]Adams, op. cit.

4. *"Ability is what will help you get to the top* if *the boss doesn't have a daughter."*
5. *"Workers aren't willing to do an honest day's work any more—if they can't get a week's pay for it."*

23-32 ■ Read the following items,[13] each containing an **if** clause, and say whether you think the clause is an **"only if"** type (paraphrasable with **as long as, provided that,** and **on condition that**), a **"negative if"** type (paraphrasable with **unless**), or a **"straight if"** type (no paraphrase).

1. *Sign in Bar: "If you drink to forget—please pay in advance."*
2. *"Knowledge is power—if you know the right things about the right people."*
3. *"If you look like your passport photo—you're not well enough to travel."*
4. *"You have a perfect right to express your opinion here—if it agrees with mine."*
5. *"Ability is what will help you get to the top if the boss doesn't have a daughter."*
6. *"If you tell him life begins at forty, he answers 'So does arthritis.'"*

23-33 ■ Say the following sentences[14] with **if, although,** or **unless** in the blank, whichever seems grammatical and/or plausible. Some of the examples are intended to be funny.

1. *"_____ I'm studying when you come in, please wake me up."*
2. *"Does this train stop at San Francisco?"*

   "Well, _____ it does there will be a big splash."
3. *"I'll never forget the first day I met my wife, _____ I've tried many times."*
4. *The mother said to her daughter, "Marriage is a matter of give and take; _____ he doesn't give what you want, take it!"*
5. *"Nobody wants to hear a man's troubles—_____ a woman is involved."*
6. *"_____ you really want to lose weight, put the scales in front of the refrigerator."*

---

[13]Ibid.
[14]Ibid.

23-34 ■ The two halves of a "hypothetical" sentence with **otherwise** can usually be reversed using **but** or **only**: **I have to go to class;** *otherwise* **I'd stay and have coffee with you** ↔ **I'd stay and have coffee with you,** *but/only* **I have to go to class**. The version with **only** is very informal. Read the following little dialog,[15] inserting **otherwise** and **only** in their proper places; then finish the partial sentences below with something starting with **otherwise** or **only**, whichever is correct.

PASSENGER	*What makes this train go so slow?*
CONDUCTOR	*If you don't like it, get off and walk.*
PASSENGER	{*I would, _____ I'm not expected till train time.* *I'm not expected till train time; _____ I would.*

1. I wasn't born in an English-speaking country; _____

2. I'd speak English fluently, _____

3. I don't have any extra money; _____

4. I'd offer to buy you lunch, _____

5. I'm too tired; _____

6. I'd suggest we go to a movie, _____

23-I • (See page 251.)

23-J • (See page 252.)

23-K • (See page 252.)

[15]Ibid.

23-L • **CLOZE** (See page 253.)

> Condition, Wishes, and the Subjunctive
>
> —I *wish I were* living back in the Stone Age . . .
>
> . . .
>
> —*If only* the bank *would* lend you some money . . .

23-35 Hypothetical **if** clauses (23-10) mention states or events that are not true or that have not happened:

> **If she were right, she'd be happier.** (She isn't right.)

Present wishes also concern what is not true or real and, like hypothetical **if** clauses, require that the verb be in the past subjunctive:

> **She wishes she *were* right.** (She isn't right.)

Wishes can also be expressed with **if only**, where the "main clause" is then unnecessary. However, an **if only** expression can be interpreted as a wish only on the part of the person who is speaking:

> **If only she were right.** (= *I* wish she were right.)

Only can also be shifted to the position before main verb or adjective:

> **If she were only right.**

23-36 Conditional clauses with **if** are restatable in the form of noun phrases:

> **The bank will give you the money . . .**
> . . . *if* (and *only if*) you can prove your identity.
> . . . subject to ⎫
> . . . conditional (up)on ⎬ proof of (your) identity.
> . . . contingent (up)on ⎭

Sentence/noun-phrase matches also occur with "closed" condition (**no matter, regardless of**), "eventuality" (**in case of**), and "concession" (**in spite of**):

> **We help them *whether they're young or old*.**
> . . . *regardless of* ⎫
> . . . *no matter what* ⎬ their age.

> **Call the fire department** *in case there's a fire.*
> *. . . in case of fire.*
>
> **I like her** *even though we disagree.*
> *. . . in spite of our disagreement.*

23-37 ■ Retell each of the following,[16] replacing the portion in *italics* with an **if only** construction.

1. "There are only two things you can be sure of: death and taxes—*too bad* they can't come in that order."
2. "*What a shame* Christmas always comes when the stores are most crowded."
3. WIDOW "I've had so much trouble collecting the money from my husband's estate—now *I wish* he hadn't died."
4. TOURIST "Are you content to spend your life walking around the country begging?"
   BEGGAR "No, lady. *I wish* I had a car."

23-38 ■ Make some wishes concerning the topics listed below. Remember that what is wished for has to be something that is not or was not true.

1. weather

   I wish { it would rain/stop raining.
   it weren't so cold/hot.
   it hadn't snowed last week.
   . . .

2. school
3. money
4. family
5. travel
6. English

23-39 ■ Some of the following **if** clauses are hypothetical, some not. (That is, the verb in the hypotheticals is subjunctive.) Which are which?[17]

1. "Well, *if I was speeding,*" the driver said to the policeman who finally caught up with her, "so were you."
2. "She's so fashionable that *if she were going to shoot her husband* she'd wear a hunting outfit."
3. "*If you looked like your passport photo* you weren't well enough to travel."

[16] Ibid.
[17] Ibid.

4. "She would run away from home *if she could figure out a way to take the phone with her.*"
5. "For tax purposes I used to list eight of my relatives under "contributions"—*if they were not an organized charity*, I don't know what is."

23-40 ■ What do you think of Sir Winston's reply to Lady Astor?[18]

Lady Astor once said to Winston Churchill: "*If you were my husband, I'd poison your coffee.*"
Churchill answered: "*If you were my wife, I'd drink it.*"

23-M • (See page 254.)

23-N • (See page 254.)

23-O • (See page 255.)

23-P • (See page 256.)

23-Q • (See page 257.)

[18]Ibid.

WRITING EXERCISES

23-A • Each of the following pairs of related words has blanks for one set of corresponding consonants. As the pairs are pronounced for you write in the missing consonants.[19] Some pairs will have the same consonant letter, some not. Which word in number 14 requires *two* consonant letters? Which *pair* requires two consonant letters?

1. résiden _t_   residén _t_ ial
2. coincidén _t_ al   coínciden _c_ e
3. óffi ___ e   offí ___ ial
4. diví ___ e   diví ___ ive
5. sof ___   sóf ___ en
6. brea ___   brea ___ e
7. revó ___ e   revo ___ átion
8. mús ___ le   mús ___ ular
9. demócra ___ ic   demócra ___ y
10. invén ___   invén ___ ion
11. condém ___   condem ___ átion
12. scíen ___ e   scien ___ ífic
13. presí ___ e   prési ___ ent
14. pícni ___   pícni ___ ing
15. malí ___ n   malí ___ nant
16. accúmula ___ e   accumulá ___ ion
17. proo ___   pro ___ e
18. precí ___ e   precí ___ ion
19. píra ___ e   píra ___ y
20. evén ___   evén ___ ual
21. undóu ___ tedly   indú ___ itably
22. absór ___   absór ___ tion

---

[19] The full pairs are to be found in the Instructor's Manual.

23-B • Each of the following verbs can occur naturally with either **out** or **off**, the choice determined by the meaning of the verb. Write what you think is the right particle for each verb, but check the dictionary first if you're not sure of the meaning.

1. dig _out_
2. shave _____
3. carve _____
4. hollow _____
5. level _____
6. scoop _____
7. flush _____
8. skim _____
9. gouge _____
10. drill _____
11. shear _____
12. root _____

23-C • In each of the blanks below write **this** or **that**, whichever is appropriate.[20]

1. The minister was preaching to his congregation: "Remember _____(1)_, my good friends. There will be no buying and selling in Heaven . . . ."

   "_____(2)_ is not where business has gone," mumbled a salesman in the rear.

2. A store that went bankrupt after only a few weeks displayed _____(3)_ sign: "Opened by mistake."

3. The salesman was upset by the prospective nonbuyer who asked, "And what does the 320 H.P. mean?"

   "_____(4)_ is horsepower."

   "_____(5)_ means it's got a lot of horsepower?"

   "Let's put it _____(6)_ way; if you get a flat, you've got to shoot it."

[20] Adams, op. cit.

4. "He's money-mad. He hasn't got a cent—_____ is why he's mad."
   (7)

23-D • Read the following story and in each of the blanks write the proper verb form.

A poor man _____ complaining to his grocer. "There _____
         (1) be   (2) be
no justice in this world," he cried. If I _____ rich and _____
                                          (3) be   (4) have
a lot of money, I _____ buy all I _____ on credit, but since I
                  (5) can   (6) want
_____ poor I _____ pay for everything in cash. If there _____
(7) be   (8) must   (9) be
any justice on earth, the rich _____ pay cash, and the poor _____
                               (10) will   (11) will
buy on credit."

"In theory, that _____ all very well," _____ the grocer's
                 (12) be   (13) be
reply, "but if I _____ to extend credit to all the loafers in this
                 (14) be
neighborhood, I _____ soon be poor myself."
                (15) will

"Why, then, you _____ have nothing to worry about," _____
                (16) will   (17) be
the poor man's quick reply. "You _____ be able to get everything on
                                 (18) will
credit!"[21]

23-E • Complete each of the following by writing whatever comes naturally to mind.

A. 1. If there were no humor in our lives, _____
   _____

   2. If we can't laugh at ourselves once in awhile, _____
   _____

   3. If I had not been able to laugh as a child, _____
   _____

[21]B. A. Botkin, *A Treasury of American Anecdotes,* (New York: Crown Publishers, 1957). Reprinted by permission of Curtis Brown, Ltd. Copyright © 1957 by B. A. Botkin.

4. If I didn't have a sense of humor, _____

5. If I hear a joke that I don't think is funny, _____

6. If world history were not so full of tragedy and suffering, _____

B. 1. There would have been no World War II if _____

2. There would now be no conflict in the world if _____

3. There won't be a third world war if _____

4. It would have been impossible to go to the moon if _____

5. It would be possible to live on the moon if _____

6. It will be practical to travel to the moon if _____

23-F • Read the following story and in the blanks write a form of either **come** or **go**, whichever is called for. In some cases either is appropriate.

A minister _____(1)_____ to the home of one of his wealthier members. It was cold outside, so he _____(2)_____ dressed in warm clothes. The minister was invited to _____(3)_____ into the living room and remove his coat. One of the members of the family _____(4)_____ to make him a cup of hot tea. They talked awhile and then the minister prepared to _____(5)_____ away. He put on his warm overcoat and asked his host to _____(6)_____ with him to the outer hall, as he wanted to say something to him in great privacy. The host, thinking that he would be _____(7)_____ back in a minute or so, did not bother to put on his own overcoat, although he was

_____ out into the unheated hall. The minister proceeded to engage in
                8
small talk, much to the discomfort of the host. He became so cold that his teeth began to chatter. But the minister continued with his small talk. Several times the host asked the minister to _____ back into the living
                                                                         9
room, but each time the minister replied that in another minute he would be _____.
       10

Finally, the rich man said: "If you do not tell me what we have _____ out here for, I'll freeze to death."
     11

"I'll tell you what I have _____ for," replied the minister. "I need
                              12
fifty dollars to buy some coal which will _____ to some poor people."
                                                13

"Here is the money, but did we have to _____ outside for you to
                                              14
tell me this?"

"Inside, perhaps you would not have realized what it means to be cold. Now you too have _____ to know what it is like," replied the wise
                        15
minister."[22]

23-G • In each of the sentences below cross out either **went** or **came**, whichever you think is incorrect.

1. He ~~came~~ / went into a frenzy.
2. She ~~went~~ / came around to our point of view.
3. He went / came out of his mind.
4. She went / came into a lot of money.
5. He went / came into a coma.
6. They went / came to an understanding.
7. The motor went / came dead.
8. The motor went / came back to life.

[22]Mandel, op. cit.

Writing Exercises

9. They went/came to realize their mistake.

10. The meat went/came bad.

11. Her dreams went/came true.

12. She went/came blind.

13. An idea went/came to me.

14. The milk went/came sour.

15. He went/came bald.

16. He didn't go/come up tc our expectations.

17. The animals went/came astray.

18. Which team went/came in first?

19. He's about to go/come bankrupt.

23-H • Read the following story and write in quotation marks wherever you think they should be added. There is also one word that requires inverted commas.

The Chinese diplomat and philosopher, Li Hung-chang, paid a visit to New York in 1896. When his official guide hurried him off one subway train into another a few feet away, Li said to him, Why do we change?

Oh, that train was a local.

I can't hear you. What kind of train?

I said local.

And what is this?

This is an express. It makes no stops till we reach Grand Central Station. We save six minutes.

A pause.

And what, asked Ambassador Li, are we going to do with that six minutes?[23]

---
[23]Botkin, op. cit.

23-I • Cross out the conditional expressions below that don't fit the meaning or the grammar of the sentence that contains them.[24]

1. We should all live within our means, {a. provided that / b. unless / c. otherwise / d. if / e. even if / f. only} we have to borrow the money to do so.

2. {a. Provided that / b. Unless / c. Otherwise / d. If / e. Even if / f. Only} you lend him money, you never see him again, and it's worth it.

3. Workers are still willing to do an honest day's work, {a. provided that / b. unless / c. otherwise / d. if / e. even if / f. only} they want a week's pay for it.

4. And what do you want to be when you grow up, {a. provided that / b. unless / c. otherwise / d. if / e. even if / f. only} your parents let you grow up?

5. He's very old; he still chases girls, but not {a. provided that / b. unless / c. otherwise / d. if / e. even if / f. only} it's downhill.

6. I don't believe him {a. provided that / b. unless / c. otherwise / d. if / e. even if / f. only} he swears he's lying.

[24]Adams, op. cit.

Writing Exercises

23-J • The sentences below all contain negative conditionals expressed with **only**. Rewrite each one more formally using **otherwise**. In the rewriting, omit from consideration the verbs **consider, think, expect, want, try,** and **be anxious**.

1. We considered coming by to see you, only we thought you were out of town.
   We thought you were out of town; otherwise we might have come by to see you.

2. We thought there might have been a bigger audience, only it was raining that day.
   _____

3. We really expected to do better, only we didn't get much help.
   _____

4. We wanted to do some shopping, only it was a holiday and the stores were closed.
   _____

5. We tried our best to stay awake, only the lecture wasn't very inspiring.
   _____

6. We were anxious to get a good seat, only we got there late.
   _____

23-K • Complete each of the following by writing whatever comes naturally to mind. Let the sentence state some kind of condition, and finish the sentence using one of the following: **provided that, as long as, on condition that, or else, unless, otherwise,** or **even if**. Be careful of the different punctuation requirements for some of these.

1. There will be plenty of food for everybody, *provided that nobody takes more than his share.*

2. Tell the truth _____

3. Tell a lie _____

4. He would never tell a lie _____

5. He was let out of prison _____

_____

6. He promised to report to the authorities once a week _____

_____

7. They wouldn't let him out of prison_____

_____

8. He'll never get out of prison _____

_____

9. His lawyer will defend him_____

_____

23-L • CLOZE

(In each blank space write a word that you think fits naturally.)

An interesting new theory _____(1)_____ economics is demonstrated by the Head _____(2)_____ of a small Mexican Indian tribe. _____(3)_____ seems that this tribe was very _____(4)_____ at making a straw mat that _____(5)_____ great sales potential in the United _____(6)_____. The representative of an American company _____(7)_____ down to visit the tribe and _____(8)_____ to make a good business deal. _____(9)_____ spoke to the Head Man and _____(10)_____ that his company would like to _____(11)_____ several thousand pieces. The Head Man _____(12)_____, but announced that the price per _____(13)_____ would be higher on such a _____(14)_____ order than it would be if _____(15)_____ a smaller order were placed.

The _____(16)_____ was more than a little shocked _____(17)_____ the business sense of the Indian _____(18)_____ insisted that the price should be _____(19)_____, because of the large volume, and _____(20)_____ not higher.

"No," replied the Indian.

"_____(21)_____ why not?" asked the American.

"Because _____(22)_____ is so tiresome to make the _____(23)_____ article over and over," answered the _____(24)_____ Man.[25]

[25]Mandel, op. cit.

Writing Exercises 253

23-M • Rewrite the clauses below as noun phrases.

1. The airport was still in operation {even though the weather was bad.
   in spite of *the bad weather.*

2. He's saving all his ten-cent stamps {in case the letter rate drops.
   in case of _____

3. Whether he's old or not,
   Regardless of _____, } I still say he *looks* old.

4. Put the scale in front of the refrigerator, {in case you decide to lose weight.
   in case of _____

5. Married men do not live longer than single men, {even though it *seems*
   in spite of _____ longer.
   _____

6. They say he married her because her aunt left her a lot of money. That's not true. He would have married her {whether *anybody* left her
   no matter _____ the money.[26]
   _____

23-N • Each of the following sentences, taken from student compositions, contains an error concerning the use of conditional or concessive clauses. Rewrite them in such a way as to remove the error.

1. *He wouldn't give me the money even I beg him for it.

2. *She likes America very much despite only knows Los Angeles.

3. *If he had gone to the concert, he would enjoy it.

4. *Even it rains, there won't be enough water for the crops.

[26]Adams, op. cit.

23-O • Only a slight difference in form distinguishes certain "possible" and "hypothetical" **if** clauses. In hypotheticals using **would** the speaker considers fulfillment of the condition as desirable. In future possibles using **should** the speaker is neutral in that respect:

If it *would (only)* rain again, the flowers would bloom.
If it *should (happen to)* rain again, the flowers will drop.

In the sentences below cross out either **would** or **should**, whichever you think does not fit the meaning of the sentence.

1. If she would/~~should~~ finish her degree, she'd have a better chance of finding a job.
2. If she would/should finish her degree, would she have a better chance of finding a job?
3. If war would/should break out again, it might be the end of civilization.
4. If peace would/should come to the Middle East, the world would be better off.
5. Even if peace would/should come to the Middle East, many problems would still remain to be solved.
6. If Mexico would/should beat Hungary, they'd become world champions. Then we could celebrate.
7. If Mexico would/should beat Hungary, they'd become world champions. Then we couldn't celebrate.
8. If they would/should serve me American food, . . . [Finish the sentence.]

23-P • Suppose you overheard the following half of a telephone conversation. Write down what you think the other person might be saying.

  CLERK Hello. Robinson's.
1. MRS. HOBBS *Did you say "Robertson's"?*
  CLERK No, this is Robinson's. If you want Robertson's, ...
2. MRS. HOBBS _____
  CLERK In that case, what can I do for you?
3. MRS. HOBBS _____
  CLERK I'm sorry to interrupt. What did you say your name was?
4. MRS. HOBBS _____
  CLERK If it's a complaint you're making, let me ring Customer Service for you.
5. MRS. HOBBS _____
  CLERK [ring] Customer Service. May I help you?
6. MRS. HOBBS _____
  CLERK I can't hear you unless you speak a little louder.
7. MRS. HOBBS _____
  CLERK Did you buy something here?
8. MRS. HOBBS _____
  CLERK Check the position of the batteries. The radio wouldn't work if the batteries were in backwards.
9. MRS. HOBBS _____
  CLERK I see. Well, I wish I could tell you what's wrong, Madam.
10. MRS. HOBBS _____
  CLERK But I <u>am</u> the person to talk to. Do you know what I would do if I were you?
11. MRS. HOBBS _____
  CLERK I'd bring it back here to the store.
12. MRS. HOBBS _____
  CLERK No, as long as you return it within thirty days; otherwise you'll have to send it to the factory.

13. MRS. HOBBS _____

    CLERK *I don't blame you. I wouldn't want to either. I'm sure everything will be all right if you'll just bring the radio to me.*

14. MRS. HOBBS _____

    CLERK *Jack Saunders, but if I'm not here someone else can take care of you.*

15. MRS. HOBBS _____

    CLERK *Provided you make it Monday. That's the only evening we're open, and we close at 9:00.*

16. MRS. HOBBS _____

    CLERK *Whatever you wish.*

17. MRS. HOBBS _____

    CLERK *You're welcome. Goodbye.*

18. MRS. HOBBS _____

23-Q • Write out a humorous story that you are familiar with. If it involves dialog, be sure to observe the conventions for reported speech. Refer to one of the models (e.g. 23-18) for guidance. After you have finished writing, tell the story to the rest of the class.

Unit 24

24-1 DIALOG

THE SCIENCE SEMINAR

DR. FALK So it's clearly not just a matter of giving dates for the discovery of oxygen or the invention of the telephone, or saying when Aristotle lived or when Newton was born. What we really want to look at is the scientific thought of those various times, and since we aren't likely to have more time to . . . Yes, Mr. Carr?

MR. CARR I'm a little confused. Wasn't earlier scientific thought to a large extent mixed up with myth and superstition?

DR. FALK That's an interesting question, but it's a hard one to answer. It's based on two assumptions that need some clarification. You're assuming for one thing that "unscientific" myth and superstition can be separated from so-called "pure" science. Some of us wouldn't be willing to accept that. In fact, . . . uh, Miss Moreno?

MISS MORENO Why can't pure science, in a historical sense, be referred to as whatever has been useful?

DR. FALK What do you mean by "useful"?

MISS MORENO Well, for science it would apply to a theory that hasn't been disproved.

DR. FALK But seldom has a theory *not* been disproved. So by your definition there has been a great deal of "impure" science over the ages . . . , mostly mythology and superstition perhaps, as suggested by Mr. Carr.

MR. CARR But what is it, Dr. Falk, that we call science today, if not a collection of theories that are said by the scientific community to be valid?

DR. FALK Now we're getting to the heart of the matter. Your other assumption that I said needs to be clarified is contained again in this last question of yours. That question implies that science has developed in something like a straight line and that making up today's science is an accumulation of the inventions and discoveries of past ages.

MR. CARR And that's not true?

DR. FALK Let's just say for now that there is more than one way to view the history of science. Our next couple of sessions will be taken up with precisely this issue, of how science has, shall we say, "developed." If you can wait, you'll eventually be able to answer your own question.

VOCABULARY

mix up
refer to (reference, referral)
disprove
clarify (clarification, clear)
contain (content)
imply (implication)
develop (development)

seminar
oxygen
invention (invent)
myth (mythology, mythical)
superstition (superstitious)
clarification (clarify, clear)
sense
theory
definition (define)
community
accumulation (accumulate)
session
issue

scientific (science)
pure (purify, purity, purification)
impure
valid (validity)

clearly
perhaps
precisely
eventually

for one thing
so-called
in a _____ sense

24-2 ■ DIALOG VARIATION

1. *What we really want to look at is the scientific thought of those times.*
   We really want to look at the scientific thought of those times.
   It's the scientific thought of those times that we really want to look at.
2. *Wasn't earlier scientific thought . . . mixed up with myth and superstition?*
   Isn't it the case that earlier scientific thought was mixed up with myth and superstition?
   Can't it be said that earlier scientific thought was mixed up with myth and superstition?

3. *That's a hard question to answer.*
   That question is hard to answer.
   It's hard to answer that question.
4. *Some of us wouldn't be willing to accept that.*
   For some of us that wouldn't be acceptable.
   That wouldn't be acceptable for some of us.
5. *. . . theories that are said by the scientific community to be valid.*
   . . . theories that the scientific community says are valid.
6. *And that's not true?*
   And isn't that true?
   And that's not the truth?
7. *Our next couple of sessions will be taken up with precisely this issue . . . .*
   Our next couple of sessions will deal with precisely this issue . . . .
   Our next couple of sessions will be concerned with precisely this issue . . . .
   Our next couple of sessions will involve precisely this issue . . . .

24-3 ■ QUESTIONS

1. What area of science does Dr. Falk prefer to examine?
2. Why is Mr. Carr confused?
3. What are the two assumptions that Mr. Carr makes?
4. How does Dr. Falk feel about myth and superstition?
5. How does Miss Moreno define pure science?
6. What does her definition imply, according to Dr. Falk?
7. How does Mr. Carr define science?
8. What feeling do you have about the way Dr. Falk looks at science? How do you think of science?

24-4 SOUND PATTERNS

—Wasn't earlier scientific thought . . . mixed up with *myth* and superstition?

• • •

—. . . there has been a great deal of "impure" science . . . , mostly *mythology* perhaps, . . .

We have seen in previous units how certain kinds of affixes affect the stress patterns of the words that they attach to (**lócate ~ locátion, áctive ~ actívity, prefér ~ préfer*ence*, pérson ~ persón*ify*)**. There is another large class of words whose stress pattern is also affected by affixation: learned words that are of Greek origin, words ending in **-ology** and **-ography**, for example. Listen to the pronunciation of the following groups of words, each member of a group having the main stress on a different syllable:

Section A

NOUN (THING)	NOUN (CONCEPT)	ADJECTIVE
phótograph	photógraphy	photográphic
	mythólogy	mythológical
télescope		telescópic
démocrat	demócracy	democrátic

24-A • (See page 283.)

24-5 ■ Match word-parts from the two columns below to make up words that you are familiar with. Pronounce them.

A	B
baro-	
thermo-	
micro-	
kilo-	
anthropo-	-thesis
geo-	-logy
bio-	-graph(y)
theo-	-scope
philo-	-meter
socio-	-phone
psycho-	-gram
chrono-	-sophy
tele-	
phono-	
photo-	
biblio-	

24-6   PHRASAL VERBS

—Why can't pure science . . . *be referred to* as whatever has been useful?
—Our next couple of sessions will *be taken up* with precisely this issue.

Most phrasal verbs that take direct objects can occur in the passive. In this form, however, particles are stressed, whereas prepositions are not:

When will it be taken úp?
How will it be reférred tò?

24-B • (See page 283.)

24-7 SPEECH ACT

—... can be separated from *so-called* "pure" science.

• • •

—Why can't pure science, *in a historical sense,* be referred to as ...

• • •

—... of how science has, *shall we say,* "developed."

Speakers or writers often find it necessary to avoid making a flat statement or assertion. They frequently choose to qualify a remark by suggesting that its truth is limited to a certain time or place, that others may not agree with it, that not enough is known about it to be absolutely sure, and so on. In order to convey these meanings they use *qualifiers*: words or expressions that allow them to back away from the full truth value of what they would otherwise be saying or writing. Many such qualifiers (including **fairly** and **rather** in 20-7) have appeared throughout the Dialogs and Readings of this volume.[1]

24-8 ■ Refer again to the Dialog for this unit. Find the sentences containing each of the qualifiers listed below, read the sentences with the qualifier removed, and decide in what way the meaning of the sentences has been changed.

just	*so-called*	*something like*
really	*in a historical sense*	*for now*
to a large extent	*for science*	*precisely*
some	*by your definition*	*shall we say*
for one thing	*perhaps*	*eventually*

---

[1] See Appendix F for a list of selected qualifiers.

24-9 ■ Look at the statements listed below, all of which have been taken from earlier Readings. Pick out those with which you basically agree but that need to be qualified in some way. Use a qualifier from the accompanying list or add another of your own.

1. It is impossible to change your psychological space needs.
2. Rocks dug up from the submerged continent of Gondwanaland are 600 million years old.
3. Large cars cause more highway accidents than small cars.
4. The present design of the oversized automobile is responsible for the increasing death toll on the highway.
5. Australia and the United States are equal in size.
6. The way to improve the appearance and content of newspapers is to improve their use of photography.
7. The United States and Canada are one country.

one of the . . . -s
largely/to a large extent
chances are that . . .
believed to be
almost
completely
about/approximately
practically

B

24-10 ■ DIALOG IMPROVISATION

(Try to re-create or even improvise a variation of the Dialog at the beginning of this unit, as you remember it.)

A What we really want to look at is . . .
B But wasn't earlier scientific thought . . .
A That's a hard question to answer. It's based on two . . .
C Why can't pure science be . . .
A What do you mean . . .
C Well, for science it would . . .
A Then by your definition there . . .
B But what is science, if not a . . .
A That question implies that . . .
B And that's . . .
A Let's just say for now that . . .

Sentence Rearrangement: Adjective Complements; **-ed** vs. **-ing**

—I'm a little *confused*. Wasn't earlier scientific thought to a large extent mixed up with myth and superstition?
—That's an *interesting* question, but it's *a hard one to answer*.

24-11 Certain adjective-complement constructions have alternate versions with word-order rearrangements:

It's *hard to answer* **that question.** = **That question is** *hard to answer.*

Where "that question" has already been introduced as a topic of conversation, either sentence is appropriate, except that in this context the version on the left has its intonation peak on the word **answer**:

It's hard to *answer* that question.

Adjectives that have a pattern like **hard** include **easy, good, fun, different, strange, impossible,** and so on.[2]

24-12 Most adjectives ending in **-ed** or **-ing** are derived from verbs, the two suffixes corresponding to those for past and present participles, respectively.[3] Therefore, the **-ed** and **-ing** adjective endings signal different relationships to the nouns they modify:

That question *interests* me.

That question is *interesting*.   **I am *interested*.**

Learners of English often make the mistake of saying things like ***I am interesting in that question.**

---

[2]See Appendix G for a longer list of such adjectives.
[3]See Appendix H for a list of verbs from which **-ed** and **-ing** adjectives can be formed.

Section B

24-13 ■ Describe your understanding of some scientific concepts that the instructor will mention. Let your comments be in the adjective-complement forms indicated.

1. A   What about the theory of relativity?
   B   That's $\begin{Bmatrix} \text{not easy (at all)} \\ \text{(rather) hard} \\ \text{(very) difficult} \\ \text{(almost) impossible} \\ \ldots \end{Bmatrix}$ (for me) to understand.

2. A   What about the multiplication table?
   B   That's $\begin{Bmatrix} \text{(very) easy} \\ \text{(comparatively) simple} \\ \text{not hard (at all)} \\ \ldots \end{Bmatrix}$ (for me) to understand.

3. (The rest of the suggestions are to be found in the Instructor's Manual.)

24-14 ■ Answer the following questions with an adjective-complement construction. In each case choose the version that lets the "old" information come first and/or "new" information come last.

1. A   What's an easy experiment to perform?
   B   **It's easy to (demonstrate that the earth has gravity).**
2. A   Is it hard to demonstrate that the moon has gravity?
   B   **No. That's easy to demonstrate (too).**
3. (The rest of the suggestions are to be found in the Instructor's Manual.)

24-15 ■ From what you know of complementation presented in this and earlier units, finish each of the examples below with the proper complement form for the sentence [**Prices (will) rise/fall . . .**].

1. It's hard . . .
   . . . for prices to fall (in this economy).
2. It's certain . . .
   . . . that prices will rise (again this year).
3. It's possible . . .
   . . . for prices to fall (on certain items).
   . . . that prices will fall (on certain items).
4. It's likely . . .
5. It's easy . . .
6. It's necessary . . .
7. It's odd . . .
8. It's impossible . . .
9. It's obvious . . .
10. It's difficult . . .

11. It's good . . .
12. It's incredible . . .
13. It's nice . . .

24-16 ■ Say "yes" or "no" according to whether each of the following is a possible sentence or not. If the answer is "no," make the sentence correct by adding a form of **be**.

1. He played with the baby.
   Yes.
2. He annoyed with the baby.
   No. He is/was annoyed with the baby.
3. He stayed with the baby.
4. He pleased with the baby.
5. He looked at the baby.
6. He surprised at the baby.
7. He disturbed about the baby.
8. He talked about the baby.
9. He talked to the baby.
10. He attracted to the baby.
11. He interested himself in the baby.
12. He interested in the baby.

24-C • (See page 284.)

24-D • (See page 285.)

24-E • (See page 285.)

24-F • (See page 286.)

24-17 READING (361 words)

ZERO

Numeral designation can also be categorized according to ease of manipulation. In this category are the Arabic numerals. Long ago Arabic numerals displaced all others because of their great convenience. They are most convenient to use because they give us a way of writing an indefinite amount of numbers while using only a small number of symbols called *digits*. This feat is accomplished by attaching different meanings to the same digit. In the number 111, three ones are used, and each has a different meaning. The 1 on the extreme right stands for the number *one*, the 1 in the second column from the right stands for the number *ten,* and the 1 in the third column stands for the number *one hundred*. The symbol 111 stands for the sum of one, ten, and one hundred. Because the meaning of a digit depends on its identifying position in the written numeral, the Arabic system of numerals is said to be a *place value* system. To represent three *hundreds* plus two *tens* plus five *ones,* we write 325.

Now suppose we want to write the symbol for three *tens*. We put a 3 into the second column from the right. But we will be unable to recognize it as the second column unless something is written down in the first column. This makes it necessary to think of three tens as three tens plus *no ones* and to introduce a symbol to represent the absence of ones. We use the symbol 0 for this purpose, and call it *zero*.

The concept of a numeral representing *none* was first hit on by the Hindus. Not until the later spread of Islam, however, was it taken over by the Arabs and built into their system of numerals. Zero became a new number in the natural number system and had to be incorporated into the addition and multiplication tables in a way that was consistent with the rest of the tables. This was done by using these rules for computation with zero: zero plus any number gives that number again; and zero times any number gives zero. The first of these rules is statable in the following terms: $0 + x = x$, for any natural number x.[4]

---

[4]Adapted from *The New Mathematics,* by Irving Adler. Copyright © 1958 by Irving and Ruth Adler; copyright © 1959 by Irving Adler. Reprinted with permission of the John Day Co., Inc., Publisher.

VOCABULARY

categorize (categorization)
displace (displacement)
accomplish (accomplishment)
attach (attachment)
stand for
hit on
incorporate (incorporation)

numeral (numerical)
designation (designate)
manipulation (manipulate)
category (categorize, categorical)
convenience (convenient)
digit (digital)
sum (sum up)
value (value, valuable)
absence (absent)
spread (spread)
multiplication (multiply)
computation (compute)
term

indefinite
extreme (extremity)
consistent (consistency)
statable (state, statement)
plus

24-18 ■ INCLUDED MEANING

(For each of the following passages pick the one statement whose meaning is part of the meaning of the passage.)

1. *They are most convenient to use because they give us a way of writing an indefinite amount of numbers while using only a small number of symbols called* digits.
   a. Indefinite numbers use small symbols.
   b. Small numbers are called *digits*.
   c. Fewer symbols means more convenience.
2. *This feat is accomplished by attaching different meanings to the same digit.*
   a. One digit can have different meanings.
   b. The feat has different meanings.
   c. Different meanings accomplish feats.
3. *Because the meaning of a digit depends on its identifying position in the written numeral, the Arabic system of numerals is said to be a* place value *system.*
   a. It is said that the Arabic system of numerals is dependent on its position.
   b. They say that the Arabic system of numerals is a *place value* system.
   c. A *place value* system says that numerals are written.
4. *Not until the later spread of Islam, however, was it taken over by the Arabs and built into their system of numerals.*
   a. Islam was taken over by the Arabs.
   b. The Arabs built it into their system of numerals.
   c. Islam took over a system of numerals.

5. *Zero became a new number in the natural number system and had to be incorporated into the addition and multiplication tables in a way that was consistent with the rest of the tables.*
   a. The natural number system had to be incorporated into the addition and multiplication tables.
   b. The addition and multiplication tables were in the way.
   c. The addition and multiplication tables had to incorporate a new number.

24-19 ■ QUESTIONS

1. What advantages do Arabic numerals have over other number systems?
2. What is the difference between a number and a digit?
3. What do the numbers 6 and 5 stand for in 3,264.53?
4. Why is zero needed in a number like 50?
5. How do you suppose 50 would have been written before the introduction of zero?
6. How would you write the second rule for computation with zero?

24-20   VOCABULARY RELATIONS

The negative prefix **in-** (**im-/il-/ir-**) was studied in 20-4. There are, however, other negative prefixes in English, most commonly **un-**. The choice between **un-** (**unable**) and **in-** (**inability**) is based on developments in the history of the language that are rather complex. Yet it is to be noted that **un-** occurs much more freely than **in-** with words ending in **-ed** or **-ing**: *un*complet*ed*/*in*complete, *un*offend*ing*/*in*offensive.

24-G   • (See page 286.)

24-21 ■ Another frequently occurring negative prefix is **non-**: **That which is not concerned with science is** *non*scientific. Often contrasting with **non-** are **un-** or **in-**: **That which fails to be scientific is** *un*scientific. Compare also *in*human (= cruel) and *non*human (e.g. animal). Notice that **un-** and **in-** are judgmental or evaluative, whereas **non-** is neutral in this respect. Make a list of words from your field of study or general knowledge that begin with **non-** (e.g. *non*-American). Do any of these have corresponding forms with **un-/in-** (e.g. *un*-American)? If so, what is the difference in meaning?

24-22 COMPOUNDS

We've already seen (24-12) that past and present participles of verbs can function as modifiers: **The meaning of a digit depends on its *identifying position* in the *written numeral*.** Constructions like these can form the nucleus of longer noun phrases with recognizable internal relationships. For example, from a sentence like

Chemicals regulate growth.
SUBJ   V   OBJ

it is possible to derive two noun phrases that preserve the same relationship of subject-verb-object:

growth-regulat*ing* chemicals
OBJ   V   SUBJ

chemical-regulat*ed* growth
SUBJ   V   OBJ

24-23 ■ Match each of the following noun phrases with a sentence that shows the same internal relationships.

1. an air-cooled engine
   Air cools the engine.
2. a time-consuming experiment
   The experiment consumes time.
3. an eye-catching display
4. laboratory-trained personnel
5. habit-forming drugs
6. city-operated transportation
7. a tax-paying citizen
8. government-owned property
9. a long-lasting effect
10. chocolate-covered peanuts
11. fast-moving events
12. a state-appointed official
13. incoming bills
14. outgoing mail

24-24 ■ RESTATEMENT

The suffix **-able** attached to a verb (verb-**able**) is equivalent to **can be** verb-**ed**:

The first of these rules $\begin{Bmatrix} \text{is stat}able \\ \text{can be stat}ed \end{Bmatrix}$ in the following terms.

Restate the following sentences using a verb-**able** construction (verb-**ible** in 3, 4, and 11). **Not** will need to be changed to a negative prefix.

1. All of these sentences *can be restated* using -able.
   All of these sentences are restatable using -able.
2. There are some questions that *cannot be answered*.
   There are some questions that are unanswerable.
3. The fraction 13/39 *can be reduced* further to 1/3.
4. One is a number that *cannot be divided*.
5. One chemical in the solution *could* still *be identified*.
6. In this solution the ingredients *cannot be separated*.
7. There was a change in color that *could be noticed*.
8. Once this substance hardens it *cannot be broken*.
9. *Can* those findings *be verified*?
10. That was a laboratory accident that *could not be avoided*.
11. What happens when the *force that cannot be resisted* meets the *object that cannot be moved*?

24-25   PUNCTUATION

The colon (:) occurs in scientific writing and elsewhere as a marker of exemplification, enumeration, or specification. For example:

   ... is statable in the following terms (:) $0 + x = x$
   ... summarized in one equation (:) hydrogen → helium + energy
   ... found uncombined in nature (:) gold, silver, and copper

24-26 ■ Scan some reading material that interests you (technical in nature, if possible) and make a list of examples where a colon is used. What different functions are performed by the constructions that follow the colon?

24-27 ■ **READING IMPROVISATION**

(Complete each of the following sentences with what you remember from the Reading.)

1. Arabic numerals displaced ...
2. They are most convenient to use because ...
3. This feat is accomplished by ...
4. Because the meaning of a digit depends on its identifying position, ...
5. It is necessary to introduce ...
6. We use the symbol ...

7. Zero had to be incorporated . . .
8. This was done by . . .
9. The first of these rules is statable . . .

> Choosing Among Sentence Rearrangements
>
> —*What* we really want to look at *is* the scientific thought of those various times.
>
> • • •
>
> —But what *is it that* we call science today, if not a collection of *theories* that *are said* by the scientific community *to be valid*?
>
> • • •
>
> —Your other assumption . . . *needs to be* clarified.
>
> • • •
>
> —But *seldom has a theory* not been disproved.

24-28 As already seen (22-31, 32), it is frequently necessary to rearrange sentences in such a way that certain elements appear earlier or later. One commonly used device for such rearrangement is the passive (see Volume I, Unit 15). Two new kinds of passive appeared in the Dialog, as shown above. Reduced to the simplest form, their correspondences would be as follows:

X *says* **that Y** *is* **valid.** ~ **Y** *is said* **(by X)** *to be* **valid.**
(X reads that Y is valid. ≁ *Y is read (by X) to be valid.)

X *needs to clarify* **Y.** ~ **Y** *needs to be clarified* **(by X).**
(X wants to clarify Y. ≠ *Y wants to be clarified (by X).)

Other verbs that have a pattern like **say** include **know, think, feel, report,** and **believe.**[5] Those that have a pattern like **need** are **start, begin, fail, continue, have, used, be going, seem, tend, happen,** and **appear.** The verbs in this group are similar in function and meaning to the modals.

---

[5]The passive construction displayed is often referred to as the "second passive." For a longer list of the verbs that can occur in this pattern, see Appendix I.

Section D

24-29 Two other devices for putting parts of a sentence into special focus use the words **it** and **what**.[6] Some of their range of focus is illustrated in the following:

Dr. Falk taught physics at Harvard until last year.

- It was *Dr. Falk* who taught physics at Harvard until last year.
- It was *physics* that Dr. Falk taught at Harvard until last year.
- It was *at Harvard* that Dr. Falk taught physics until last year.
- It was *until last year* that Dr. Falk taught physics at Harvard.

- What Dr. Falk taught at Harvard until last year was *physics*.
- What Dr. Falk did at Harvard until last year was *teach physics*.

24-30 Negative elements can also be shifted to the beginning of the sentence, which then must use question word-order:

Only after a few tests *will you* **find out.**
  (*You will* find out *only* after a few tests.)

Question word-order applies only to shift of negatives whose scope is the verb phrase or even the entire sentence. Notice the difference, therefore, between the following:

At no time (will we) **know for sure.** (= We won't know for sure at any time.)

In no time (we will) **know for sure.** (= We will know for sure in no time/soon.)

24-31 ■ Imagine that you are relaying information to a science-student friend of yours who is on the telephone. The information concerns how to perform a certain experiment and will be given to you in the form of directions. Change these directions to descriptions as you relay them.

1. A Mix a pint of soil with a quart of distilled water in a large jar.
   B **A pint of soil is mixed with a quart of distilled water in a large jar.**
2. A Pour off the liquid through filter paper and into a beaker.
   B
3. A Allow the solid that remains on the paper to dry.
   B

---

[6]The constructions in question are commonly referred to as "cleft sentence" and "pseudo-cleft sentence," respectively.

4. A Examine what is left on the paper.
   B
5. A Allow the liquid that goes through the paper to evaporate.
   B
6. A Identify some of the elements in the remaining soil sample by using the flame test.
   B
7. A Get a green flame and you have copper.
   B If you . . .

24-32 ■ Sketched out below are some supposed characteristics of someone who was seen breaking into the chemistry laboratory. Enumerate these characteristics, beginning each sentence with "he."

1. think − they − [He is about 5 feet 8 inches]
He is thought to be about 5 feet 8 inches.
2. believe − they − [He has a police record]
3. assume − they − [He is someone who knew the plan of the building]
4. know − they − [He was working alone]
5. discover − they − [He had been drinking]
6. find − they − [He was looking for drugs]
7. [Neg] consider − they − [He is dangerous]
8. expect − they − [He will try to break in again]

24-33 ■ After each of the following ask a question with **who** or **what**, as in the models.

1. His work used to be criticized.
   Who used to criticize it?
2. He seemed to be bothered by something.
   What seemed to bother him?
3. His opinions continued to be questioned.
4. He appeared to be upset by something.
5. He happened to be given the wrong job.
6. His ability began to be doubted.
7. His file has had to be checked.
8. He used to be irritated by something.
9. His problems started to be discussed.
10. His motives tended to be questioned.
11. He failed to be rehired.

24-34 ■ Say the sentence **They were able to fool the public** with the following words and phrases added at the beginning.

1. never
   Never were they able to fool the public.
2. almost always
   Almost always they were able to fool the public.
3. not even then
4. seldom
5. even then
6. only then
7. in no time
8. for a long while
9. at no time
10. not for a long while
11. until they published their research
12. not until they published their research
13. not infrequently
14. in not many years

24-35 ■ Imagine that you are having a conversation with someone who is very ignorant. Correct this person's false presuppositions by responding with a sentence beginning **It isn't/wasn't . . .**

1. A   I have to write a report about that ancient Greek philosopher Socrates, who said that the earth was the center of the universe.
   B   **(Wait a minute!) It wasn't Socrates who said that; it was Ptolemy.**
2. A   Ptolemy? Oh, right. What a genius! And then he finally discovered that the earth revolves around the sun.
   B   **(Just a second.) It wasn't . . .**
3. A   Copernicus? Yes, now I remember. Every school child knows about him and how he formulated the laws of gravity.
   B
4. A   Oh, what a mistake! I've even seen drawings of Newton dropping those weights from the Tower of Pisa.
   B
5. A   How could I forget Galileo? I mean is there anybody left who hasn't heard of *Origin of the Species*?
   B
6. A   I guess I'm not doing too well. Darwin, the father of psychoanalysis . . . Who could ever forget that?
   B
7. A   Freud. Oh course! This isn't my day. His theory of relativity has affected everybody.
   B
8. A   Einstein! I give up!

24-H • (See page 287.)

24-I • (See page 288.)

24-J • (See page 289.)

24-K • (See page 289.)

24-L • (See page 290.)

24-M • (See page 291.)

E

24-N • **CLOZE** (See page 292.)

> More on Sentence Rearrangement: Inversion
>
> —Numeral designation can also be categorized according to ease of manipulation. *In this category are the Arabic numerals.* Long ago Arabic numerals displaced all others because of their great convenience.
>
> **24-36** Decisions about what particular sentence rearrangement to use are constantly influenced by the tendency to let old or nonessential information appear toward the beginning and new information toward the end. In the above example such an arrangement (*italicized*) was possible only through *inversion* of the "basic" sentence:
>
> **The Arabic numerals *are* in this category.**
>
> **In this category *are* the Arabic numerals.**
>
> Inversion of this kind can apply to sentences whose verb phrase designates location or direction. The verb, moreover, can be any verb that includes the meaning of **be** as a final state:

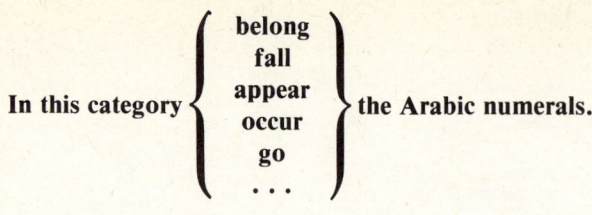

24-37 A slightly different kind of inversion applies to a wider range of basic sentences in which there is no restriction on verb type. Such rearrangement is often required by the principle of end weight:

An accumulation
of the inventions
and discoveries
of past ages makes up today's science.
~ Mak*ing* up today's science *is* an accumulation
of the inventions
and discoveries
of past ages.

Notice here that neither **be** nor **-ing** derive from the original version, nor do they together represent the present continuous, since with some verbs the continuous would normally not even be allowed:

Another layer *extends* upward from the stratosphere. { ~ Extend*ing* upward from the stratosphere *is* another layer.
+ *Another layer *is* extend*ing* upward from the stratosphere. }

24-38 ■ Invert each of the following sentences such that the verb phrase (in *italics*) appears first.

1. An accumulation of the inventions and discoveries of past ages *makes up today's science.*
   Making up today's science is an accumulation of the inventions and discoveries of past ages.
2. The symbol 100 *stands for the sum of one, ten, and one hundred.*
3. Carbon dioxide and water vapor in the atmosphere *absorb energy.*[7]
4. A very complicated equation *sums up these reactions.*[7]
5. A great many important chemical reactions *take place in the laboratory.*[7]
6. Oxygen and sulfur *also fall into this group.*[7]
7. The humid air of container A *weighs less than the dry air of container B.*[7]

[7]Adapted from *Matter: Its Forms and Changes,* by Paul F. Brandwein, Robert Stollberg, and R. Will Burnett (New York: Harcourt Brace Jovanovich, 1968). Reprinted with permission.

24-39 ■ Read the following sketches as full sentences by moving something into initial position. Let the first phrase be what, in the context of the preceding sentence, is "old" information.

1. Numerical designation can also be categorized according to ease of manipulation.
   be − the Arabic numerals − in this category
   In this category are the Arabic numerals.
2. Viruses have characteristics that make them very difficult to examine.
   be − their tiny size − one such characteristic
3. The laser has already established itself as a major scientific development.[8]
   could equal − its impact on our world − the harnessing of nuclear energy
4. Early in the 19th century the attention of archaeologists turned toward the Near East.[8]
   lie − the ruins of ancient Egypt, Assyria, and Babylonia − here
5. The computer is able to accept enormous amounts of information and make calculations at lightning speeds because it has no moving or mechanical parts.[9]
   be − electrons − the only things that move in the computer

24-40 ■ Read the following sentences, choosing the one of each pair that best fits the context of what has preceded.

1. Kinesiology has a useful purpose.
   a. In order to learn how to analyze the movements of the human body we study it.
   b. We study it in order to learn how to analyze the movements of the human body.
2. But this pyramid forms only part of a model of a molecule that is much larger than this.[10]
   a. In order to build more of the model we must show how one pyramid is joined to another.
   b. We must show how one pyramid is joined to another in order to build more of the model.
3. The glacier leaves its marks behind it.[10]
   a. Preserved in hard rock surfaces are long thin scratches made by rocks that were once embedded in the underside of the glacier.
   b. Long thin scratches made by rocks that were once embedded in the underside of the glacier are preserved in hard rock surfaces.

---

[8] Clifford D. Simak, *The March of Science,* (New York: Harper & Row, 1971).
[9] Melvin Berger, *Tools of Modern Biology,* (New York: Thomas Y. Crowell, 1970).
[10] Brandwein, Stollberg, and Burnett, op. cit.

4. In any community, climate is one of the basic determining factors.[11]
   a. But influenced to a great extent by the shape of the land is, in turn, climate.
   b. But climate, in turn, is influenced to a great extent by the shape of the land.
5. The computer improves the performance of almost every method in biology.[12]
   a. In time, the computer may even replace the microscope as the prime tool of biology, some biologists have predicted.
   b. In time, some biologists have predicted, the computer may even replace the microscope as the prime tool of biology.

24-41 ■ Much has now been said about the reasons for choosing to say or write something in one way rather than another. Very often the experienced listener or reader unconsciously expects or anticipates in very rough form the outline of what is to follow. This anticipation makes communication more rapid and efficient, clear speech and lucid writing depending to a large extent on how often the listener or reader is led to try to predict the general outline of what is coming next and how often that prediction is fulfilled. After each of the sentences below[13] choose the phrase that you think is likely to start the next sentence.

1. In the number 111, three ones are used and each has a different meaning.
   a. The 1 on the extreme right . . .
   b. The entire number stands for . . .
   c. Different meanings are also . . .
2. Now we are ready to carry out our construction step by step.
   a. Then we will examine . . .
   b. First, we take all possible ordered pairs . . .
   c. So we now have symbols like . . .
3. The 0 class has some interesting properties.
   a. Therefore, . . .
   b. Notice first that . . .
   c. Even more can be said . . .
4. The type of structure that they represent is not just a mathematical curiosity. In fact,
   a. it has an important . . .
   b. they are called . . .
   c. we will conclude by . . .

---

[11] Simak, op. cit.
[12] Berger, op. cit.
[13] Adler, op. cit.

5. This number system has some properties that it shares with the natural number system.
   a. These include . . .
   b. The natural number system will be the . . .
   c. Nevertheless, these properties do not . . .
6. The 0 class differs in one very important respect from the ring of integers.
   a. We have now seen that . . .
   b. It does not contain . . .
   c. So far we have merely . . .
7. Actually, it is not necessary to give this special proof.
   a. Once this fact is established . . .
   b. To prove that the two systems are . . .
   c. All we have to do . . .

24-O • (See page 292.)

24-P • (See page 294.)

24-Q • (See page 295.)

24-R • (See page 295.)

24-S • (See page 296.)

WRITING EXERCISES

24-A • As you hear the following words pronounced, identify by number the syllable that carries the main stress, and write the stress mark (´) over the appropriate vowel letter. Then practice pronouncing the words.

1. télephone
   1 2 3

2. telephónic
   1 2 3 4

3. diameter
   12 3 4

4. diametric
   12 3 4

5. speedometer
   1 2 3 4

6. mimeograph
   1 23 4

7. bibliography
   1 23 4 5

8. bibliographic
   1 23 4 5

9. geometry
   12 3 4

10. hypothesis
    1 2 3 4

11. hypothetical
    1 2 3 4 5

12. microscope
    1 2 3

13. microscopic
    1 2 3 4

14. symphony
    1   2 3

15. symphonic
    1   2 3

16. aristocrat
    1 2 3 4

17. aristocracy
    1 2 3 4 5

18. aristocratic
    1 2 3 4 5

19. philosophy
    1 2 3 4

20. philosophical
    1 2 3 4 5

21. paragraph
    1 2 3

22. methodology
    1 2 3 4 5

23. methodological
    1 2 3 4 5 6

24. antithesis
    1 2 3 4

25. oceanography
    1 2 3 4 5

26. oceanographic
    1 2 3 4 5

24-B • Write appropriate stress marks (´ = strong; ` = weak) over each of the following particles/prepositions, all of which have appeared in previous units. Then practice pronouncing the sentences.

1. That's what we want to look àt.

2. That's what we want to look úp.

3. When is the issue to be brought *up*?

4. A few of the methods have been objected *to*.

5. Some of the scientists have been discriminated *against* . . .

6. . . . and their privileges taken *away*.

7. A solution is being looked *for*.

8. Inquiries will probably be sent *out*.

9. The curtains have been pulled *back*.

10. A lot of things have been thought *about*.

11. All the equipment has been brought *in*.

12. The "scientific method" is generally believed *in*.

13. The research proposal has been turned *down*.

14. A large audience is being planned *on*.

15. A new concept has been hit *upon*.

24-C • The following sentences display different kinds of adjective complementation. The subject of each sentence and the verb within each complement are in *italics*. Draw an arrow between the two to show the relationship as either subject→verb or object←verb.

1. *The scientist* was now free to *talk* . . .

2. . . . and *she* was also interesting to *talk to*.

3. *She* was eager to *explain* . . .

4. . . . but *she* wasn't always easy to *understand*.

5. Sometimes *she* was entertaining to *watch*, as she demonstrated something...

6. . . . and *she* was always careful to *do* only one thing at a time.

7. *Her voice* happened to be pleasant to *listen to*, . . .

8. . . . and *it* seemed to be able to *carry* to the back of the room.

9. On the whole, *the conference* was very worth while *attending*.

24-D • In the following paragraph[14] cross out one word of each bracketed pair, whichever is ungrammatical.

Nature still has a number of $^1\begin{Bmatrix} unsolved \\ unsolving \end{Bmatrix}$ puzzles, but without more $^2\begin{Bmatrix} survived \\ surviving \end{Bmatrix}$ evidence, many of them are likely to remain puzzles. The $^3\begin{Bmatrix} overwhelmed \\ overwhelming \end{Bmatrix}$ natural forces that leave behind $^4\begin{Bmatrix} shaped \\ shaping \end{Bmatrix}$ forms are the very same forces that also eventually destroy them. Although an $^5\begin{Bmatrix} unfolded \\ unfolding \end{Bmatrix}$ geological panorama has characterized earth since time began, the $^6\begin{Bmatrix} observed \\ observing \end{Bmatrix}$ portion of that panorama has been comparatively small.

24-E • Write appropriate forms with **-ed** or **-ing** in each of the blanks below.

1. *During construction of the Grand Coulee Dam on the Columbia River,* a slowly _____ mass of _____ sand and silt created
   (1) flow   (2) saturate
   _____ problems until the _____ engineers decided to
   (3) alarm   (4) frustrate
   run pipes through the wet mass and circulate a _____ mixture.
                                                    (5) freeze
   As a result, the _____ ground remained stable until the construc-
                    (6) freeze
   tion was _____.[15]
            (7) finish

2. *Green plants make glucose through a _____ series of*
                                          (1) complicate
   chemical reactions _____ to as "photosynthesis." Animals eat
                       (2) refer
   green plants and make use of the glucose through another _____
                                                              (3) interest
   series of chemical reactions _____ "cell respiration." For these
                                 (4) call
   _____ processes it is possible to write a _____ equation
   (5) differ   (6) clarify
   that sums up the series of _____ reactions.[16]
                               (7) occur

[14]Adapted from *Introduction to Physical Geology,* by Chester R. Longwell and Richard F. Flint. Copyright © 1962 by John Wiley & Sons, Inc. Reprinted by permission of John Wiley & Sons, Inc.
[15]Ibid. [16]Brandwein, Stollberg, and Burnett, op. cit.

24-F • Each of the following sentences, taken from student compositions, contains an adjective error. Change each sentence in such a way as to remove the error.

1. *I am interesting in taking another course.

2. *Water is composed with hydrogen and oxygen.

3. *I think they satisfied with their progress.

4. *There are more problems in this country comparing with that one.

5. *When she asked the question I suddenly confused.

24-G • The previous vocabulary lists of these two volumes have included many words beginning with **un-** and **in-**. For how many of these words below can you write in the correct prefix, **un-** or **in-** (and its variants **im-/ir-/il-**)?

1. _un_ able   _in_ ability
2. _____equality   _____equal
3. _____legal   _____lawful
4. _____thinkable   _____conceivable
5. _____readable   _____legible
6. _____literate   _____lettered
7. _____justice   _____just
8. _____attended   _____attention
9. _____edible   _____eatable
10. _____dependent   _____dependable
11. _____expensive
12. _____clear
13. _____true
14. _____personal

15. _____ grammatical

16. _____ convenient

17. _____ polite

18. _____ kind

19. _____ interesting

20. _____ popular

21. _____ practical

22. _____ familiar

23. _____ possible

24. _____ definite

25. _____ certain

26. _____ formal

27. _____ necessary

28. _____ natural

29. _____ usual

30. _____ perfect

31. _____ likely

32. _____ important

24-H • The numbered sections below are intended to be sequences of naturally connected sentences. Write each of the sketches as a complete sentence by moving something into subject position, choosing an appropriate verb tense, and making any other necessary changes. Let conditions of appropriateness determine choice of subject.

1. *Of the many tools of the biologist one stands alone.*[17]
    a. advance more than any other tool — it — biological research

    It has advanced biological research more than any other tool.

    ~~*Biological research has been advanced by it more than any other tool.*~~

    b. happen to be — this tool — the microscope

    _____

[17]Berger, op. cit.

c. be — the heart of the microscope — a convex lens

   _____

   d. know for about 3000 years — the convex lens

   _____

2. *Scientists are engaged in many different kinds of activity.*[18]
   a. find necessary — some scientists — [Some scientists use very large numbers]

   _____

   such as the distances to stars and galaxies. On the other hand,
   b. often encounter — very small numbers

   _____

   such as the dimensions of atoms and molecules.
   c. be — one way to handle such numbers — [One expresses them as powers of 10]

   _____

   d. form — the expression of numbers as powers of 10 — the basis of a kind of *shorthand* [*The shorthand* is known as "standard notation"]

   _____

   _____

24-I • A sentence like **Mathematicians know that prime numbers have certain properties** can be rearranged in two different ways, both of which enable us to avoid mentioning the less essential word **mathematicians,** and one of which allows the sentence to begin with **prime numbers**:

Prime numbers are known (by mathematicians) to have certain properties.
It is known (by mathematicians) that prime numbers have certain properties.

Rewrite the sketches below as full sentences by moving into subject position the noun phrase in *italics*. Choose an appropriate verb tense and make any other necessary changes.

1. discover — [*Arabic numerals* have great convenience]

   Arabic numbers were discovered to have great convenience.

2. know — [*They* displaced all other number systems]

   _____

[18]Simak, op. cit.

3. certain — [*Roman numerals* would live a short life]

4. say — [*The Arabic system of numerals* is a "place value" system]

5. very likely — [*The concept of zero* was first conceived by the Hindus]

6. think — [*It* was later taken over by the Arabs]

7. believe — [*Arabic numerals* have universal acceptance for calculation]

24-J • Each of the following sentences, taken from student compositions, contains an error stemming from faulty sentence arrangement. Change each sentence in such a way as to remove the error.

1. *They are possible to have finished the experiment.

2. *An extra atom was noticed to be in the molecule.

3. *I was necessary to do the experiment a second time.

4. *The research was decided not to have been necessary.

5. *Recognition was belong to the scientist with the best theory.

24-K • Each of the following is the beginning of a paragraph containing a definition. Write the sketched-out definition as a full sentence by moving something into subject position. Let the choice of subject be determined by the content of the previous sentence.

1. *We next turn our attention to the concept of efficiency.*
   mean — efficiency — output power divided by input power

Writing Exercises

2. *Here is a photograph of the sun taken with a special telescope.*
   call — the dark patches — sunspots

   _____

3. *Although the word "humidity" is in everyone's vocabulary, very few people have a clear idea of what it means.*
   may define as — humidity — the amount of water vapor in the air

   _____

4. *Metal has been in continuous use since the end of the Stone Age.*
   say — [A mineral or rock [The mineral or rock
                            contains a useful
                            amount of metal] is an ore of that metal]

   _____
   _____

24-L • The second sentence within each of the following sentence pairs needs to be rearranged in order to achieve a smoother connection between the two. This can be accomplished in each case by rewriting the second sentence with the negative element first. After you have done this, cross out the original.

1. *The concept of a number representing none was first conceived by the Hindus.* ~~It wasn't taken over by the Arabs and built into their system of numerals, however,~~ *until the later spread of Islam.*

   not until the later spread of Islam, however, was it taken over by the Arabs and built into their system of numerals.

2. *It was no wonder that the ancients thought the stars were in fixed position.* The stars' proper motions would change the patterns seen in the sky *only over many thousands of years.*[19]

   _____
   _____

3. *Radio waves that would travel out into space are bounced back to earth by the ionosphere.* We can communicate by radio around the curve of the earth's surface *only in this way.*[19]

   _____
   _____

---

[19]Brandwein, Stollberg, and Burnett, op. cit.

4. *Place a small amount of sulfur in a test tube about half full of carbon tetrachloride.* The carbon tetrachloride vapors should *not* be breathed *under any circumstances.* [20]

5. *The oceanographer needs to know just where the ship is positioned at any given moment.* Electronic navigation systems have made this kind of accuracy possible *only in the last few years.* [20]

6. *When hydrogen and chlorine are mixed there is a combustion reaction.* You can*not* actually see the reaction between the two *at any time during the combustion process,* however.

24-M • The sentences listed below[21] make up a paragraph. They are scrambled, however. Reorder the sentences to make up a coherent paragraph by giving them the appropriate sequential numbers.

1. *On the other hand, genera of carnivores survive only about eight million years on the average.*
2. *For example, genera of clams seem to have persisted for far longer intervals on the average than have genera of mammalian carnivores (cats, dogs, bears, and so forth).*
3. *From such studies it is also possible to conclude that since the origin of life probably one hundred million to two hundred million species of animals and plants have disappeared.*
4. *Clam genera have an average endurance of nearly eighty million years before becoming extinct.*
5. *Paleontologists have been able to determine from the fossil record the average duration of various kinds of animals.*
6. *Studies of this kind indicate that animal species, on the average, survive only about five million years.*

---

[20]Ibid.
[21]Simak, op. cit.

Writing Exercises

24-N • CLOZE

In each blank write **a**, **the**, or **X** (for nothing), whichever is grammatical.

_____(1) piece of _____(2) apple was heated in _____(3) test tube over _____(4) Bunsen burner with _____(5) gentle flame. _____(6) care was taken to hold _____(7) test tube with _____(8) mouth facing away from _____(9) experimenter. Soon _____(10) drops of _____(11) water began collecting on _____(12) inside of _____(13) tube. _____(14) heating continued. Then _____(15) apple turned black, showing that _____(16) carbon was present.[22]

24-O

• Using the principles of word rearrangement based on weight, focus, and new and old information, read the following sequences[23] and choose the member of each row that most naturally completes the sequences. Draw a connecting line from the end of one sentence to the beginning of its proper successor.

A. *Weathering and erosion of rock exposed to the atmosphere constantly remove particles from the rock.*

	a	b	c
1.	These rock particles are called sediment.	Sediment is what these rock particles are called.	What these rock particles are called is sediment.

	a	b
2.	The upper layers press down on the lower ones as sediments accumulate.	As sediments accumulate, the upper layers press down on the lower ones.

	a	b
3.	Sediments that stick together form sedimentary rocks.	Sedimentary rocks are formed by sediments that stick together.

	a	b
4.	Such rocks have been able to survive the test of time only in this way.	Only in this way have such rocks been able to survive the test of time.

---

[22] Brandwein, Stollberg, and Burnett, op. cit.
[23] Ibid.

B. *Nuclear fusion occurs when the nuclei of certain atoms join together.*

a	b
1. Simpler nuclei fuse into more complex nuclei during a fusion reaction.	During a fusion reaction, simpler nuclei fuse into more complex nuclei.

a	b	c
2. For example, a nucleus of helium-4 will be formed from fusion of a hydrogen-2 nucleus and a hydrogen-3 nucleus.	For example, fusion of a hydrogen-2 nucleus and a hydrogen-3 nucleus will form a nucleus of helium-4.	For example, formed from fusion of a hydrogen-2 nucleus and a hydrogen-3 nucleus will be a nucleus of helium-4.

a	b
3. One place where nuclear fusion (or thermonuclear) reactions take place is in the sun.	The sun is one place where nuclear fusion (or thermonuclear) reactions take place.

a	b
4. Present also in thermonuclear bombs may be fusion reactions.	Fusion reactions may also be present in thermonuclear bombs.

a	b
5. Not until scientists learn how to control nuclear fusion will we be able to make constructive use of energy from fusion reactions.	We won't be able to make constructive use of energy from fusion reactions until scientists learn how to control nuclear fusion.

Writing Exercises

24-P • The *italicized* sentences in the following passages are grammatically correct but not quite appropriate. Without changing their meanings, rearrange these sentences structurally in such a way that they fit more naturally into their contexts.

1. Air coming up from the lungs causes the vocal cords to vibrate. ~~Stretching across the larynx are the vocal cords.~~ *The vocal cords stretch across the larynx.* The larnyx is the upper part of the respiratory tract.

2. The upper part of the respiratory tract is called the larynx. *The vocal cords stretch across the larynx. The vocal cords are caused to vibrate by air coming up from the lungs.*

3. Many university campuses today have service vehicles with electric engines. *For example, some of the vehicles at the University of California use this kind of engine.* The main reason for the increasing use . . .

4. Seismographic stations keep their instruments operating all the time. *Scientists at each station can determine the distance of their station from the source of any earthquake by timing the arrival of the shock waves.* This distance is used as the radius of a circle around the station.[24]

5. Other metals were unknown because they are found combined in compounds with other elements. *The Stone Age gave way to the Age of Copper only after man discovered how to use fire to extract metals from their compounds.* In estimating how long ago the Age of Copper emerged . . .[24]

6. Some nuclei decay, however, by giving off beta particles. *We need, first, a symbol for the beta particle in order to write an equation for an example of beta decay.* To form the symbol we begin with the letter e.[24]

---

[24]Ibid.

24-Q • Discussions of technical subjects in English sometimes include a set sequence of (1) stated facts, (2) generalization based on the facts, and (3) implications of the generalization. Steps two and three can be introduced by familiar stock phrases. For example:

(1) [statistics, reports, research findings, and so on]
(2) *From this we conclude* that large cars cause more accidents than small cars.
(3) *If this is the case,* then as these facts become more widely understood we can expect the sales of small cars to climb.

Drawing on your own knowledge of some technical subject, write a set of sentences similar in form to those above. Merely hint at step number one, if you wish, but write out steps two and three in full.

24-R • Rewrite the sketches below[25] as two paragraphs by moving elements into initial position and making any other necessary changes. The first sentence of both paragraphs is already supplied. Let conditions of appropriateness determine the forms of the rest of the sentences.

A. *Most rocks, like other solid substances, expand when they are heated.*

   mean − this − [The molecules that make up the solid tend to move apart from each other]

   Therefore,

   take up − the whole mass of material − more room

   move farther apart − the particles − when the temperature reaches the melting point

   In this way

   change into a liquid − the substance

_____
_____
_____
_____
_____
_____

[25]Ibid.

B. *When an atom combines with another it tends to acquire enough electrons to fill its outer shell.*

    be full — when they hold eight electrons — the outer shells of most atoms

    be — in the outer shell of the oxygen atom — six electrons

Therefore,

require — two hydrogen atoms — to form a molecule of water

give — the hydrogen atoms — the oxygen — a full outer shell of electrons

Thus

be — H_2O — the formula for the compound

_____

_____

_____

_____

_____

24-S • Write a detailed description of a technical or scientific process with which you are familiar. Be especially careful to have sentence form be influenced by the conditions of appropriateness already studied.

APPENDIXES

APPENDIX A

17-6 Verb-particle: intransitive

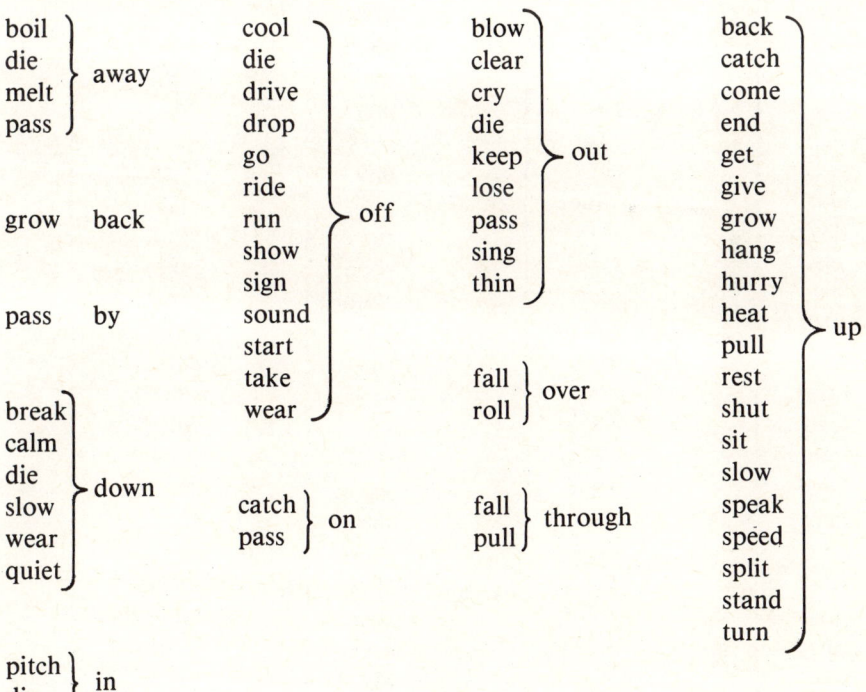

Verb-particle: transitive

bring	about	beat ⎫		beat ⎫	act ⎫	
		break		block	blow	
		bring		break	bring	
put ⎫	across	burn		bring	call	
get ⎭		chop		brush	carry	
		count		buy	clean	
		drink		call	cross	
		fasten		carry	crowd	
lay ⎫	aside	flag		check	cut	
set ⎬		force		clear	dig	
put ⎭		hand		clip	drown	
		hunt		cut	dry	
blow ⎫		jot		dash	empty	
clean		keep		dry	even	
clear		lay		even	figure	
give		let		fence	fill	
keep		mark		fight	find	
lay		narrow ⎬ down		finish	give	
pack		note		head	hand	
put	away	pin		hold	help	
roll		play		laugh	hold	
rub		put		let	keep	
send		rub		mark	lay	
sign		run		pass	let	
sweep		set		pay ⎬ off	measure ⎬ out	
tear		shoot		pull	move	
throw		shut		rinse	pick	
wipe ⎭		take		rope	point	
		tear		round	pour	
		throw		rub	pull	
cut ⎫		turn		run	rip	
drive		vote		send	round	
feed		wash		set	rule	
hold		wear		shake	send	
keep		write ⎭		shave	set	
play ⎬ back				shoot	sort	
read				show	spread	
set		put ⎫ forth		shut	stamp	
take		set ⎭		sweep	straighten	
turn				take	stretch	
win ⎭				tell	take	
		bring ⎫		throw	thin	
		cash ⎬ in		tip	tire	
pass	by	push		top	throw	
		take ⎭		touch	turn	
				ward	wash	
				wash	wear	
				write ⎭	work ⎭	

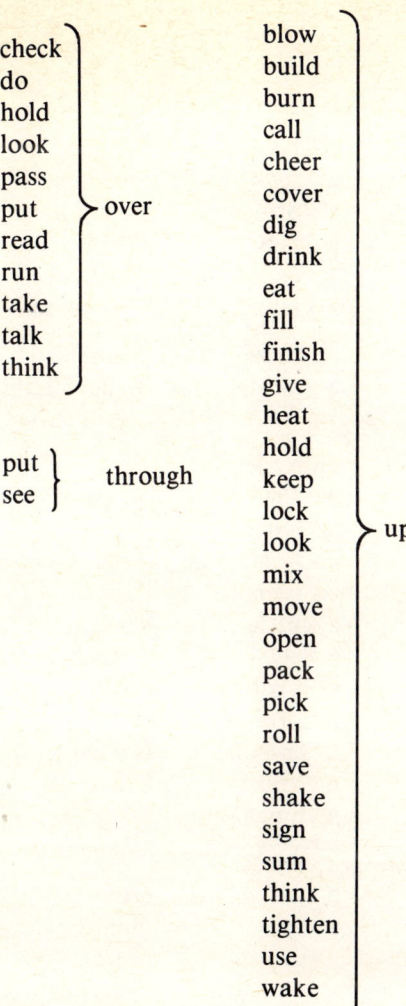

check		blow	
do		build	
hold		burn	
look		call	
pass		cheer	
put	over	cover	
read		dig	
run		drink	
take		eat	
talk		fill	
think		finish	
		give	
put	through	heat	
see		hold	
		keep	up
		lock	
		look	
		mix	
		move	
		open	
		pack	
		pick	
		roll	
		save	
		shake	
		sign	
		sum	
		think	
		tighten	
		use	
		wake	
		wrap	

APPENDIX B

17-10

country/continent	adjective	person	language
China	Chinese	a Chinese	Chinese
Japan	Japanese	a Japanese	Japanese
Portugal	Portuguese	a Portuguese	Portuguese
Switzerland	Swiss	a Swiss	(German/French/Italian)
Vietnam	Vietnamese	a Vietnamese	Vietnamese
Israel	Israeli	an Israeli	(Hebrew)
Pakistan	Pakistani	a Pakistani	(Urdu/Sindhi/Punjabi)
Africa	African	an African	
America	American	an American	(English)
Asia	Asian	an Asian	
Australia	Australian	an Australian	(English)
Italy	Italian	an Italian	Italian
Russia	Russian	a Russian	Russian
Belgium	Belgian	a Belgian	(French/Flemish)
Brazil	Brazilian	a Brazilian	(Portuguese)
Europe	European	a European	
Germany	German	a German	German
Greece	Greek	a Greek	Greek
Hungary	Hungarian	a Hungarian	Hungarian
Norway	Norwegian	a Norwegian	Norwegian
Denmark	Danish	a Dane	Danish
Finland	Finnish	a Finn	Finnish
Poland	Polish	a Pole	Polish
Spain	Spanish	a Spaniard	Spanish
Sweden	Swedish	a Swede	Swedish
Arabia	Arabian	an Arab	Arabic
England	English	an Englishman	English
France	French	a Frenchman	French
Holland / the Netherlands	Dutch	a Dutchman	Dutch
Ireland	Irish	an Irishman	(English/Gaelic)
Britain	British	a Briton	(English)
Scotland	Scottish	a Scot/Scotsman	(English)

APPENDIX C

PRESENT TENSE

Tense	Voice	Simple	Continuous
Simple Present	active	he teaches	he is teaching
	passive	he is taught	he is being taught
Present Perfect	active	he has taught	he has been teaching
	passive	he has been taught	(he has been being taught)
Expressions of Future Time	active	he will teach he is going to teach	he will be teaching (he is going to be teaching)
	passive	he will be taught he is going to be taught	(he will be being taught) (he is going to be being taught)
Future Perfect	active	he will have taught	(he will have been teaching)
	passive	he will have been taught	(he will have been being taught)

PAST TENSE

Tense	Voice	Simple	Continuous
Simple Past	active	he taught	he was teaching
	passive	he was taught	he was being taught
Past Perfect	active	he had taught	he had been teaching
	passive	he had been taught	(he had been being taught)
Expressions of Future Time in the Past (Conditional)	active	he would teach he was going to teach	he would be teaching (he was going to be teaching)
	passive	he would be taught he was going to be taught	(he would be being taught) (he was going to be being taught)
Future Perfect in the Past (Conditional Perfect)	active	he would have taught	(he would have been teaching)
	passive	he would have been taught	(he would have been being taught)

Adapted from "The System of Tense and Aspect in English," by Dietrich Nehls. *International Review of Applied Linguistics in Language Teaching,* vol. 13, no. 4, November, 1975. Reprinted by permission of the author and the publisher.

APPENDIX D

22-5 Complementation: verb preposition + sentence

(reliance)	rely ⎫	(allusion)	allude ⎫	
(insistence)	insist	(objection)	object	
(dependence)	depend	(confession)	confess	
(agreement)	agree	(reference)	refer	
(settlement)	settle		take	⎬ to + [S]
	plan ⎬ (up)on + [S]		admit	
	figure		get around	
	count		look forward ⎭	
	decide			
	center ⎭			

		(decision)	decide ⎫	
		(warning)	warn	
(thought)	think ⎫	(argument)	argue	⎬ against + [S]
(approval)	approve	(discrimination)	discriminate ⎭	
(dream)	dream			
	hear ⎬ of + [S]			
	get out	(wonder)	wonder ⎫	
	speak	(worry)	worry	
	tell ⎭	(thought)	think	
		(talk)	talk	
		(lie)	lie	⎬ about + [S]
(hint)	hint ⎫	(dream)	dream	
(balk)	balk ⎬ at + [S]		forget	
	work ⎭		speak	
			tell	
			care ⎭	

(success)	succeed ⎬ in + [S]			
(belief)	believe			

	feel	like + [S]		

			keep ⎫	
			stop	
			prevent	⎬ NP from + [S]
			block	
			bar	
			dissuade ⎭	

APPENDIX E

22-25 Simple complementation

$$\left.\begin{array}{r}\text{consider}\\ \text{feel}\\ \text{believe}\\ \text{know}\\ \text{find}\\ \text{hold}\\ \text{assume}\\ \text{judge}\\ \text{imagine}\\ \text{understand}\\ \text{acknowledge}\\ \text{discover}\end{array}\right\} \text{NP to be} \left\{\begin{array}{l}\text{NP}\\ \text{Adj}\end{array}\right.$$

$$\left.\begin{array}{r}\text{consider}\\ \text{regard}\\ \text{think of}\\ \text{know}\\ \text{describe}\\ \text{accept}\\ \text{welcome}\\ \text{admit}\\ \text{picture}\\ \text{imagine}\\ \text{remember}\\ \text{recognize}\\ \text{see}\\ \text{count}\\ \text{acknowledge}\\ \text{label}\\ \text{rate}\\ \text{classify}\end{array}\right\} \text{NP as} \left\{\begin{array}{l}\text{NP}\\ \text{Adj}\end{array}\right.$$

$$\left.\begin{array}{r}\text{consider}\\ \text{call}\\ \text{find}\\ \text{imagine}\\ \text{pronounce}\\ \text{hold}\\ \text{picture}\\ \text{believe}\\ \text{make}\\ \text{leave}\\ \text{keep}\\ \text{judge}\\ \text{rate}\\ \text{prove}\\ \text{label}\end{array}\right\} \text{NP} \left\{\begin{array}{l}\text{NP}\\ \text{Adj}\end{array}\right.$$

APPENDIX F

24-7 Qualifiers

sort of	typical(ly)
kind of	almost
loosely/strictly speaking	to a large extent
more or less	so-called
roughly	of sorts
pretty (much)	shall we say
relatively	in one sense
somewhat	in a (real/important/historical/ . . .) sense
rather	in a way
fairly	in a manner of speaking
mostly	details aside
technically	so to say/speak
essentially	virtually
in essence	practically
basically	all but a
principally	anything but a
particularly	in name only
largely	actually
for the most part	really
very	-like
especially	-ish
exceptionally	can be looked (up)on/viewed as
literally	

APPENDIX G

24-11

It is { hard, nice, easy, good, strange, useless, useful, wonderful, convenient, possible, difficult, fun, sad, all right } to verb X

X is { hard, nice, easy, good, strange, useless, useful, wonderful, convenient, possible, difficult, fun, sad, all right } to verb

APPENDIX H

24-12 Verbs with -ed and -ing adjectives

please	thrill
disgust	alarm
excite	amuse
intrigue	disappoint
frighten	disturb
shock	satisfy
irritate	stun
interest	bore
fascinate	convince
annoy	confuse
amaze	embarrass
move	reassure
strike	exhaust
upset	tire
surprise	frustrate

Verbs with other than -ing adjectives

please	(pleasant)	inform	(informative)
scare	(scary)	abuse	(abusive)
inconvenience	(inconvenient)	provoke	(provocative)
impress	(impressive)	appreciate	(appreciative)
delight	(delightful)	exhaust	(exhaustive)
respect	(respectful)	tire	(tiresome)
attract	(attractive)	bother	(bothersome)
offend	(offensive)	worry	(worrisome)

APPENDIX I

24-28 Verbs occurring in the second passive

think
expect
fear
feel
discover
consider
observe
assume
suspect
acknowledge
suppose
believe
know
understand
see
find out
imagine
hear
say
reveal
prove
declare
admit
whisper
report
demonstrate

APPENDIX J

Vocabulary

The number and letter in square brackets refer to the unit and section containing the Dialog or Reading in which the vocabulary item first appeared.

abandon [20C]
absence [24C]
accept [22C]
accident [18A]
accomplish [24C]
accumulation [24A]
accurately [20C]
action [20C]
activity [22C]
adapt [22C]
advertize [20A]
affair [22A]
allotment [21C]
alone [16C]
along with [17C]
amaze [21A]
angle [20C]
announce [17C]
approach [20C]
arrogant [21C]
as a matter of fact [19A]
attach [24C]
attempt [21C]
attend [22C]
audience [23C]
auditorium [23C]
automobile [18C]
avoid [18C]

bankrupt [23A]
barren [19C]
bath [16A]
bathtub [16A]
bear, v [19C]
benefit [21C]
besides [16A]
bicycle [18A]
bitterness [22C]
blame [18A]

blow, n [21C]
borrow [23A]
bottom [17C]
bow, n [20C]
brake [18A]
brief [20C]
bring up [17C]
button [21A]
by now [17A]

careless [18A]
categorize [24C]
category [24C]
cause [18C]
cautious [20C]
chance [16C]
cheap [20A]
claim [18A]
clarification [24A]
clarify [24A]
classify [18A]
clean out [23A]
clearly [24A]
cluster [16C]
collection [17A]
collision [18C]
community [24A]
compartment [21A]
computation [24C]
congestion [18C]
confirm [20C]
conformity [22C]
confrontation [22C]
conquer [22C]
conservative [20C]
consider [20A]
considerable [22C]
consistent [24C]
contain [24A]

contour [17C]
contribute [18C]
convenience [24C]
conversation [23C]
convert [23C]
convict, n [19C]
crib [16C]

danger [20C]
deadline [20C]
deal with [21C]
death [18C]
deductive [20C]
deep [17C]
definition [24A]
denunciation [23C]
denounce [23C]
depletion [18C]
deprive [22C]
designation [24C]
determine [16C]
develop [24A]
die [18C]
dig [17C]
digit [24C]
dinosaur [18C]
disaster [20C]
discontinue [21C]
displace [24C]
disprove [24A]
distiller [23C]
distress [20C]
divide [18C]
dollar [20A]
drill [17C]
due to [18A]

early [19A]
eastern [19C]

Appendix J 307

eastward [17C]
echelon [22C]
editor [20C]
electrify [21A]
emphasize [18A]
encounter [21C]
enormous [18A]
ensure [21C]
enthrall [23C]
escape [20C]
evangelist [23C]
eventually [24A]
evidence [17C]
evil [23C]
exclusive [23C]
expand [19C]
expansion [19C]
extension [17C]
extreme [24C]

fair [22A]
fairly [20A]
fascinate [23C]
faulty [18A]
feat [20C]
feature [20C]
fence [18C]
fiery [23C]
file suit [21C]
financial [21C]
finger [17C]
flatly [20C]
fleet [20C]
fool, v [18A]
foot [18A]
force [18C]
former [19C]
for one thing [24A]
frenzy [23C]
funny [19A]

gamble [20C]
geology [17A]
give rise to [22C]
go to war [19C]
gold [19C]
grant [19C]

grasp [23C]
gravitate [16C]
greasy [21A]

haircut [21A]
headline [20C]
heart attack [18C]
hemisphere [22A]
henceforth [22C]
highway [18C]
hit [18A]
hit upon [24C]

iceberg [20C]
identify [17C]
illegal [20A]
immigrant [22C]
impassioned [23C]
imperialism [22A]
imply [24A]
impossible [20A]
impure [24A]
in a _____ sense [24A]
inconvenience [18C]
incorporate [24C]
indefinite [24C]
indicate [21C]
influence [16C]
in place [17C]
injury [18C]
inquiry [21C]
insane [20A]
insert [20C]
inspire [23C]
instruction [22C]
interfere [22A]
invention [24A]
irreplaceable [20C]
issue [24A]

jewel [23C]
jigsaw [17C]
journalism [20C]

label [22C]
landlord [23C]
laughable [23A]

lay [16A]
legally [21C]
lend [23A]
lifeboat [20C]
light, adj [18C]
light up [21C]
limp [18A]
liner [20C]
liquor [23C]
live, adj [23A]
lizard [16A]
look like [19A]
look up [17A]
lovable [23A]
luxury [23A]

mail [19A]
make out [21C]
manicure [21A]
manipulation [24C]
mark [20C]
member [16C]
message [20C]
mile [17C]
million [17C]
mink [23C]
misery [23A]
miss [18A]
mix up [24A]
mobile [22C]
moderate [22C]
modify [16C]
mute [21C]
multiplication [24C]
myth [24A]

narrow [20C]
neighborhood [23C]
next door [22A]
niche [16C]
norm [22C]
numeral [24C]

obligation [21C]
obstacle [21C]
obvious [18A]
occur [19C]

ocean [17C]
official [22A]
once [17C]
optimistic [20C]
originally [19C]
otherwise [18A]
ovation [23C]
oversized [18C]
own, v [20C]
oxygen [24A]

packed [23C]
pal [23A]
parallel [19C]
parent [16C]
passport [22A]
pay back [21A]
paycheck [23A]
pay off [23A]
penny [20A]
perhaps [24A]
permanent [19C]
persistent [19A]
petroleum [18C]
physical [19C]
piece [17C]
platform [23C]
plus [24C]
point [17C]
pollution [18C]
portion [19C]
practically [22A]
precisely [24C]
press, n [20C]
pressure [16C]
pride [20C]
priority [22C]
private [16C]
probably [18A]
prohibit [22C]
proper [21C]
protest [21C]
prove [17C]
provide [16C]
provoke [23A]
pure [24A]

push [21A]
put out [20A]
put up with [16A]
puzzle [17C]

quarters [16A]

rapid [18C]
rare [16C]
rather [20A]
reach [17C]
rear [16C]
recently [18C]
reduce [18C]
refer to [24A]
reflect [20C]
release [20C]
remain [18C]
rent out [23A]
reptile [16A]
resemblance [19C]
resist [22C]
resource [18C]
respect [22C]
responsible [18C]
reveal [16C]
revolution [19C]
right [22C]
risk [20C]
rock, n [17C]
route [21A]
rumor [20C]

sad [23A]
scientific [24A]
sea [17C]
search [19C]
secession [22C]
sediment [17C]
seminar [24A]
sense [24A]
separate, adj [16C]
serious [18C]
sermon [23C]
session [24A]
settle [19C]

settlement [19C]
shape [17C]
sharp [19C]
sheep [19C]
ship [17C]
shock [20C]
shoeshine [21A]
shower [21A]
sight [19C]
signal [20C]
sinful [23C]
sink, v [20C]
site [17C]
slight [23A]
smash [18A]
so-called [24A]
space [16A]
sprain [18A]
sprawl [18C]
spread [24C]
staff [20C]
stand for [24C]
statable [24C]
stock market [23A]
Stone Age [23A]
striking [19C]
strongly [16C]
submerge [17C]
subway [21A]
sum [24C]
superpower [22A]
superstition [24A]

take for granted [22C]
take place [19A]
take up [16A]
tense [22C]
term [24C]
terminal [21A]
testimony [21C]
thanks to [18A]
theory [24A]
thoroughly [20C]
throw [20C]
thunder [23C]
tireless [20C]

Appendix J   309

toll [18C]
train [16C]
turn out [20C]
typical [22A]

unsinkable [20C]
unthinkable [20C]
urban [18C]
usually [17A]

vacation [21A]
valid [24A]
value [24C]
vast [17C]
virtual [22C]

wash [16A]
watch, n [19A]
west [19C]

western [19C]
westward [19C]
wheat [19C]
wireless [20C]
work, v [17A]
wrong [19A]

INDEX

In hyphenated references, the first element is the unit number; the second element is the discussion or exercise. Page numbers refer to the Preparatory Unit or to footnotes.

Vocabulary items appear in bold roman type.

Items marked by a dagger (†) have an entry in the index to Volume One.

†**a**, indefinite article, 17-9
†**-able**, 24-24
†adjective
   in **-able/-ible**, 24-24
   in causation, 18-24
   complement, 24-11
   in **-ed**, 24-12, 24-22
   in **-ing**, 24-12, 24-22
   opposites, 19-D
   with possessive **-ed**, 17-18
   referring to country, 17-10
†adverbial
   in causation, 18-24
   time, 20-22
†affix, *see* prefix, suffix
after, 20-22
agent noun, *see* noun
alter, 16-F
although, 19-24, 19-25
an, *see* **a**
†**and**
   punctuation with, 18-22, 20-20
   in sentence conjunction, 21-22, 21-28, 23-15
appear, 24-36
†article
   with count noun, 17-13, 17-D
   definite, 17-19, 17-B
   indefinite, 17-9
   omission of, 17-29, 20-Q

†**as**, 18-10
   as a result, 18-10
   ascend, 17-E
†**ask**, 21-18
   as long as, 23-29
   attribute, 18-24
   avoid, 22-F

back, 21-5
†**be**
   contraction with, 21-4
   as final state, 24-36
   omission of, 20-Q
   in sentence inversion, 24-36, 24-37
   subjunctive of, 23-10
†**be able to**, 20-11
†**be allowed to**, 20-11
   because, 18-10, 18-11, 18-15, 18-29, 18-30, 18-O, 23-30
   because of, 18-15
   before, 20-22
   begin, 24-28
†**be going (to)**, 20-11, 24-28
belong, 20-F, 24-36
†**be supposed to**, 20-11
blame, 18-24
†**both**, 19-12
bring up, 17-E
†**but**, 18-22, 19-24, 19-27, 23-34
†**by**, 17-L

†**can('t)**, 20-10, 20-11, 24-24
capital letter, 17-19, 20-20
caption, 17-29, 20-19, 20-Q
†causation
   with adjective phrase, 18-24
   with **as**, 18-10
   assignment of, 18-24
   with **because**, 18-10, 18-11, 18-29
   with **due to**, 18-10
   with **for**, 18-29
   with **for the reason that**, 18-10
   with **how come**, 18-8, 18-11
   with **-ify**, 18-4
   indirect, 18-28
   with **-ize**, 18-4
   with preposition, 18-24, 18-26
   questioning of, 18-8, 18-29
   with **since**, 18-10
   with **thanks to**, 18-10
   with verb, 18-20, 18-24
   with **why**, 18-29
cause, 18-20
change, 16-18, 16-F
change of state, 23-22
clarification
   expression of, 22-7
   punctuation, 22-22
climb, 17-E
collective noun, *see* noun
colon, *see* punctuation
†**come**, 23-21, 23-22
come up, 17-E
†comma, *see* punctuation
common noun, *see* noun
comparative, *see* comparison
†comparison
   with **both**, 19-12
   in causation, 18-24
   complex, 19-21
   double, 19-21
   incomplete, 19-23
   as intensifier, 19-8, 19-21
   with **neither**, 19-12
   with opposites, 19-18, 19-D
   in single word, 19-F
   with **so**, 19-8
   superlative, 19-G
   with **too**, *see* negation
   see also contrast

†complement
   adjective, 24-11
   in causation, 18-21
   with **consider** type verb, 22-25, 22-26
   noun, 22-11
   with sentential object, 22-26, 22-J
   verb, 22-5, 22-10, 22-25, 22-26
†complementizer
   absence of, 22-12
   for to, 22-10, 22-11, 22-26, 22-F
   's -ing, 22-10, 22-11
   that, 22-10, 22-11, 22-F
   wh-, 22-10, 22-11
†compound
   with agent noun, 23-23
   in headlines, 20-19
   noun, p. 11
   with possessive **-ed**, 17-18
   with verb-**ing**, 22-20
concession, 23-26
condition
   with **as long as**, 23-29
   closed, 23-36
   with conjoined sentences, 23-15
   formal, 23-26
   future possible, 23-10, 23-15, 23-O
   hypothetical, 23-10, 23-15, 23-26, 23-35, 23-O
   with **if**, 23-10, 23-15, 23-26, 23-35, 23-36, 23-O
   with **in case**, 23-36
   negative, 23-30
   with **on condition that**, 23-29
   with **only if**, 23-29
   with **or else**, 23-30
   with **otherwise**, 23-30, 23-34
   with **provided that**, 23-29
   with **unless**, 23-30
conditional (up)on, 23-36
†conjunction
   as condition, 23-15, 23-30
   punctuation with, 18-22
   of sentences, 21-22, 21-28, 23-15
†**consequently**, 18-10
†consonant, doubling of, 22-4
contingent (up)on, 23-36
continue, 24-28
continuous, *see* tense

†contraction
    of **be**, 21-4
    of **have**, 20-24, 21-4
    of modals, 20-24, 21-4
†contrary to fact, *see* condition, hypothetical
contrast, 19-24, 19-25, 19-27, 19-29. *See also* comparison
conversely, 19-24
convert, 16-F
correlative punctuation, *see* punctuation
†**could**, 20-10, 20-11
†count noun, *see* noun
credit, 18-24

†definite article, 17-19, 17-B
deixis, *see* reference
deny, 22-F
deprive, 22-F
desire, 20-15
†direct object
    of phrasal verb, 17-6, 18-6, 20-6, 24-6
    as sentence, 22-26
due to, 18-10

each other, 16-26
echo question, 16-4
-ed
    in adjective, 24-12, 24-22
    with negative prefix, 24-20
    in participial clause, 21-M
    in passive with **can**, 24-24
    as possessive suffix, 17-18
effect, 18-10. *See also* causation
ellipsis, *see* shortening
end focus
    with cause/effect, 18-24
    through cleft sentence, 24-29
    through passive, 24-28, 24-I
    through pseudo-cleft sentence, 24-29
    through sentence inversion, 24-36
    with **there**, 22-32
end weight
    through cleft sentence, 24-29
    through **it** replacement, 22-31, 22-32, 24-I
    through passive, 22-31, 24-28, 24-I
    through pseudo-cleft sentence, 24-29
    through sentence inversion, 24-36, 24-37

†**enough**, 19-14, 19-D
equal, 19-F
even, 19-6
even though, 23-36
exceed, 19-F
excess, *see* negation, with **too**
exclamation, 21-6. *See also* punctuation
extension expression, 22-7
†extraposition, *see* **it** replacement

fail, 24-28
fairly, 20-7
fall, 24-36
feel, 22-12
focus principle, *see* end focus
for
    expressing reason/purpose, 18-29, 18-30
    as sentence connector, 18-22
forbid, 22-F
force, 18-20
†**for to**, *see* complementizer
†**for example**, 22-7
from, in causation, 18-26
full stop, *see* punctuation, period

†generic expression, 17-9
get, 18-20
†**go**, 23-21, 23-22, 24-36

happen, 20-11, 23-0, 24-28
†**have**
    in aspectual passive, 24-28
    in causation, 18-20
    with complement, 22-12
    contraction with, 20-24, 21-4
    -ing form of, 21-9
    of possession, 20-F
†**have to**, 20-11
headline, *see* caption
hear, 22-12
hedge, *see* qualifier
help, 22-12
how + adjective, 19-D
how come, 18-8, 18-11
†**however**, 19-24
hyphen, *see* punctuation
†**if**, 22-7. *See also* condition
if only, 23-35, 23-O
in-, *see* prefix

Index   313

†**in case (of)**, 23-36
 in contrast, 19-24
†infinitive, *see* **to** verb
 inflection, *see* suffix
 information question
    intonation in, 16-4, 21-6
    with **what**, p. 3, 16-4, 16-7
    see also **how, how come, what for, why**
†**-ing**
    in adjective, 24-12, 24-22
    as complementizer, 22-10
    in compound, 22-20
    with negative prefix, 24-20
    in participial clause, 21-27, 21-M
    in relative clause, 21-9, 21-22
    in sentence inversion, 24-37
    in sentential forms, 22-5
 in order to/that, 18-30
 in other words, 22-7
 instead of, 19-24
 in spite of, 23-36
 intensifier
    with comparative, 19-8, 19-21
    own, 16-30
    very, 19-8
†intonation
    in adjective complement, 24-11
    in echo question, 16-4
    in exclamation, 21-6
    in information question, 16-4, 21-6
 in that, 18-0
 inversion, sentence, 24-36, 24-37
 inverted comma, 23-27, p. 238n. *See also* punctuation
 invitation, 21-18
 it
    in cleft sentence, 24-29
    as pronoun, 16-9
†**it** replacement, 22-26, 22-31, 22-32, 22-J, 24-I

 keep, 20-F, 22-F
†**know**, 21-9

†lax vowel, *see* vowel
 let, 22-12
 letter
    of application, 21-O
    business, 21-N
    formal, 21-15, 21-L, 21-N

    open, 21-L
    personal, 21-1, 21-E, 21-K
    thank-you, 21-K
 lift, 17-E
†**like**, 21-9
 likely, 20-11
 listen (to), 22-12

 make
    in causation, 18-20
    with complement, 22-12
 maximum, 19-F
†**may**, 20-10, 20-11
 might as well, 20-15
†modal
    in conditional, 23-10
    contraction of, 21-4
    meaning of, 20-10, 20-11, 24-28
    past forms of, 20-11
    perfect form of, 20-11
    in relative clause, 21-4
    see also **can, could, may, might, must, should, will, would**
†modification, *see* adjective, adverbial, relative clause
 modify, 16-18, 16-F
†**more**, 19-21
†**must**, 20-10, 20-11

†**namely**, 22-7
 need, 21-9, 24-8
†negation
    in condition, 23-30
    with prefix, 20-4, 20-5, 24-20, 24-21
    preposed, 24-30
    scope of, 24-30
    with **too**, 19-8, 19-14, 19-D
†**neither**, 19-12
 no matter, 23-36
 non-, 24-21
†noun
    agent, 23-23
    choice of article with, 17-9
    collective, 17-C
    common, 17-9
    complement, *see* complement
    compound, *see* compound
    count, 17-9, 17-13, 17-D
    ending in **-(ific)ation**, 18-5
    generic, 17-9

in geography, 17-B
head, 17-27
as name of country, 17-10
as name of language, 17-10
in possessive expression, 17-21, 17-25
proper, 17-9, 17-19
reference, 16-25, 16-26
see also noun phrase
†noun phrase
in condition, 23-36
definite/indefinite, 16-9
internal relationship of, 24-22
in possessive expression, 17-27
singular/plural, 16-10

†object, *see* direct object
occur, 24-36
†of
as alternate of 's, 17-21, 17-25, 17-27
in causation, 18-26
off, 23-5
on condition that, 23-29
†one(s), 16-9
only, 23-34
only if, 23-29
†on the contrary, 19-24, 19-27, 19-29
on the other hand, 19-24, 19-29
†or
punctuation with, 18-22
+ rather, 22-7
in sentence conjunction, 23-15
otherwise, 18-10, 23-30, 23-34
out, 23-5
out of, in causation, 18-24
own
as possessive intensifier, 16-30
as verb, 20-F

parentheses, *see* punctuation
participial clause, *see* **-ing, -ed**
participle, *see* **-ing, -ed**
particle, in phrasal verb, *see* verb + particle
†passive
for **-able** paraphrase, 24-24
aspectual, 24-28
for end weight, 22-31, 24-I
with phrasal verb, 24-6

second, 24-28, 24-I
†past participle, p. 146n
†period, *see* punctuation
phrasal verb, 16-6, 17-6, 24-6. *See also* verb + particle, verb + preposition
possess, 20-F
†possession
with **-ed**, 17-18
with noun phrase, 17-27
with **of**, 17-21, 17-25, 17-27
with **own**, 16-30
questioning of, 17-22
relationship expressed by, 17-21, 17-26
with **'s**, 17-21, 17-25, 17-27, 22-10
†possessive, *see* possession
predication, with **'s/of**, 17-25
preference, 20-15
prefix
in-/im-/il-/ir-, 20-4, 20-5, 24-20, 24-21
non-, 24-21
un-, 24-20, 24-21
†preposition
in causation, 18-24, 18-26
in phrasal verb, *see* verb + preposition
in possessive expression, 17-21
in relative clause, 21-10, 21-23, 21-C
sentential object of, 22-5
see also **of**; prepositional phrase
†prepositional phrase, 17-B. *See also* preposition
†presupposition
with **but**, 19-28
with **even**, 19-6
prevent, 22-F
†pro-adverb, 16-21
progressive tense, *see* tense, continuous
prohibit, 22-F
†pronoun
definite/indefinite, 16-9
with following modifier, 16-D
as object of phrasal verb, 18-6
reciprocal, 16-26
reference, 16-9, 16-10
reflexive, 16-25, 16-29
singular/plural, 16-10
proper noun, *see* noun
provided that, 23-29
†punctuation
colon, 16-19, 24-25

comma, 16-19, 18-22, 19-19, 20-20, 21-20, 21-22, 22-22
correlative, 21-20, 22-22
dash, 21-20, 22-22
exclamation point, 16-19
hyphen, 16-19
inverted comma, 23-27
parentheses, 16-19, 21-20, 22-22
period, 16-19, 18-22, 20-20
question mark, 16-19
quotation mark, 20-26, 23-27
in relative clause, 21-22
semicolon, 16-19, 20-20
with subordinate clause, 19-25
purpose
with **because**, 18-29
with **for**, 18-29, 18-30
with **in order to/that**, 18-30
questioning of, 18-8, 18-29
with **what for**, 18-8
with **why**, 18-29

qualifier, 20-7, 24-7
†question
echo, 16-4
as sarcasm, 18-C
see also information question
question mark, see punctuation
quotation mark, see punctuation

raise, 17-E
rather, 20-7
reason, see causation
reference
in change of state, 23-22
of nouns, 16-9, 16-10, 16-25, 16-26, 17-13
of pronoun, 16-9, 16-10
in spatial relations, 23-21
of **this/that**, 23-7
of **which**, 21-22
regardless, 23-36
relationship
within compound, 17-18, 22-20, 23-23, 24-22
of **-ed/-ing**, 24-12, 24-22
shown through punctuation, 22-22
sound, through spelling, 23-4
subject-verb, 21-9, 21-D, 24-22

verb-object, 21-10, 21-D, 22-20, 23-23, 24-22
of words, 17-4, 23-4
†relative clause
formality, 21-C
with **-ing**, 21-9, 21-22, 21-27
modifying complex noun phrase, 17-27
nonrestrictive, 21-22, 21-27, 21-28
object, 21-10
of possession, 17-22, 21-23
preposition in, 21-10, 21-23
with proper noun, 17-9
with sentence antecedent, 21-22
subject, 21-9, 21-22
with **to** verb, 21-10, 21-D
use of, 21-28
†relative marker, 21-10, 21-23
†request, 21-18
result, see effect
rise, 17-E

†sarcasm, 18-C
see, 22-12
seem, 20-11, 24-28
-self/-selves, 16-25
semicolon, see punctuation
sentence
as complement, 22-10, 22-11, 22-12, 22-J
as object of preposition, 22-5
as subject, 22-26
†shortening, 16-21, 16-22
†**should**, 20-10, 20-11, 23-0
since, 18-10
†**so**
in comparison, 19-8, 19-11, 19-G
as replacement for **that**-S, 16-21
as sentence connector, 18-10, 18-22, 18-0
†**some**, 16-10
†spelling
of consonants, 23-4
doubling of consonants, 22-4
of tense/lax vowels, 17-4, 22-4
of verb-**ed**, 22-4
of verb-**ing**, 22-4
split, 22-31
start, 24-28
†stress
on conversation topic, 19-4

in phrasal verb, 24-6
in possessive, 16-30
with prefix, 20-4
with suffix, 18-4, 18-5, 22-4, 24-4
in verb phrase, 16-22
subject to, 23-36
subjunctive, *see* tense
subordination, *see* individual listings (**although, because,** etc.)
substitution, 16-21, 16-22. *See also* pronoun
†**such**, 19-G
†suffix
 -**ation**, 18-5
 -**ed**, *see* -**ed**
 -**ed**, possessive, 17-18
 -**er/-or/-ar**, 23-23
 -**ification**, 18-5
 -**ify**, 18-4
 -**ing**, *see* -**ing**
 -**ize**, 18-4
 for learned words, 24-4
 for name of language, 17-10
 plural, 17-C
summons, 17-7
†**superlative**, *see* comparison
switch, 16-F

take, 19-5
telegraphic English, 17-29
tend, 24-28
†tense
 continuous, 20-22, 21-9, 24-37
 in headline, 20-Q
 historical present, 20-M
 past perfect, 20-22, 20-26
 past perfect continuous, 20-22
 perfect, 20-11, 20-22, 23-10
 shift, 20-26
 simple past, 20-22, 21-9, 23-10
 simple present, 21-9
 subjunctive, 23-10, 23-35
tense vowel, *see* vowel
than, 19-21
thanks to, 18-10
†**that**
 as complementizer, 22-10, 22-11, 22-F
 as pronoun, 16-D
that is, 22-7

†**the**, 17-9
there, 22-32
†**therefore**, 18-10
those, 16-D
†time
 past, 20-11, 20-22, 20-26
 present, 20-26, 20-M
 relationship, 20-22
†**too**, *see* negation
to verb, 21-10, 21-C. *See also* **for to**
transform, 16-F
turn (into), 16-F

un-, 24-20, 24-21
used (to), 24-28

†verb
 -**able/-ible**, 24-24
 adjective derivation from, 24-12
 complement, *see* complement
 -**ed**, *see* -**ed**
 ending if -**ify**, 18-4, 18-5
 ending in -**ize**, 18-4, 18-5
 -**ing**, *see* -**ing**
 + particle, 17-6, 18-6, 19-5, 20-6, 21-5, 23-5, 24-6
 in passive, *see* passive
 + preposition, 17-6, 19-5, 22-5
 tense, *see* tense
 transitive, *see* passive
†verb phrase
 of location/direction, 24-36
 substitution and shortening in, 16-22
†**very**, 19-8
†**vowel**, 17-4, 22-4

†**want**, 21-9
watch, 22-12
weight principle, *see* end weight
†**what**
 as complementizer, 22-10
 in pseudo-cleft sentence, 24-29
 see also information question
what for, 18-8
†**when**, 20-22
whereas, 19-24, 19-25
while, 19-24, 19-25
†**who**, 21-C
whom, 21-C

†**wh**-question, *see* information question
whose
    in information question, 17-22
    as relative marker, 17-22, 21-23
†**why**, 18-8, 18-11, 18-29
†**will/won't**, 20-10, 20-11, 20-12, 23-10
  wishes, 23-35

†**would**, 20-10, 20-11, 20-12, 20-24, 23-10, 23-0
would just as soon, 20-15
would rather, 20-15

yet, 18-22, 19-24